GROWTH

TIME LIFE ®
BOOKS

Other Publications:

PLANET EARTH

COLLECTOR'S LIBRARY OF THE CIVIL WAR

LIBRARY OF HEALTH

CLASSICS OF THE OLD WEST

THE EPIC OF FLIGHT

THE GOOD COOK

THE SEAFARERS

THE ENCYCLOPEDIA OF COLLECTIBLES

THE GREAT CITIES

WORLD WAR II

HOME REPAIR AND IMPROVEMENT

THE WORLD'S WILD PLACES

THE TIME-LIFE LIBRARY OF BOATING

HUMAN BEHAVIOR

THE ART OF SEWING

THE OLD WEST

THE EMERGENCE OF MAN

THE AMERICAN WILDERNESS

THE TIME-LIFE ENCYCLOPEDIA OF GARDENING

LIFE LIBRARY OF PHOTOGRAPHY

THIS FABULOUS CENTURY

FOODS OF THE WORLD

TIME-LIFE LIBRARY OF AMERICA

TIME-LIFE LIBRARY OF ART

GREAT AGES OF MAN

THE LIFE HISTORY OF THE UNITED STATES

TIME READING PROGRAM

LIFE NATURE LIBRARY

LIFE WORLD LIBRARY

FAMILY LIBRARY:

   HOW THINGS WORK IN YOUR HOME

   THE TIME-LIFE BOOK OF THE FAMILY CAR

   THE TIME-LIFE FAMILY LEGAL GUIDE

   THE TIME-LIFE BOOK OF FAMILY FINANCE

*This volume is one of a series that explores the world of
science, from the crude observations of the first
astronomers to 21st Century technology.*

GROWTH

by James M. Tanner, Gordon Rattray Taylor
and the Editors of **TIME-LIFE BOOKS**

Revised Edition

TIME-LIFE BOOKS   ALEXANDRIA, VIRGINIA

CONTENTS

LIFE SCIENCE LIBRARY

Staff for the First Edition:
Text Editors: Nancy E. Gross, Alfred Lansing
Picture Editor: Wilbur L. Jarvis Jr.
Associate Designer: Edwin Taylor
Staff Writers: Timothy Carr, Peter M. Chaitin,
Jonathan Kastner, Harvey B. Loomis,
John Stanton
Chief Researcher: Thelma C. Stevens
Researchers: Valentin Y. L. Chu,
Mollie Cooper, Leah Dunaief, Alice Kantor,
Robert R. McLaughlin, Marianna Pinchot,
Susanna Seymour, Rachel Tyrrell,
Victor H. Waldrop

Staff for the Revised Edition:
EDITOR: Rosalind Stubenberg
Chief Researcher: Barbara Levitt
Text Editors: Sarah Brash, Lee Greene
Researcher: Deborah Rose
Editorial Assistant: Mary Kosak

EDITORIAL PRODUCTION
Production Editor: Douglas B. Graham
Operations Manager: Gennaro C. Esposito,
Gordon E. Buck (assistant)
Assistant Production Editor: Feliciano Madrid
Quality Control: Robert L. Young (director),
James J. Cox (assistant), Daniel J. McSweeney,
Michael G. Wight (associates)
Art Coordinator: Anne B. Landry
Copy Staff: Susan B. Galloway (chief), Ann Bartunek,
Brian Miller, Celia Beattie
Picture Department: Rebecca Christoffersen
Traffic: Jeanne Potter

Correspondents: Elisabeth Kraemer (Bonn); Margot
Hapgood, Dorothy Bacon, Lesley Coleman (London);
Susan Jonas, Lucy T. Voulgaris (New York); Maria
Vincenza Aloisi, Josephine du Brusle (Paris); Ann
Natanson (Rome). Valuable assistance was also
provided by: Katrina van Duyn (Copenhagen);
Carolyn T. Chubet, Miriam Hsia, Christina
Lieberman (New York); John Scott (Ottawa); Mimi
Murphy (Rome); Mary Johnson (Stockholm).

ABOUT THIS BOOK

THE COMPLEX, INTRICATE PROCESS of human growth is the subject of this book. An understanding of this process calls for insights from all the sciences concerned with man—from medicine to anthropology—and from experiments on insects, rats and apes. Text chapters and picture essays trace the timetable of human development from conception to maturity, describe the many patterns that growth displays and explore the frontiers of new research which may enable man to influence growth.

The alternating text chapters and picture essays can be read independently, although each essay supplements the chapter it follows. For example, Chapter 6, "Genes, Hormones and Environment," is followed by an essay which pictures in some detail the operation of the endocrine system, which manufactures the hormones that regulate growth.

THE AUTHORS

JAMES M. TANNER is Professor of Growth and Development at the University of London's Institute of Child Health and is Physician-in-Charge of the Growth Disorder Clinic of The Hospital for Sick Children in London. Dr. Tanner, who holds an M.D. from Johns Hopkins Medical School, wrote *Foetus into Man*, an account of human growth for the layman. He is also the author of numerous technical books and articles.

GORDON RATTRAY TAYLOR, educated at Trinity College, Cambridge, is a British writer noted for his popularizations of scientific topics. Among his books are *The Biological Timebomb*, *The Doomsday Book*, *The Science of Life* and *The Natural History of the Mind*. Mr. Taylor has also been an advisor for science programs seen on BBC-TV.

ON THE COVER

The small hand of a child rests on the palm of an adult, dramatizing the changes wrought in time by growth.

1
A 20th Century Challenge

JOURNEY TOWARD ADULTHOOD
Approaching the swiftest years of growth, pre-adolescent playmates frolic on a Saturn-shaped jungle gym in a Los Angeles park. The period that lies close ahead of them is not only a time of tremendously swift increase in size but also years during which a bewildering departure is made from childhood and a start begun on the momentous journey toward adulthood.

OF ALL THE CHALLENGES that confront 20th Century biology, the study of growth is among the greatest and the most exciting. The process meets the eye at every turn. Plants sprout, eggs hatch, and the overalls that fit four-year-old Johnnie in the spring are up above his ankles by winter. But these events, far from being commonplace, are a continual wonder to behold, and many of them still mystify scientists.

Growth is an extraordinarily complicated business, at least in living things. In the realm of inanimate matter, it is relatively easy to understand. There it consists of an increase in size: Crystals grow, for example, and so do icicles and stalactites and stalagmites. But the mechanisms of their enlargement are very different from those that make organic growth possible. The inanimate object grows from the outside, by simple accretion. It merely adds on to its surface more and more of the material of which it is composed.

The living organism, on the other hand, grows by metabolism, from within. It takes in all kinds of substances, breaks them down into their chemical components to provide energy and then reassembles them into new materials. All living things, no matter what their specific natures, have to work in order to grow. This phenomenon is as true of the single-celled amoeba as it is of man.

In addition to an increase in size, organic growth involves differentiation and change in form. The oak tree bears no more resemblance to the acorn from which it sprang than a baby does to the fertilized egg. Living things become more complex as they grow. They acquire specialized parts that they did not have to begin with, and they arrange these parts in a more elaborate way.

The three elements—increase in size, differentiation of structure and alteration of form—constitute something more than simple growth. Together, they comprise development, the series of orderly stages that every organism goes through from the beginning of its life to the end. In everyday speech, the words "growth" and "development" are used almost interchangeably. To the scientist, however, growth is only one aspect of the larger process of development.

No two living organisms are exactly alike. Each grows and develops in a unique fashion within the limits that its environment permits. Every species, however, has its own way of growing, and each has its own rate of growth. The range of variations is overwhelming. In as little as three months, for example, one variety of bamboo that grows in tropical Sri Lanka may shoot up to a height of 120 feet (36.6 m), as tall as a 12-story building, by growing at an average rate of 16 inches (41 cm) a day. A eucalyptus native to Uganda has been known to grow 45 feet (13.7 m) in two years, whereas dwarf ivy generally grows only one inch (2.54 cm) a year. The majestic sequoia of California, which starts out as a seed weighing only one three-thousandth of an ounce (0.0095 g), may end up 270 feet (82.3 m) tall, with a base diameter of 40 feet (12.2 m) and a weight estimated at 5,623.4 metric tons. It takes more than 1,000 years for the sequoia to multiply its mass 600 billion times.

The animal kingdom, too, has its growth champions. The blue whale, found in the oceans from the North to the South Pole, begins life as a barely visible egg weighing only a fraction of an ounce. At birth, it weighs from 1.8 to 2.7 metric tons. When it is weaned, at about seven months, it is 52 feet (15.8 m) long and weighs 21 metric tons, having gained about 200 pounds (90.7 kg) a day. A full-sized blue whale may weigh more than 130 metric tons and reach 100 feet (30.4 m) in length.

Facts and figures of growth, however, are far less interesting to the scientist than the investigation of the many processes involved in growth and development. It is the multiplicity of these processes, the intricacy of some of them, and the recurrence of many of them in all kinds of different things that attract his attention. For example, tapeworms, human hair and animal fur all lengthen according to a similar scheme. Their growth is initiated from one major point. The tapeworm's body develops from front to back, starting from a spot just behind its head. Fur and hair grow from one point, the root. Plants, on the other hand, have at least two growing points, one just behind the tip of the root, the other just behind the tip of the stem.

Sometimes growth proceeds in many directions at once, and at different rates in different parts of the same structure. The inner ear, which transmits aural messages to the brain, begins as nothing more than a thickened mass of tissue in the embryo. In a brief six weeks, by a complex pattern of differential growth, it transforms itself into a closed sphere and then into an elaborate, labyrinthine system of fluid-filled chambers and canals.

Geometry in growth

Rigid objects show another pattern of growth. The shells of marine animals increase in width as well as length, retaining their shapes all the while. Shells are rigid, and cannot be stretched or twisted. How nature solves the problem of retaining shape while expanding size can be seen in a clam shell. The material between any two of the crescent-like lines across its width is one growth unit. Each of these gnomons, as they are called, is a trifle larger in all its dimensions than the one that preceded it. Gnomons permit objects to increase in size without changing in form. They are the growth units for many kinds of rigid things, including marine shells, horns and tusks.

Not all rigid objects grow by the addition of gnomons. If the proportions of the long bones of the body are not to be radically altered as they grow, the diameters of their marrow-filled cavities must increase at the same time that the bones as a whole widen. This kind of growth requires destruction as well as construction. As new deposits are laid down on the outer surface of the growing bone, old ones are destroyed on its inner surface. One group of cells, the osteoclasts, destroys the old bone while another group, the osteoblasts, is building the new.

Cells: the fundamental unit

Bone, shells and nails are essentially secretions, like tears and sweat. They are among the metabolic products of the cells. It is the cells that are the fundamental units of life, and it is in them that the basic mysteries of growth and development are hidden.

All cells are tiny blobs of the kind of matter known as protoplasm. All are made on the same basic plan. A membrane surrounds every cell, defining its limits and containing the cytoplasm, the body of the cell. In the cytoplasm are the nucleus and a variety of specialized parts called organelles and inclusions. The cell functions as a whole, all of its elements interacting with one another. However, each element has its own function. The membrane determines which materials can enter the body of the cell and which materials synthesized within can depart. The cytoplasm is primarily a manufacturing plant. Here the organelles do the work of converting material from the environment into usable form. And the nucleus, through the chromosomes and genes that it contains, is the control center for all the processes of growth and development.

The body of the average adult human being contains perhaps 100 trillion cells. All have developed from one fertilized egg. To produce this fantastic increase in number, cells divide over and over, creating daughter cells that are identical with one another and with their parent. Each daughter cell initially contains half the mass of the parent. But the chromosomes have not been divided in half. Before the cell divided, the chromosomes began reproducing themselves. After division each daughter cell contained precisely the same number and kind of chromosomes as did the parent.

The division process can be seen by examining a stained section of a living plant under a special microscope. As the cell prepares to divide, the chromosomes, which were previously almost invisible and distributed throughout the nucleus in a loosely coiled form, begin to tighten their coils and to appear as distinct rods or V-shaped objects. When all the chromosomes become distinct, each one separates lengthwise into two. Then one set of chromosomes migrates to one pole of the cell, another to the opposite pole. Each set establishes itself within a new nucleus, and a new cell membrane appears in the middle of the old cell. When the cell divides, a full set of chromosomes is available for each daughter cell.

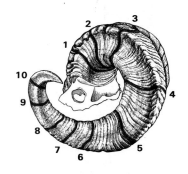

ANNUAL GROWTH RINGS occur in the horn of a ram *(above)* in much the same way as they do in a tree trunk *(below)*. The number of rings that form indicates the age of the organism, while the size of any one ring reflects its growth rate during a particular year. For its species, the 11-year-old ram, whose horn is shown, grew at a normal rate. The 42-year-old tree, however, began life in an unfavorable environment, and so developed slowly at first in its rise to maturity.

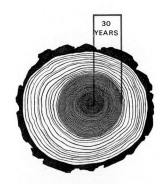

The chromosomes contain all the information needed to construct a complete organism. Every form of life has its own number of chromosomes. The fruit fly has eight, the human being 46. Science has known of the existence of the chromosomes since the end of the 19th Century, but it was not until the 1940s that biochemists began to discover the chemical composition of their genetic material, a substance called deoxyribonucleic acid, or DNA. By 1953 the chemical composition of DNA had been established, and in that same year James D. Watson and Francis H. C. Crick were able to create a model revealing its structure. Their work, which earned them a Nobel Prize in 1962, showed DNA to be a "double helix"—a twisted molecule resembling a spiral ladder. The two sidepieces of the ladder are chains composed of simple sugars alternating with phosphate compounds. "Rungs" running between sugar segments connect the two chains. Each rung consists of a pair of bases, or nitrogen compounds, flanking a hydrogen bond. The order of these bases determines the physical characteristics of the organism containing them.

The processes by which cells grow are reflected in the patterns of growth of the larger structures, such as tissues and organs, that they make up. In some of these structures, the cycle of cellular growth and reproduction continues throughout life, although it proceeds at a particularly rapid pace during the early years. An adult has more skin cells than a baby, and more blood cells too. In contrast with the structures that grow by increasing their total number of cells, others grow after their initial formation only by increasing the size and complexity of their cells. This is the pattern of growth followed by the most specialized organs of the human body. The heart of a newborn baby boy is only one sixteenth as large as the heart of a grown man, but it contains exactly the same number of cells. The same thing is true of the brain. Before birth, every individual has a full complement of nerve cells. With growth, the cells become larger, developing the extensions, axons and dendrites, which interconnect nerve cells. As time goes on, the axons and dendrites become longer, and their interconnections more complex.

Sometimes growth begins again long after it would normally have stopped. When disease requires the removal of one of the two adrenal glands, the other enlarges to compensate for the loss. Similarly, if the heart pumps against abnormal pressure, as it has to in a person who suffers from hypertension, the added work will stimulate an increase in its size and strength.

From flower to fruit

In many forms of life, from plants to man, increases in size and complexity are accompanied by spectacular changes in form. An apple begins as a blossom. Near the base of the flower is the ovary containing

A MOMENTOUS MASTERPIECE, William Harvey's *De generatione animalium* helped launch embryology as a science with its painstakingly accurate descriptions of the stages in the development of the chick embryo. This title page from the first edition of 1651 shows Zeus freeing animals from an egg which bears the inscription "Ex ovo omnia," Harvey's famous, but not entirely accurate, belief that "everything comes from the egg."

ovules, the precursors of seeds. As the blossom transforms itself into a fruit, the skin of the ovule becomes the hard coat of the pip. At the same time, the ovary and other nearby sections of the flower expand enormously, by cell division, until they become the flesh of the apple. The petals die and fall away.

Equally spectacular are the processes that transform a fertilized egg into a baby, the baby into a child, an adolescent, and finally an adult. The changes that occur in the womb are, of course, the most extraordinary, and the forces that lie behind them are still only partly understood.

Some elemental questions

What stimulates a cell to divide? What starts cell specialization? How do these blobs of matter learn to differentiate, to have different forms and to perform different functions? What are the forces that impel similar cells to come together to form tissues and organs? What sets the timetable for the emergence of structures and functions in the embryo? And what can happen in those nine precarious months to upset the delicate balance and cause a distortion of development? What governs the growth of the child after he is born? Why does he grow proportionately more in the first year of his life than in the sixth? Why does his head reach its full size more quickly than his feet? Why do 20th Century girls reach puberty earlier than did those of the 19th?

What are the roles that heredity and environment play in directing growth? And how do they work together with those major body chemicals, the hormones, to determine the child's differing rates of growth at different times of life? How are the changes galvanized that take place at puberty? What turns a boy into a man, and a girl into a woman?

These are some of the questions that science has been asking and investigating, and their answers make up part of this book. Not all of the basic questions can be answered with full confidence, but science is pushing ahead anyway to experiment in much more esoteric and possibly fateful areas. Some of the work being done with animals may sound to many laymen like out-and-out science fiction. Experiments have already produced some fairly bizarre results. Embryologists have circumvented sexual reproduction and created frogs by the technique of cloning, replacing the nucleus of a frog egg with one taken from a tadpole intestinal cell and then stimulating the egg to divide and develop into a physically normal-looking adult. Zoologists have made it possible for inferior strains of livestock to give birth to purebred offspring. Psychologists have derailed normal behavioral growth and development in monkeys and have then set it back on the track.

One day it may be possible to apply this kind of new knowledge for the benefit of man. Then it may be possible to control human growth, not to breed a race of supermen but to guarantee that every child is born healthy and has the opportunity to achieve his maximum potential.

At present, these opportunities are determined in large part by his parents. The environment into which they bring him sharply influences the future course of his growth, and his heredity plays a large part in determining the characteristics he will have. Much of his future is established at the very moment sperm and egg unite. A number of physical characteristics are set at this time: sex, eye color, color and quality of hair, and blood type. At conception he may also be doomed to disease. All of these characteristics are set by the genes contained in the chromosomes. The single cell representing the first stage of development is itself produced by the fusion of two cells. From the father comes the sperm, one of billions continually mass-produced in the testes. From the mother comes the egg, one of which is normally released every month from the ovaries. These two kinds of cells are different from each other, and different, too, from all the other cells in the human body.

The seeds of life

The sperm is the active member of the pair; it has to travel to meet the egg, and it is admirably constructed for this job. The human sperm is a stripped-down cell, shaped something like a tadpole. The oval head, the heaviest part of the cell, contains very little cytoplasm. It is composed primarily of chromosomes tightly packed together. Behind the head is the small midpiece, or body, filled with structures called mitochondria. The mitochondria are power units, which are found in all cells that have a nucleus. They are, however, particularly abundant in the sperm, which needs considerable energy to travel its course. At the end of the sperm is a long, thin tail which whips from side to side to propel the cell. The sperm's streamlined shape and its economy of structure permit it to move at a relatively rapid rate. It travels at an average speed of an estimated one tenth of an inch (0.25 cm) per minute, no small feat for a cell so light and tiny that 100,000 of them tightly packed together would still be barely visible. The sperm are manufactured in almost astronomical quantity: It has been estimated that from 300 million to 500 million are released to meet each egg.

Compared to the sperm, the egg is enormous. It is one of the largest cells in the body, so large that it is visible to the naked eye. Although it weighs only a millionth of a gram, it contains a considerable amount of cytoplasm and a small amount of yolk used to nourish the fertilized egg in its earliest stages. The ovaries contain an estimated 400,000 eggs; from 300 to 400 are released during a woman's fertile years.

When sperm and egg fuse, the father's contribution to his offspring is primarily in the genetic material contained in the head of the sperm.

And it is this contribution that determines the infant's sex. All the cells of the human body, except the sperm and the egg, contain 46 chromosomes, arranged in the nucleus in 23 pairs. One of these pairs is associated with the individual's sex. In women, the members of this pair are identical with each other, both being the so-called X chromosome. In men, however, the members of this pair are not identical. Male cells have one X chromosome and one of a very different type, known as Y.

Not only is there a difference in the chromosomal composition of men's and women's body cells, but the sperm and the egg are different in their chromosomal numbers from all the other cells in the body. The sperm and the egg contain only 23 chromosomes apiece—one member of each pair. This reduction in number, a necessity if the fertilized egg is to have only 46 chromosomes, is accomplished by a special form of cell division called meiosis. Since the precursor cell from which the eggs develop contained two X chromosomes, every egg contains one X chromosome. But the sperm precursors contain one X and one Y. When meiosis occurs, each newly formed sperm may therefore contain either an X or a Y chromosome. Chance seems to determine which members of the chromosome pairs meiosis will give to any egg or sperm—in other words, which of a parent's characteristics the child will inherit. This explains the often startling differences among offspring of the same parents. Chance also seems to determine whether the sperm that finally penetrates the egg is one that carries an X or a Y chromosome. But once the penetration is accomplished, there is no more room for chance. If the chromosome is an X, a female has been conceived. If it is a Y, a male has been conceived.

The parents' equal roles

The facts that the father determines the sex of his child and that both parents contribute equally to its inheritance were not always appreciated. Aristotle recognized that both play a role, but his interpretation of those roles was entirely incorrect. He believed that the embryo developed from a "coagulum" of menstrual fluid; the mother supplied the material, the father the form. But many of his contemporaries disagreed with his view. They held that the father played the only active role. He sowed the seed, and the woman provided the fertile ground in which it was nourished. As the Greek playwright Aeschylus wrote in the *Eumenides:* "The mother of what is called her child is no parent of it, but nurse only of the young life that is sown in her." In the 18th Century, when embryology was still in its infancy, opinion was sharply divided between the spermists and the ovists, between those who believed, with the ancients, that the father was the child's only true parent and those who believed that the mother was, with the corol-

FOLLOWING HARVEY, William Langly published in 1674 his studies on the growing chick embryo. Unlike Harvey's *De generatione*, Langly's work was illustrated with carefully executed drawings like these, which show the rapid changes that occur in the first three days of the chick's embryonic development.

NEW-LAID EGG

BLOOD VESSELS FORMING

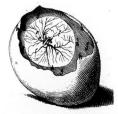

ENLARGING EMBRYO

lary that the father's role was merely to stimulate the growth process.

Although both exclusive viewpoints had been abandoned by the early 19th Century, it was not until 1944 that Harvard University gynecologist John Rock, who later helped develop the birth-control pill, actually witnessed the fertilization of a human egg. Dr. Rock and his assistant, Miriam F. Menkin, took a human egg that had been surgically removed from a woman's ovary and put it in a small dish. Then they put in some live male sperm. After letting the mixture stand for an hour at room temperature, they placed it in a culture of human blood serum. In 40 hours, the single fertilized egg had split into two cells.

It is difficult to tell how long the fertilization process takes in humans, from the moment the sperm begin their journey to the uterus to the moment one of them joins with the egg in the Fallopian tube. Experiments suggest, however, that the time lapse may be about six hours.

Science does not know as yet what the properties are that permit one particular sperm among all the millions finally to succeed, and to make an entry into the egg. It does know, however, that once this entry is accomplished, the nuclei of sperm and egg unite into one. At that moment the fertilization process is completed. And then there begins the long sequence of complex events which, if all goes well, will result nine months later in the birth of a baby.

The Manufacture
of
Building Blocks

The key to growth is the production of protein molecules. During its long journey to maturity, the human body must produce trillions of new cells for its growing tissues, organs and organ systems. The new cells, in turn, are made of new molecules. A majority of the molecules are proteins, whose name is derived from a Greek word meaning "holding first place." Apart from water, proteins are the most important group of substances in the body, accounting for three quarters of its dry weight. Because each species of plant and animal possesses its own unique set of proteins, man cannot utilize directly the proteins he consumes in animal or plant foods. Instead, his body must act as a chemical factory, transforming the food into a set of proteins made to his own measure. This process is growth at its most fundamental level, for without the steady mass production of new molecules, none of the other processes of growth could take place.

WHAT THE CELL NEEDS
As shown on the opposite page, three classes of chemical substances are involved in the growth of cells and thereby the growth of human beings. Nutrients from outside the body—food, water and oxygen—supply raw materials for cell growth, which is the basis for the growth of the body. Genes direct the processing of the materials; hormones speed the processing and stimulate genes.

16

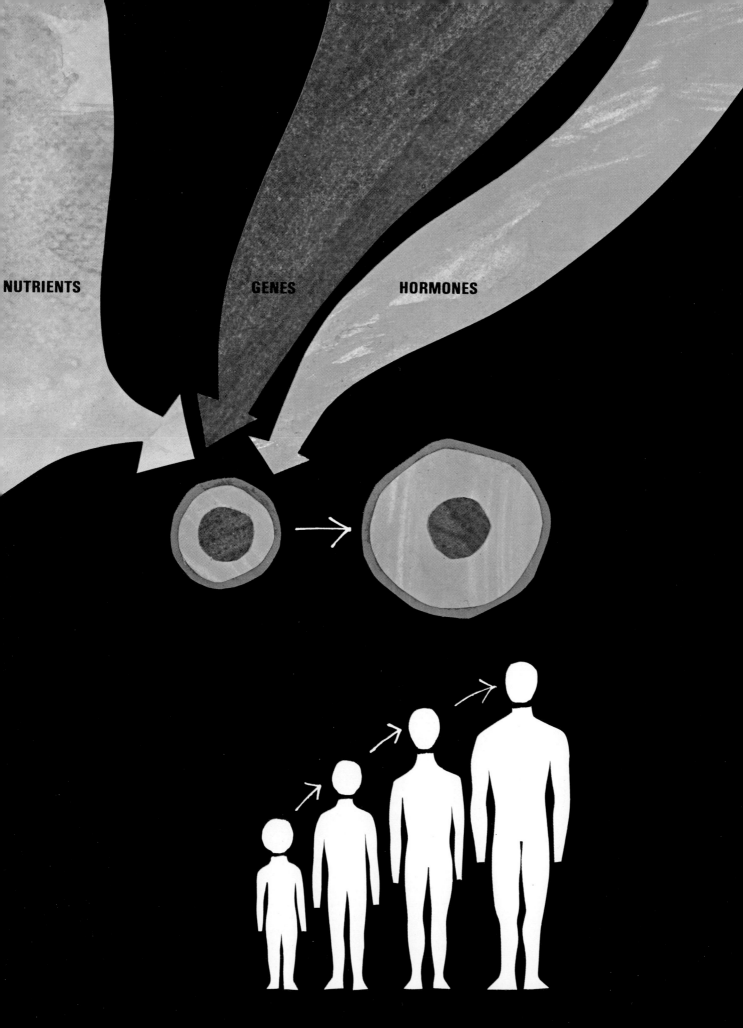

NUTRIENTS   GENES   HORMONES

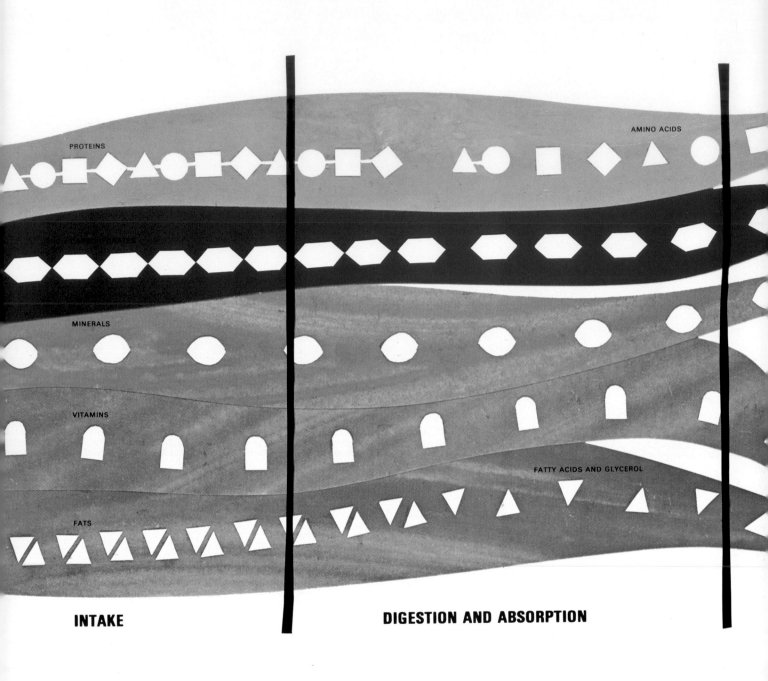

PROTEINS

AMINO ACIDS

CARBOHYDRATES

MINERALS

VITAMINS

FATTY ACIDS AND GLYCEROL

FATS

INTAKE

DIGESTION AND ABSORPTION

The First Step: Raw Materials

Five kinds of chemicals from food, along with water and oxygen, constitute the raw materials for growth. Of these foodstuffs, two—vitamins and minerals—come ready for immediate use. The other three must be chemically broken down into simpler substances before individual cells can admit and utilize them. Until this process has been carried out, these nutrients are as useless to the cell as a whole tree would be to a carpenter. Digestion, starting in the mouth but taking place chiefly in the stomach and small intestine, accomplishes this necessary transformation of large nutrients into acceptably small units. Proteins are split into amino acids (there are 20-odd kinds), carbohydrates into simple sugars, fats into fatty acids and glycerol. From the digestive sites in the alimentary canal, the processed chemicals, as well as the unprocessed vitamins and min-

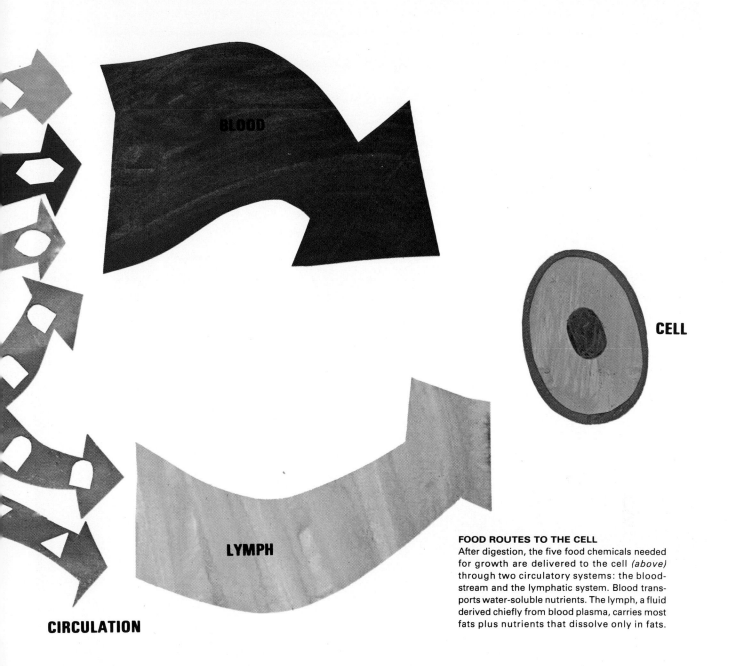

BLOOD

CELL

LYMPH

CIRCULATION

FOOD ROUTES TO THE CELL
After digestion, the five food chemicals needed for growth are delivered to the cell *(above)* through two circulatory systems: the bloodstream and the lymphatic system. Blood transports water-soluble nutrients. The lymph, a fluid derived chiefly from blood plasma, carries most fats plus nutrients that dissolve only in fats.

erals, are absorbed into the bloodstream or the lymph and carried to the cells. There, the amino acids, fatty acids, glycerol and minerals will be assembled into new compounds that will form structural components such as cell membranes. The sugars will be used mostly to supply energy for the assembly process. The vitamins will serve as chemical expediters, or catalysts, which will speed the synthesis of the new compounds.

PROCESSING SITES IN A CELL

This view of a portion of a human cell, magnified 27,000 times by an electron microscope, shows the four basic components that maintain cell life and growth. *(Components labeled above are described in the captions on the opposite page.)* The cell, taken from a human salivary gland, manufactures proteins of the sort called enzymes. These particular enzymes begin to split carbohydrates such as starch into sugars.

20

A

NUCLEAR PATTERNS FOR GROWTH

The nucleus contains genetic "blueprints" that supply the patterns *(symbolized at right)* that govern the cell's assembly of proteins—each kind differently patterned—and other molecules.

B

ACTIVE CELL MEMBRANE

The cell membrane permits some chemicals to seep directly through it, but must actively assist others, such as amino acids. These are conveyed into the cell by "carrier" molecules *(right)*.

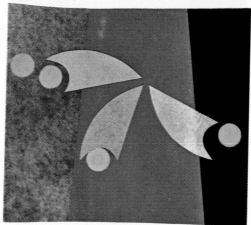

C

MITOCHONDRIAL POWER PLANT

Within the mitochondria, sugars are broken down, releasing energy *(right)*. Packed into storage molecules, this energy will then serve to power growth and all other cellular processes.

D

THE SYNTHESIZING RIBOSOMES

Throughout the cell, ribosomes, using power provided by the mitochondria and acting under nuclear instructions, link separate amino acids into the long chains that are proteins *(right)*.

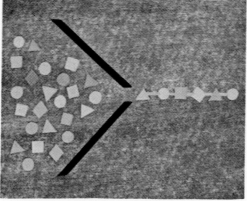

A Microscopic Chemical Factory

The chemical synthesis on which all growth depends takes place in the cell. Programming the activities of this microminiature chemical plant is the nucleus, which contains the instructions for manufacturing proteins and other vital compounds. The raw materials for the manufacturing process enter the cell through an outer membrane about half a millionth of an inch (0.0000012 cm) thick. The cell membrane is a living filter that accepts certain substances and excludes others. When necessary, it can speed up or slow down the entry of molecules from the blood and the lymph. Within the cell, sausage-shaped organelles, called mitochondria, generate, store and supply energy on demand. Depending upon its specific function, a cell may have from one to 500,000 of these power plants. High-production cells, such as those found in the muscles or the pituitary gland, have an especially large complement of mitochondria. The actual work of protein synthesis—assembling amino acids into large molecules —is done by the ribosomes, organelles a millionth of an inch (0.0000025 cm) or less in diameter. Ribosomes are found all through the cytoplasm, usually attached to the membranes comprising the endoplasmic reticulum.

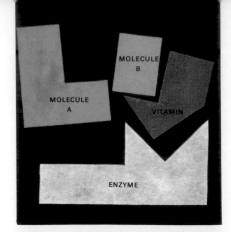

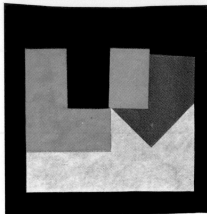

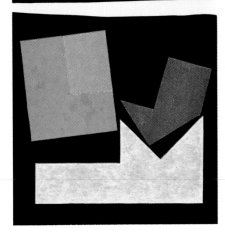

MEETING, JOINING, LEAVING

In the drawings above, an enzyme and a vitamin act as efficient chemical matchmakers, marrying two separate molecules, A and B, into a new compound. The enzyme serves as the one and only common meeting place where this union can occur. A vitamin, acting as temporary escort to molecule B *(top),* is chemically attracted and exactly fitted to a particular site on the enzyme surface. Meanwhile, molecule A drops into an adjacent slot on the enzyme *(middle).* Brought close together, molecules A and B now are so strongly attracted to each other that they quickly merge to form a new substance *(bottom).* As they leave together, the enzyme and the vitamin break apart, preparing themselves to perform their matchmaking task all over again.

The Body's Vital Expediters

For living things to maintain themselves and grow, chemical reactions have to be carried out rapidly. The speedup is performed by chemical expediting agents called catalysts. With the assistance of these catalysts, cells can accomplish in seconds changes that would otherwise require days or even centuries.

The human body uses four kinds of catalysts: enzymes, hormones, minerals and vitamins. Enzymes are by far the most important. Of the body's thousands of different chemical reactions, every one is expedited by a specific enzyme. Assisting the enzymes are approximately 20 minerals, vitamins and hormones.

Enzymes are at work all through the process by which ingested food is transformed into new protein. In the digestive tract, they help to convert foodstuffs into compounds that cells can utilize. Enzymes within the cell membrane help to transport nutrients through it. In the mitochondria, enzymes preside over each step of the intricate process by which sugars are broken down to yield energy. Finally, enzymes play a critical role in the protein assembly line, attracting, clasping and joining small molecules to construct bigger ones *(left).*

Enzymes themselves are classified as proteins—chains of from 124 to 10,000 or more linked amino acids. Thus enzymes help produce more of themselves, in addition to everything that is manufactured by the cell.

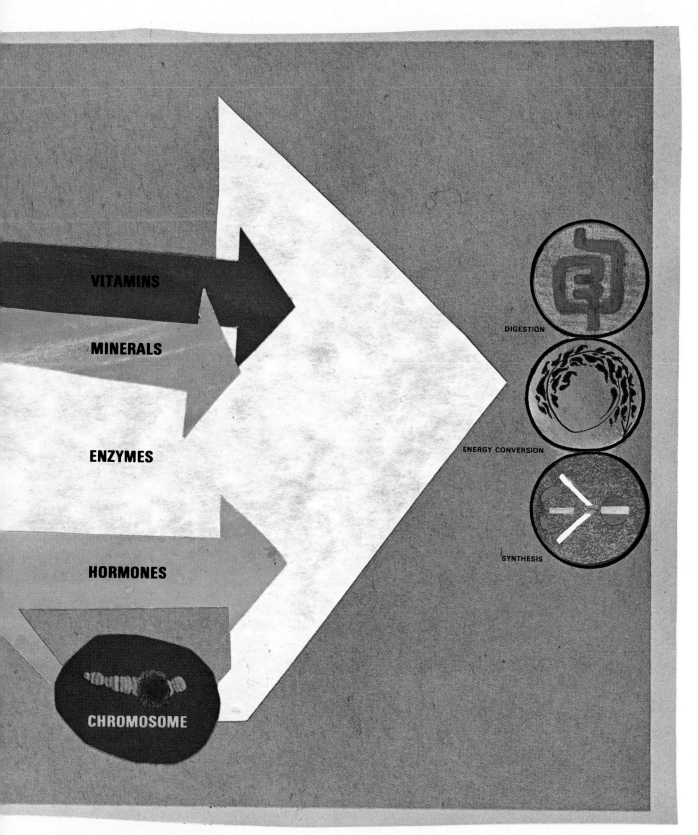

VITAMINS

MINERALS

ENZYMES

HORMONES

CHROMOSOME

DIGESTION

ENERGY CONVERSION

SYNTHESIS

QUARTET OF CHEMICAL BOOSTERS

Four catalytic agents speed virtually all life and growth processes. The enzymes, pre-eminent among these catalysts, sometimes act on their own to quicken such processes as digestion, energy conversion and synthesis *(above, right)*. More often, however, they are assisted by "cofactors": vitamins, minerals or hormones. The hormones also act in league with special proteins, called receptors, to stimulate portions of the chromosomes. In invertebrate animals, a bit of chromosome may respond noticeably to the stimulus by puffing up *(bottom, center)*.

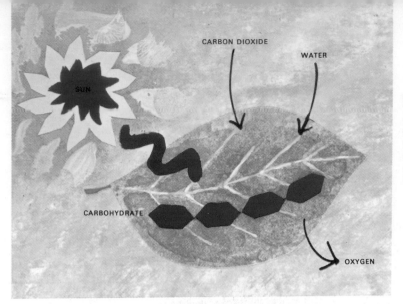

ENERGY PACKAGED BY PLANTS

Through photosynthesis, plants *(left)* convert the energy of sunlight into a form accessible to man. The energy serves to join carbon dioxide from the air with water from the earth, and reassembles their atoms into carbohydrates, energy-rich chains of sugar molecules. Oxygen is a by-product of the photosynthetic process.

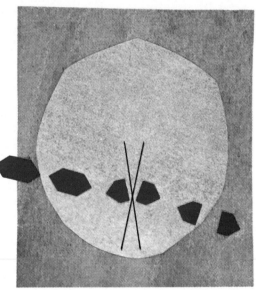

BREAKING UP THE PACKET

In the digestive tract, carbohydrate molecular chains formed by plants are broken up by enzymes into simple sugars, chiefly glucose, that can then be directly utilized by individual cells.

SPLITTING UP THE FUEL

Within the cell, glucose molecules are snipped in two *(above)* in a process known as glycolysis. Each of the 10 or so steps in this process of division is catalyzed by a specific enzyme.

Power for the Protein Factory

Protein synthesis, like every other manufacturing process, requires energy. This energy, like nearly all the forms of energy utilized by man, ultimately derives from the sun. Solar energy, incorporated into chemical compounds by plants, comes to man in the form of plant foods or the meat of plant-eating animals. But these substances, unmodified, are useless to the cell. Like coal shipped to a factory powerhouse, the fuel molecules must be "burned" so that their energy can be converted into a usa-ble form. In this process, food energy is transferred to the compound adenosine triphosphate (ATP), the universal currency of cellular energy transactions. The conversion takes place through a complex sequence of reactions called the Krebs cycle, after its discoverer, Sir Hans Krebs, who won a Nobel Prize for his discovery. The cycle, which "burns" food as a power plant burns coal, harnesses about one third of the energy in food. This efficiency is as great as that of the newest man-made power plants.

ENERGY-CONVERSION CYCLE

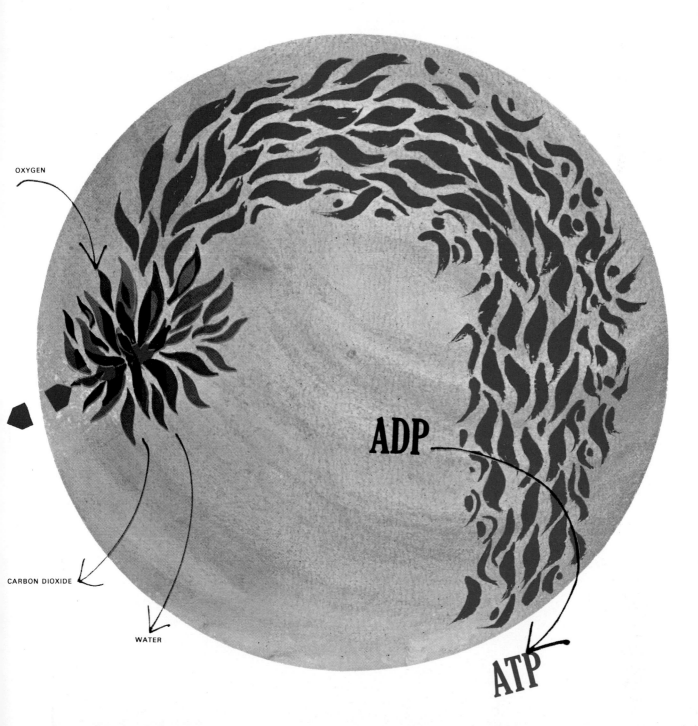

OXYGEN

CARBON DIOXIDE

WATER

ADP

ATP

ENERGY CONVERTED FOR USE
Within the mitochondrion, split glucose molecules are "burned" as fuel in the Krebs cycle *(above)*, which reverses the process of photosynthesis. In photosynthesis, carbon dioxide plus water plus energy yield carbohydrates plus oxygen; in the Krebs cycle, carbohydrates plus oxygen yield carbon dioxide, water and energy. The energy converts molecules of adenosine diphosphate (ADP) into adenosine triphosphate (ATP). During the Krebs cycle, which includes some 20 stages, energy from one molecule of glucose is used to form 36 molecules of ATP.

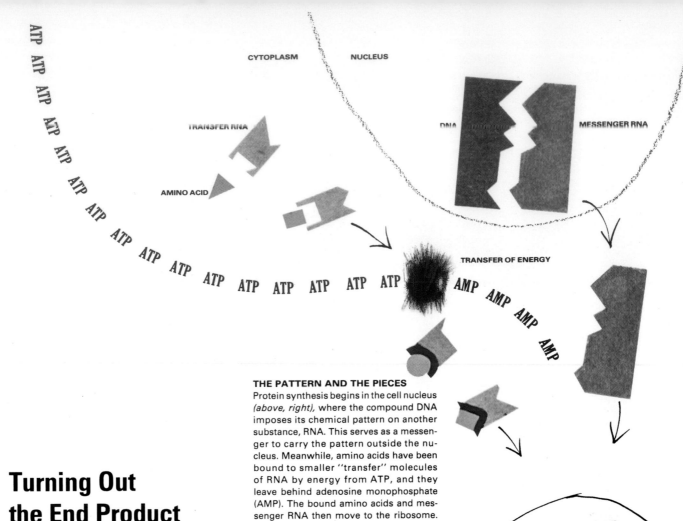

CYTOPLASM   NUCLEUS

TRANSFER RNA

DNA   MESSENGER RNA

AMINO ACID

ATP ATP ATP ATP ATP ATP ATP ATP ATP ATP ATP ATP ATP ATP ATP ATP ATP

TRANSFER OF ENERGY

AMP AMP AMP AMP

Turning Out the End Product

A protein is like a long string of beads, each bead being an amino acid; the sequence of amino acids determines the specific properties of the protein and thus its function. The stringing together of amino acids into proteins, in sequences determined by the cell nucleus, as diagramed on this page, is the key chemical step in the growth process.

The body produces a prodigious variety of proteins, which serve it in all sorts of capacities. They are the major components of hair, skin, muscle, blood vessels and internal organs. Enzymes, the blood's hemoglobin, and some hormones, such as insulin, are all proteins. From birth to age 20, a human being synthesizes an estimated 500 to 1,000 pounds (226.8 to 453.6 kg) of protein, but nearly all of this enormous quantity is required to replace aged or damaged cells. The net build-up in body protein is a very modest 20 to 40 pounds (9.1 to 18.1 kg). In muscle, protein makes up 80 per cent of the nonwater weight; in blood, 90 per cent. Even in bone, the dry weight is 35 per cent protein.

THE PATTERN AND THE PIECES
Protein synthesis begins in the cell nucleus *(above, right),* where the compound DNA imposes its chemical pattern on another substance, RNA. This serves as a messenger to carry the pattern outside the nucleus. Meanwhile, amino acids have been bound to smaller "transfer" molecules of RNA by energy from ATP, and they leave behind adenosine monophosphate (AMP). The bound amino acids and messenger RNA then move to the ribosome.

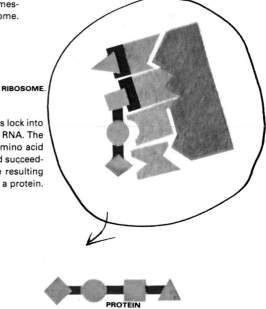

RIBOSOME

THE ASSEMBLY LINE IN ACTION
On the ribosome *(right),* transfer RNAs lock into the patterned structure of messenger RNA. The energy that first served to bind the amino acid to the transfer RNA now shifts to bind succeeding amino acids to one another. The resulting chain of amino acids *(below, right)* is a protein.

PROTEIN

PROTEINS BY THE THOUSAND
The diversity of body proteins is suggested by the permutations of symbols in the painting opposite; each symbol represents an amino acid. Many thousands of different proteins are required in the body. The smallest contains 50 amino acids, others contain tens of thousands.

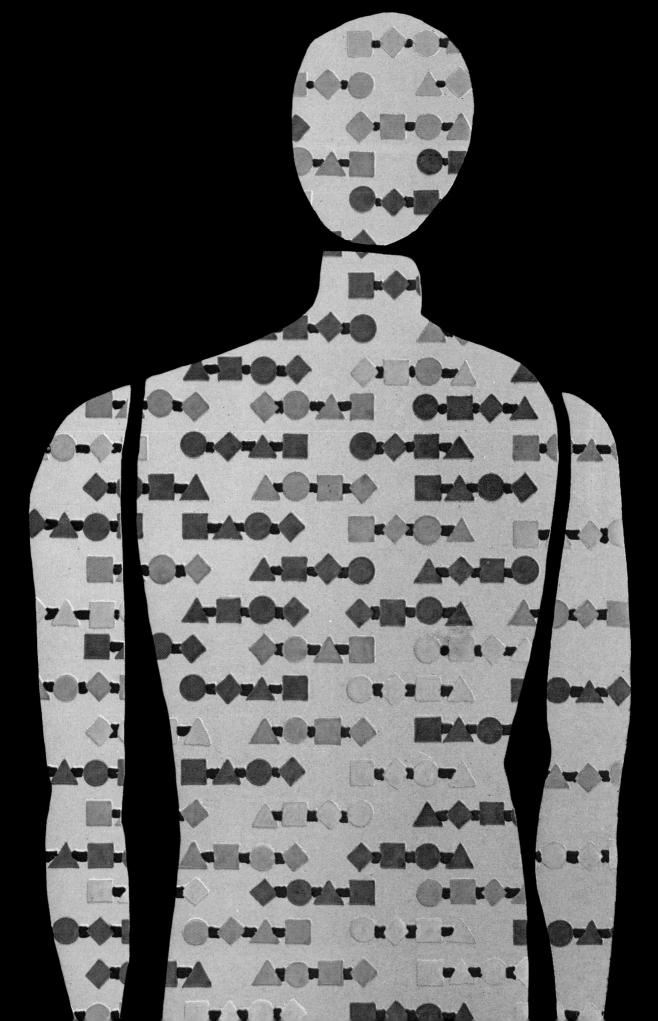

2
The First
Two Months

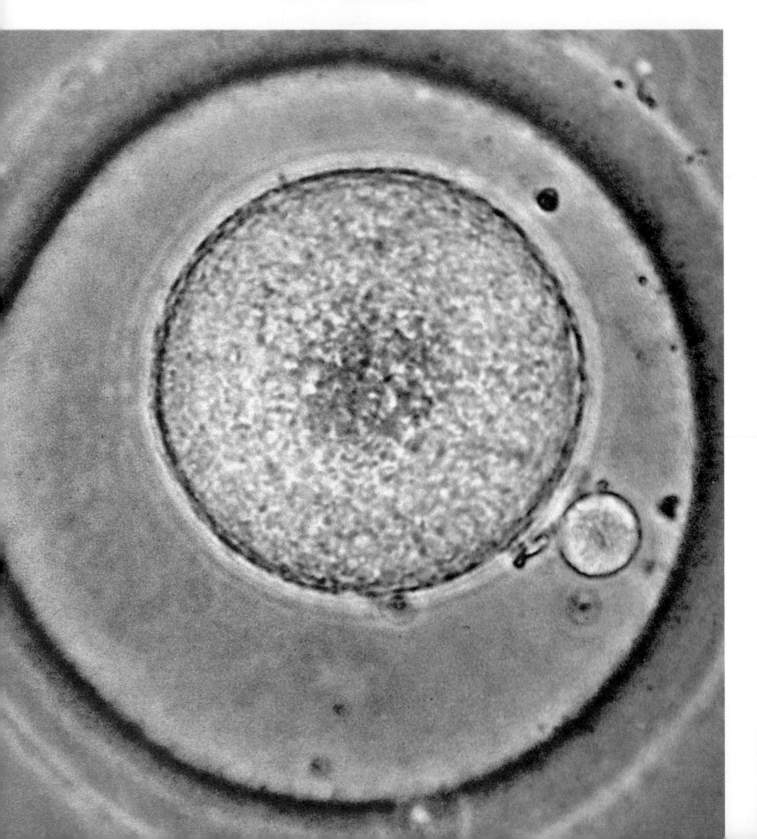

THE PARENTS of a strapping teen-age son may find it hard to remember that their offspring was once a tiny seven-pounder (3.1 kg). In less than a score of years, he has increased in height about three and a half times and in weight more than 20 times, at the same time changing from an infant to a man. But this visible growth and transformation are infinitesimal compared with those that take place in the first two months the embryo spends in the mother's womb. There, in eight brief weeks, the embryo increases in length about 240 times and in weight one million times; it grows from a single fertilized egg into a miniature fetus.

From its mother's body the embryo absorbs the raw materials with which it builds the structures that are needed for life. Elaborate and little-understood mechanisms guard the delicate embryo against harm —even from its own mother. The startling fact is that normal processes of the mother's body should seemingly abort every developing embryo; biologists are still trying to discover why abortions are not the rule rather than the exception. Other researchers are working out the details of how the growing embryo develops, guided by submicroscopic "blueprints" in its cells and further shaped by still-obscure interactions among its own parts. Human growth and development are, from the very beginning, rigorously patterned and controlled.

First come the more vital necessities. The most obvious of these is a nutritional system to supply the embryo with the raw materials for growth. This need the mother's body regularly anticipates. Every month the wall of the uterus grows a thick, spongy lining, rich in blood vessels. If the egg that has been released during this period is not fertilized by a sperm, the lining is sloughed off in menstruation. But if fertilization occurs, the lining remains and grows thicker, readying itself to receive the embryo and to supply it with nutrients from the mother's body.

The sperm and egg unite in one of the Fallopian tubes, the ducts that lead from the ovaries to the womb. The fertilized egg takes three or four days to travel down into its future home, dividing steadily all the time. By the time it arrives in the uterus, it has grown to a spherical cluster of several dozen cells and has begun to change from a solid, spherical cluster of cells to a hollow ball, the blastocyst, with a tiny protuberance at one spot on its inner wall. Most of this little bump, known as the inner cell mass, is destined to become the embryo proper. But the cells that make up the greater part of the blastocyst play no direct part in building the embryo. They, with bits of the inner cell mass, form the embryo's contribution to the structures that will protect and nourish it for the next nine months: the chorion, the outer membrane that surrounds the embryo; the amnion, the fluid-filled sac in which it floats; and the placenta, or afterbirth, where the exchange of materials takes place between mother and embryo.

THE BEGINNING
The growth of every human being begins with a special cell, the ovum, shown on the opposite page magnified 2,000 times. The dark nucleus within the nutritive, yellow cytoplasm contains chromosomes from the mother. Within the protective membrane encircling the egg is a small polar body, a nonproductive sister cell which was formed as the egg matured in the ovary.

On the fourth or fifth day after fertilization, the blastocyst begins to burrow its way into the lining of the uterus, attaching itself in such a fashion that the side on which the inner cell mass lies is in contact with the uterine lining. Almost immediately thereafter, its outer portion, which is known as the trophoblast, begins to grow rapidly. As it does it sends out finger-like extensions, called villi, which also work their way into the wall; simultaneously the outer portion forms the chorion. Other trophoblast cells begin to join with part of the inner cell mass to produce the amnion, the fluid content of which serves to cushion the embryo, and later the fetus, against shocks or pressure from the outside world.

Protection: the first necessity for growth

During the third week, the villi proliferate enormously, and small blood vessels begin to form within them. At one end, these vessels are connected to the embryo through four larger vessels; these, with their surrounding tissues, will later become the umbilical cord. At the other end, the vessels of the villi lie within the uterine lining in close contact with the mother's bloodstream. The interlocking network of villi and uterine tissues, both profusely supplied with blood vessels, makes up the placenta. To this structure, the mother's bloodstream carries foodstuffs and oxygen, while the embryo's carries the waste products of its metabolism. All these substances pass through the placenta: foodstuffs and oxygen from mother to embryo; wastes from embryo to mother, who excretes them through her lungs and kidneys. In addition to serving as a distribution center, the placenta also acts as a barrier, blocking harmful substances that may be present in the mother's bloodstream. But the placenta does not hold back every noxious substance every time. The German-measles virus may pass it, for instance, and so may some drugs, such as thalidomide. If these agents reach the embryo at crucial periods in its development, its growth may be seriously disturbed, and the baby may be born with irreparable mental or physical defects.

The first few weeks after fertilization are a risky time, when perhaps as many as 50 per cent of all embryos are spontaneously aborted. Miscarriages early in pregnancy are generally the result of abnormalities of development, either of the embryo or of the protective and nutritive structures derived from the trophoblast. If the sperm or egg is defective, the embryo is doomed from the moment of fertilization. Heredity may also doom the embryo. Genetically speaking, nobody is perfect: The sex cells of virtually every human being contain some abnormal genes, and if those of both parents carry the same serious abnormality, the embryo may not survive. For example, the fertilized egg may develop to the blastocyst stage, but the inner cell mass may fail to emerge. Or, if it does, it may become nothing more than a disorganized bundle of tissue,

THE EMBRYO'S BRAIN rapidly evolves in complexity as it grows in size *(right)*. During the fourth week of life, the primary areas, fore-, mid-, and hindbrain, become faintly visible. Then within a period of three more weeks, the brain bulges to form its five major subdivisions *(1 through 5)*. By this time the developing brain has become sufficiently elaborate to control the embryo's first simple movements.

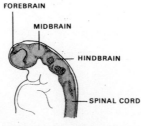

THREE AND A HALF WEEKS

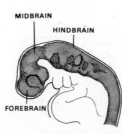

FOUR WEEKS

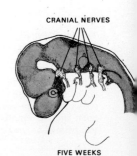

FIVE WEEKS

whose cells have multiplied but have not differentiated properly or arranged themselves into structures. Even if the embryo develops normally, the trophoblast may not. If the villi do not form properly, the embryo will not receive adequate nourishment or oxygen, and it will die. On the other hand, if the uterine lining is imperfect, the blastocyst will be unable to implant itself firmly enough, and growth will cease.

Illness of the mother is a relatively infrequent cause of miscarriage. Only such serious disorders as severe malnutrition, chronic high blood pressure, pneumonia or typhoid fever are likely in themselves to produce an abortion. Contrary to popular belief, physical or emotional shock rarely makes a mother miscarry. The cushion of the amnion, plus the chorion and the mother's own tissues, wards off all but the most extreme physical shocks. In 1963 a pregnant woman in Wales was struck by lightning—and gave birth to a normal baby six months later. Emotional shock seldom upsets the mother's system sufficiently to halt prenatal development.

From the biologist's point of view, the question of why miscarriages sometimes occur is far less interesting than why they do not invariably occur. There are seemingly good biological reasons why every pregnancy should end in miscarriage. Physiologically, the embryo is a foreign substance inside its mother. Since half its genes come from the father, its genetic makeup is different from hers. And the human body does not normally tolerate the presence of tissue that differs from it genetically. Even with special medication, transplants of organs such as kidneys may fail to "take," although the donor and recipient may be closely related, sharing many of the same genes. If a piece of skin from a child—or even fetal tissue —is grafted onto the mother, the graft will degenerate in about two weeks. Yet during the nine months of pregnancy the mother's body tolerates the presence of tissue that is, in part, foreign.

The paradox of tolerance

Since the early 1950s, scientists have been trying to discover the nature of this paradoxical tolerance. The problem is interesting in itself, but also has eminently practical implications. If the tolerance can be reproduced artificially, organs and tissues could be transplanted successfully from any human being to any other.

Two lines of study, each approaching the problem from a different direction, have offered important clues. One school believes that the trophoblast—the group of cells that is the precursor of the chorion and placenta—seems to have some special quality which permits the mother's body to accept it as a nonforeign tissue. And if the trophoblast fails to evoke a "foreign body" reaction, the chorion and placenta, which are derived from it, will presumably follow suit. These structures would

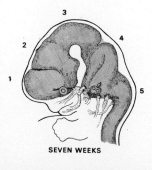

SEVEN WEEKS

thus serve to insulate the embryo against rejection by the mother. Several experiments support this theory. In one, a fertilized mouse egg was implanted on the kidney of another mouse, of a genetically different strain. Though placed in an alien environment, the embryo thrived. In a second experiment, the trophoblast of an early mouse embryo was carefully separated from the embryo proper, and each was grafted onto one of the kidneys of a second mouse, again of a different strain. The embryo quickly perished, but the trophoblast continued to grow and develop, apparently completely unaffected by its peculiar surroundings.

Blocking the mechanism of rejection

Tackling the problem from the opposite direction, a number of scientists are now focusing on the role of the mother rather than the trophoblast in maintaining successful coexistence with the embryo. This approach gained additional validity when it was found that lymphocytes —the cells that cause rejection of foreign tissue—are in fact not warded off completely by the placental barrier but that some, at least, do find their way across it. In response, the mother's body presumably forms a substance—a "blocking factor"—that prevents her lymphocytes from doing harm to the developing fetus.

Somewhat incongruously, this very startling idea of a blocking factor to protect a budding life comes from research work probing the immunology of cancer cells. When Karl Erik and Ingegerd Hellström of the University of Washington grew animal tumor cells in tissue cultures, they observed that lymphocytes impeded the growth of these diseased cells but that this inhibition was overcome by adding to the culture medium serum from the animal that had provided the tumor. Pursuing their investigation further, they were able to isolate factors from the sera that could stick to the cancer cells, preventing the lymphocytes from completing their task of attacking and destroying foreign tissue.

The Hellströms postulated that a similar set of circumstances might exist in normal pregnancy to ensure the survival of the embryo. To test this idea, they grew embryonic cells from pregnant mice in tissue cultures and found that the cells' growth was indeed inhibited by lymphocytes. Furthermore, the embryonic cells returned to normal growth when serum from the pregnant animals was added to them. The Hellströms and other investigators have gathered evidence that "suppressor cells," a type of lymphocyte from the thymus gland, produce a blocking factor that regulates the body's response to embryonic and tumorous tissues. Their work—which not only is of great theoretical interest but also has important implications for the practice of medicine—raises a strange paradox: Immunological processes that permit a tumor to invade the body also produce an environment safe for a growing embryo.

Given this environment, the embryo develops rapidly. By the start of the fourth week, it has already acquired a primitive nervous system with a two-lobed brain. By that time, too, a U-shaped heart has formed. The heart pumps blood through a simple system of vessels within the embryo's body as well as through the blood vessels of the umbilical cord to the placenta, which is now functioning. The embryo has not yet developed any internal apparatus to manufacture its own blood. This job is performed by the yolk sac, a structure which had emerged from the embryo before the heart went into action, had developed blood vessels and begun to produce red blood cells. Until the end of the sixth week, all the embryo's blood will be manufactured by the yolk sac. Then the developing liver will take over the bulk of the job, but will itself gradually be displaced by the bone marrow, which will produce red cells for the rest of the life of the individual.

With the circulatory system set up and functioning, other major structures soon emerge. In the fifth week, the arms and legs begin to develop. In another three weeks fingers and toes will be clearly visible. By the end of the seventh week, the head is recognizably human: Eyes, ears, nose and mouth are present. The embryo has also become much more sensitive to stimuli, a change which reflects the phenomenal growth of its nervous system. The brain by now has developed all five of its major subdivisions, though its surface still lacks the characteristic convolutions. The stomach, which first appeared about three weeks earlier, begins to secrete gastric juices, though it contains no food. The major musculature has also formed, and the skeleton, originally made of elastic cartilage, has begun to turn to bone.

The genetic blueprints

The gross structural changes that take place during the first eight weeks of prenatal life reflect equally profound alterations in the cells that make up the embryo. The blastocyst which first implanted itself in the uterine wall has not only expanded enormously, creating millions of cells from only a few dozen; it has also given rise to cells that are entirely different in appearance and in function both from one another and from the original fertilized egg. In the eight-week embryo, liver cells are clearly distinguishable from cells of the heart; muscle cells and blood cells are not interchangeable; bone cells cannot do the work of brain cells, or brain cells act as bone.

Yet all these cells contain exactly the same genes. Except for the sperm and the egg, every cell in the body has a full complement of hereditary material and thus is potentially capable of performing the functions of any kind of cell. As the embryo develops, however, the cells begin to specialize, "learning" to act on only one of these many possible sets of instructions. This process takes place gradually; little by little the possibilities are narrowed down until at last the cell achieves its permanent and, for the most part, irreversible character.

The embryonic sandwich

Cellular specialization progresses with a speed paralleling that of the structural changes. A mere two weeks after fertilization, the inner cell mass has already developed three distinct groups of cells, neatly arranged in a three-layered sandwich, which have, so to speak, divided up the body's structures among them. The top layer (the ectoderm) will give rise to the nervous system and all the outer coatings of the body: the epidermis, the hair, the fingernails. The middle layer (the mesoderm) will form the musculature, the bones and the cartilage, as well as the heart, veins and arteries. The bottom layer (the endoderm) will produce glands and the linings of such internal organs as the stomach and lungs.

Along with differentiation come two other equally basic cellular processes which shape the body's structures. Cells may change their position or migrate from one embryonic site to another; they may also multiply at different rates, producing a bulge at one place, a hollow at another. Like differentiation, these processes take place gradually. The shifting and multiplying of cells first block out rough shapes, then refine and elaborate them into finished organs.

An early step in this sculpturing process is the formation of the notochord. This structure, a rodlike, primitive spine, develops from a group of mesodermal cells. Above the notochord, ectodermal cells multiply furiously to create a thickened strip, which then curls up into a tube that is the precursor of the spinal cord and brain. Meanwhile, cells from the mesoderm arrange themselves on either side of the notochord in paired blocks, called somites, which will eventually develop into the vertebrae and muscles of the back. Together, these changes provide the embryo with a back and a front, as well as a fore-and-aft axis along which organ systems can arrange themselves. These organ systems, in turn, are formed by the same interweaving of processes of differentiation, movement and growth (described in more detail in the picture essay following this chapter). The digestive system, for example, begins as a tube of mesodermal cells that is lined with cells from the endoderm. As the tube is forming, groups of cells along its length begin to specialize. These cells give rise to the esophagus, the stomach, the liver, the pancreas and the intestines. A pocket branching off from the same tube develops into the lungs and trachea.

The whole process of development seems so extraordinary that early investigators in embryology, studying it under the microscope, refused to credit the evidence of their own eyes. It seemed more reasonable to

"PREFORMED" EMBRYOS, published in 1671 by the Dutch physician Theodore Kerckring, were supposed to represent, from left to right, an opened egg at two weeks, and the skeletons of three- and six-week-old embryos. Kerckring subscribed to the theory of preformation, prevalent in the 17th and 18th Centuries, which held that the human embryo was completely formed at the moment to of fertilization.

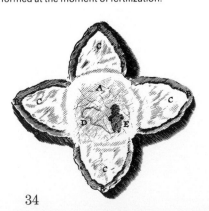

suppose that the parts of the embryo did not develop but rather were present at the moment of fertilization, and simply unfolded, like a Japanese paper flower in water. Charles Bonnet, an 18th Century Swiss scientist, put it this way: "All the constituent parts of the body are so directly, so variously, so manifoldly intertwined as regards their functions . . . their relationship is so tight and so indivisible, that they must have originated all together at one and the same time. The artery implies the veins, their operation implies the nerves, which in their turn imply the brain and that by consequence the heart, and every single condition a whole row of other conditions."

This point of view, known as preformationism, dominated scientific thought throughout the 18th Century, even though the evidence to refute it was already on hand at the time Bonnet was writing his statement. In 1759 a young German zoologist, Kaspar Friedrich Wolff, had published a report on the development of chick embryos, which he had observed under the microscope. His work made it eminently clear that the fertilized egg does not contain a minuscule chicken, and that the embryo changes radically in form as it grows. But Wolff's findings were attacked by the preformationists, and the point of view he espoused—that the structures of the embryo develop in succession—did not achieve general acceptance until early in the 19th Century. And even when Wolff's concept, which came to be called epigenesis, was accepted, the mechanisms through which epigenesis comes about were a long way from being understood. First, embryology had to be transformed from a largely descriptive to a truly experimental science.

The birth of experimental embryology

The transformation was not easy. Living organisms of any kind are difficult to work with: They change constantly, literally under the experimenter's hands. And the living organisms with which embryology deals are the most difficult of all to manipulate. They are so vulnerable that even the slightest damage can completely upset the course of their development. The development of a mammalian embryo cannot readily be followed in its normal uterine environment without risk, and abnormal surroundings in themselves can distort the pattern of growth. Not until the 1920s did refinements of technique make it possible to keep monkey and rabbit embryos alive briefly outside the mother's body, and thus to watch the early stages of their development in the laboratory. Even today no artificial environment has yet been devised that will allow the embryos of any mammalian species to develop to full gestational maturity.

In 1887, when the first systematic experiments in embryology were begun, the techniques available were still extremely crude, and the only

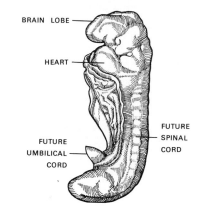

AN ACTUAL EMBRYO, three weeks old, disproves the preformationists' notion that it contains all the body's parts fully developed in miniature. Actually, it is a soft, bulging lump of tissue without any kind of skeleton and composed of only rudimentary parts *(above)*. A mere tenth of an inch (0.25 cm) long, the budding embryo nonetheless has a pulsating heart and two-lobed brain. Other portions will later form the spinal and umbilical cords.

BRAIN LOBE

HEART

FUTURE UMBILICAL CORD

FUTURE SPINAL CORD

embryos that could be worked with were those of creatures such as sea urchins or frogs, which normally develop outside the mother's body in a watery environment that could be duplicated in the laboratory. Frogs' eggs were used by the pioneer experimental embryolgist, a German named Wilhelm Roux. One of Roux's initial aims was to find experimental support for one of the then-current theories of how heredity shapes embryological development. According to this theory, advanced by another German, the biologist August Weismann, the hereditary material in the fertilized egg is progressively divided up in the process of cell division, so that by the time the organism is born, each cell carries only one piece of hereditary information. This information consists of the instructions required to produce one particular type of cell. A heart cell would thus carry only heart-cell information, a brain cell only instructions to build a brain cell. Only the sex cells would retain a complete set of instructions.

Carrying Weissman's hypothesis further, Roux theorized that of the two cells produced by the first cleavage of the fertilized egg, one should contain determinants for all the structures on the right side of the body, while the other should contain determinants for structures on the left side. The second cleavage, occurring at right angles to the first, would then segregate the determinants for the upper half of the body from those of the lower half. Each successive division would reduce the number of determinants per cell and, at the same time, segregate them from one another. Roux also believed that the developments in each cell took place independently of what was happening in every other cell; that is, no part of the developing embryo was in any way influenced by events occurring in any other part.

Wilhelm Roux's tadpoles

To put this theory to the test, Roux took fertilized frogs' eggs immediately after their first cleavage and pierced one of the two cells in each with a red-hot needle. Though only 20 per cent of the eggs survived this drastic treatment, all of the survivors appeared to confirm his point of view. For the brief period that they continued to develop they resembled nothing so much as half-embryos—developing tadpoles split down the middle.

Roux's experiments fascinated the scientific world, and other investigators hastened to try to duplicate them. One of them, Hans Driesch, a German working in a Naples laboratory, undertook a somewhat different version of the same work. Driesch experimented on sea-urchin eggs, using a technique for separating them that was somewhat less drastic than Roux's. Instead of piercing the cells with a hot needle, Driesch put a group of eggs that had reached the two-cell stage into a

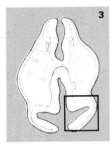

FOREBRAIN AT 24 DAYS

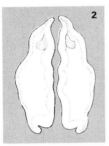

CROSS SECTION

BRAIN AT 25 DAYS

FORMATION OF THE EYE is shown here, beginning with the swelling that appears on the embryo's forebrain (1—front view) around the 24th day. In cross section (2) the swelling is seen as a slight projection on the surface. It enlarges to form a bulge called the optical vesicle (3), which eventually will form the optic nerve, retina, iris and coatings of the eyeball. The vesicle continues to bulge outward from the brain (4), then folds in upon itself (5) to make a cradle for the future lens, now forming on the surface of the head. The cradle deepens to surround the lens (6). By the end of the sixth week, the lens has separated from the surface (7). A week later (8), eyelids have started to form and the main elements of the eye have been established.

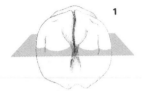

30 DAYS

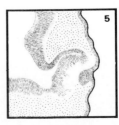

34 DAYS

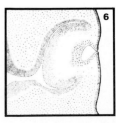

38 DAYS

bottle and shook them until the clusters separated into individual cells. "In order to obtain results," he noted, "one must shake as vigorously as possible for five minutes or more." He then placed the cells in small dishes filled with sea water and left them overnight.

Hans Driesch's sea urchins

"I awaited in excitement the picture which was to present itself in my dishes the next day," he later wrote. "I must confess that the idea of a free-swimming hemisphere or even a half [embryo] with its [gut] opened lengthwise seemed rather extraordinary. I thought the formations would probably die. Instead, however, the following morning I found typical, actively swimming [embryos] of half size."

Driesch repeated his experiment, using embryos that had reached the four-, the eight- or even the 16-cell stage. Shaken free, the individual cells still developed into complete embryos. Clearly, even after the fertilized egg had split several times, every cell still contained all the necessary information for the production of a complete organism. The results, of course, flatly contradicted Roux's findings, which Driesch believed to have been caused by using a primitive technique: The pierced cell, still hanging on to the live one, had somehow impeded its development.

Driesch's experiments not only cast doubt on the validity of Roux's theory, but also raised some new and fundamental questions. How could half of an embryo, or three quarters or even $^{15}/_{16}$, proceed to a normal development? If the hereditary material was not parceled out to the different cells, how did they "learn" to differentiate and form themselves into structures?

It was still another German, Hans Spemann, who provided the first answers to these questions. Spemann proved conclusively that the development of the fertilized egg is determined not merely by the genetic material in its nucleus, but also by an interplay between this material and the rest of the cell. Moreover, he discovered, the principle of interplay operates throughout the development of the embryo. Each successive step in cell differentiation and the development of structure is influenced by surrounding cells and is the result of steps taken before.

Spemann died in 1941, only six years after he received the Nobel Prize in medicine for his "discovery of the organizer effect in embryonic development." To the study of this principle he devoted more then 30 years of his professional career. Viewed superficially, his experiments seem very narrow in scope. Most of them concerned the development of certain organs, such as the eye in the newt embryo, but their theoretical implications were far wider.

When Spemann began his experiments on the newt eye, he already knew its step-by-step developmental timetable. The eyes begin as two

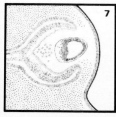

40 DAYS

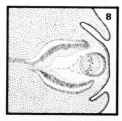

49 DAYS

small swellings on the embryonic newt's brain. These push through the surrounding tissue and press outward against the coat of ectoderm that encases the embryo. Soon the swellings change form, turning into mushroom-shaped structures with stalks running to the brain and caps close to the embryo's outer skin. The caps begin to dent inward at the center to produce a double-walled cup. The inner wall of this optic cup eventually forms the light-sensitive cells of the retina, while the outer wall forms the pigmented portion of the retina. While the retina is being formed, the outer coat of ectoderm is also changing. Moving inward to follow the shape of the eye cup, it gradually becomes transformed into the lens, which will focus light rays entering the eye. After the optic cup and the lens have been formed, the protective window, called the cornea, develops.

Development through induction

Spemann discovered that an eye can be grown in this manner virtually anywhere on the surface of the developing embryo, not just in the head. For example, when Spemann placed the eye cup from the head of a newt embryo just under the ectoderm of the animal's belly, the ectoderm cells of the belly promptly formed themselves into a lens. The embryo soon had an eye growing in its belly. Clearly, ectodermal cells far from the head region could be made to form a lens.

Further experiments showed that similar processes, which Spemann called "induction," operated at the very earliest stages of development. Making use of a technique developed by a colleague, Oscar Hertwig, Spemann looped a strand of baby's hair around a fertilized newt egg before its first cleavage and tightened the loop so that the egg was forced into the shape of an hourglass. Soon the egg cleaved and the two halves separated—but the fate of the two halves seemed unpredictable. Sometimes both developed into normal embryos. At other times one developed normally while the other produced only a disorganized blob of tissue which died. This unpredictability was not caused by Spemann's technique. The critical factor was the composition of the separated cells. When both contained a nucleus and a section of the surrounding cytoplasm called the gray crescent, both developed normally. If only one of these elements was present, development was invariably abnormal. Both were necessary, if the egg was to become an embryo.

This was Spemann's major discovery: At every stage of embryonic development, structures already present act as organizers, inducing the emergence of whatever structures are next on the timetable. In the fertilized newt egg, the gray crescent is the forerunner. As the egg divides, the group of cells derived from this area of the egg becomes the "primary organizer," galvanizing other cells to shape them-

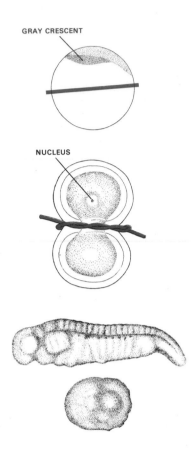

GRAY CRESCENT

NUCLEUS

A SPEMANN EXPERIMENT early in the 20th Century revealed the cellular elements that determine whether or not an egg becomes an embryo. The German zoologist divided a newt's egg in two by tying a strand of baby's hair around it, leaving a protoplasmic bridge between the halves. Nuclear material passed over the bridge, starting cell division in both halves, but only one half developed into a normal newt: the half containing an area called the gray crescent. The other half, lacking a gray crescent, became a disorganized mass of cells.

selves into specific forms. The organizer cells themselves become the notochord and the somites. The notochord and the somites induce the ectoderm to form the neural tube, from which in turn the brain and the spinal chord develop.

Spemann became certain that he was right when he found that the primary organizer will induce the formation of later structures even after the process of development is fairly well under way. In one experiment, he transplanted the organizer cells from one young newt embryo to a second embryo. The result was a set of embryonic Siamese twins. The graft induced formation of a secondary embryo upon the first, an embryo complete with spinal column, head, trunk, legs and tail. Some of its tissues came from the graft cells, but others came from the host cells. This happened even when the graft and the host were of different species.

Human development is shaped by essentially the same forces that Spemann discovered in newts. Scientists do not yet know what part of the human egg corresponds to the gray crescent in the newt, but they have tentatively identified the structure in the embryo that acts as the primary organizer. The structure, called the "primitive streak," is a group of ectodermal cells that emerges at one end of the embryo about the 14th or 15th day after fertilization. It is from the primitive streak that the mesoderm develops, and it is from the mesoderm that the first embryonic structures—the notochord and somites—are built. And as in newts, so in humans, it is the notochord and its associated structures that organize the rest of the embryo.

Obviously, then, an embryonic cell is influenced by the other cells in its environment. These other cells gradually lead it to act on only one of the many possible sets of instructions that it contains. Once these instructions have been issued, the embryonic cell tends to assume and retain a specific character. When organizer cells that would normally induce the neural tube to form are transplanted to an embryo well along in its development, nothing happens. The process of differentiation has gone too far to be changed.

The end of an eight-week journey

The interplay between the genes and their environment was demonstrated even more dramatically by a pupil of Spemann's, Otto Mangold. Mangold worked with two kinds of salamanders, the axolotl and the newt. These two creatures are somewhat different from each other even in the embryonic stage. The newt embryo has antenna-like structures, called balancers, near its mouth. The axolotl does not. When Mangold transplanted belly skin from an axolotl embryo to the face of a newt embryo, it developed into head tissue, but without balancers. On the

GRAY CRESCENT

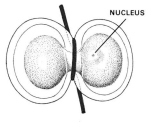

NUCLEUS

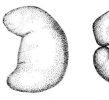

IN ANOTHER EXPERIMENT Spemann developed two perfect embryos when he tied a strand of baby's hair around a newt's egg so that part of the gray crescent fell in each half. The half containing the nucleus of the egg developed on schedule, but the other half lagged slightly behind because, at the outset, it had no nucleus. Eventually nuclear material from cell division which had occurred in the first half of the newt's egg migrated across the protoplasmic bridge to start cell division in the second half. After that, it too formed a newt.

other hand, when he reversed the process and transplanted newt belly skin onto the face of an axolotl, balancers developed. Evidently the newt embryo could make head tissue out of tissue that would normally have become belly skin, but could not force it to form balancers, because the axolotl cells did not contain instructions for doing so. But when an axolotl embryo induced newt skin to form head tissue, the balancers appeared, since instructions for them were built into the newt cells. Though inducting substances can galvanize development even outside their own species, the only kind of development they can trigger is that for which the receiving organism already has genetic blueprints.

All these experiments have shed new light on the transformation of a fertilized egg to an embryo and then a fetus. In a sense, both the epigenetic and the preformationist points of view are true. Many characteristics of each human being are determined, at the very moment of fertilization, by the united genetic material of an egg and a sperm. This material will in large measure establish the way in which the individual develops, not merely during its first eight weeks but long afterward. But the order and timing of development are determined by the interaction of this genetic material with its environment. Cells are shaped by the cells around them, and their collective, interacting development shapes the embryo.

Creating an Organism with Cells

The study of growth between fertilization and birth is remarkably well documented. Scientists know that the multiplication of cells enlarges the organism, that the movement of groups of cells helps shape the organism, and that differentiation alters the form and function of cells to prepare them for different duties. They know that some cells must die to help shape the living organism. The chromosomes, and specifically their components, the genes, are known to play the role of planners and supervisors. To gather this information, scientists have observed the growth of human fetuses where possible, and supplemented their study with experiments on animals. To illustrate their findings, they have resorted to a variety of techniques, such as the diagrams, drawings and photomicrographs shown on the following pages. Still remaining at the bottom of the ever-increasing body of knowledge is the persistent question: "How?"

A TRIUMVIRATE OF BODY BUILDERS
The three processes through which the body develops and grows—the multiplication, movement and differentiation of cells—may be thought of as lying at the points of a triangle *(opposite)*. Guided by the genes, each of the processes exerts the necessary influence at exactly the right moments of development, working, separately or in concert, steadily to complete the product, a human being.

MULTIPLICATION

MOVEMENT

DIFFERENTIATION

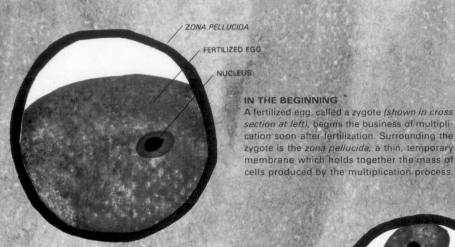

ZONA PELLUCIDA
FERTILIZED EGG
NUCLEUS

IN THE BEGINNING
A fertilized egg, called a zygote *(shown in cross section at left),* begins the business of multiplication soon after fertilization. Surrounding the zygote is the *zona pellucida,* a thin, temporary membrane which holds together the mass of cells produced by the multiplication process.

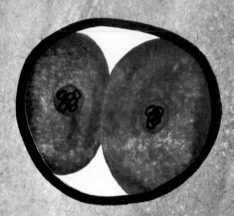

TWO CELLS FROM ONE
The first multiplication, in which the zygote splits in two, is completed within 36 hours. The daughter cells are identical to the zygote in every respect, but are only half its size.

MORE BUT SMALLER
By the fourth day, the *zona pellucida* is packed with several dozen cells. All are substantially smaller than the zygote from which they are descended, but remain otherwise identical.

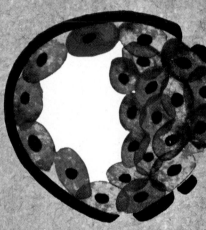

THE START OF MOVEMENT
On the fifth day, cell movement begins. Th[e] cells in the outer ring will form the placent[a]. Those clumped at the right, called the inner c[ell] mass, are the beginnings of the embryo itse[lf].

The Simple Beginnings

During the first two weeks of human development the cellular processes of growth—multiplication, movement and differentiation—are at their simplest and most comprehensible. Multiplication begins almost at the moment of fertilization, and for the first few days is the only process in operation. Cells are reproduced in a geo- metric progression, one cell divid- ing into two, then two into four and so on. As the blastocyst, as it is called, grows, cell movement begins to orga- nize the mass of cells, first into an ir- regular hollow ball, then into more elaborate shapes such as the embry- onic disc, which sets the stage for the third process, differentiation. It is

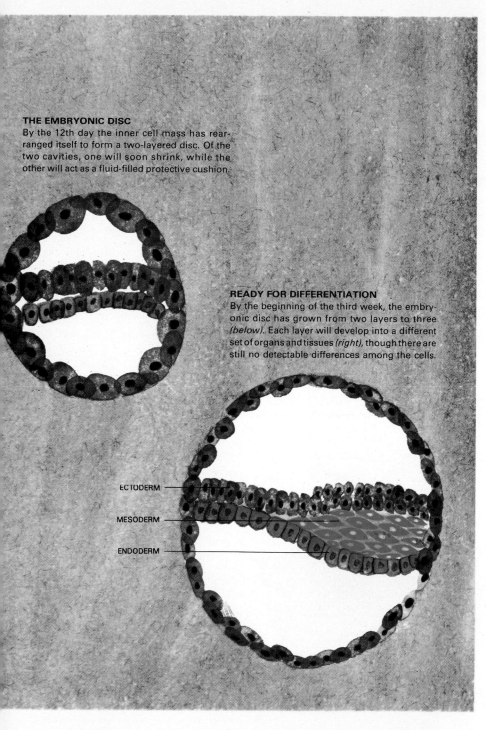

THE EMBRYONIC DISC
By the 12th day the inner cell mass has rearranged itself to form a two-layered disc. Of the two cavities, one will soon shrink, while the other will act as a fluid-filled protective cushion.

READY FOR DIFFERENTIATION
By the beginning of the third week, the embryonic disc has grown from two layers to three *(below)*. Each layer will develop into a different set of organs and tissues *(right)*, though there are still no detectable differences among the cells.

ECTODERM

MESODERM

ENDODERM

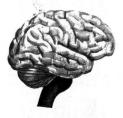

THE THREE-LAYERED DISC:
FOUNDATION OF THE MAN

ECTODERM, THE OUTER LAYER
Not surprisingly, cells from this section of the disc form the body's outermost tissues, the skin, hair and nails. But some will develop into the brain and the rest of the nervous system.

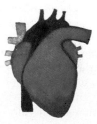

MESODERM, THE MIDDLE LAYER
This group of cells will develop into the skeleton and bone marrow, the muscles, heart and blood corpuscles, and also form the inner skin layer, the blood vessels, kidneys and gonads.

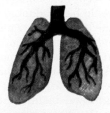

ENDODERM, THE INNER LAYER
From these cells will spring the linings of nearly all of the internal organs, including those of the lungs, trachea and pharynx, and digestive tract including the pancreas and the liver.

uncertain at just what point differentiation begins its irrevocable changes by which the cells are gradually modified for specific functions. But by the end of the second week, groups of cells have embarked on the different paths that will eventually result in the specializations necessary for the formation of the mature organism.

43

Embryonic Disc to Working Tissue

Perhaps the least understood of the various aspects of development is differentiation. In searching for an analogy to the mechanisms of development, biologist John Tyler Bonner of Princeton University has compared multiplication to the work of a sculptor "who continually adds clay to make a shape," and cell movement to the "pushing and the modeling of the clay." But there the analogy ends, for there is no process, either natural or man-made, that parallels the invisible chemical changes within developing cells that bring about vastly differing forms and functions.

Without differentiation a complex organism such as man could not exist. By producing cells with specific abilities to perform specific jobs, differentiation makes possible a division of labor within the body. The cells that form heart muscle, for example, would be ill adapted to do the work of the lungs or nervous system.

Whether differentiation is accomplished in one step or in many is unknown. Although the mechanisms of the process remain largely mysterious, its gradual manifestations are omnipresent. They are readily observable in the generation of the great variety of organs and structures, such as the heart and lungs (*right*), from different layers of the embryonic disc.

THE ENDODERM

THE LUNGS
The lungs, like many internal organs, are composed of cells that spring from more than one layer of the embryonic disc. They begin their development with the thick lining of endoderm cells *(opposite, left)* which becomes steadily thinner as the lungs grow. After birth, the air tubes are expanded *(far right),* and the lining of the tiny air sacs has become thin enough to permit inhaled oxygen to be transferred to the blood in exchange for carbon dioxide.

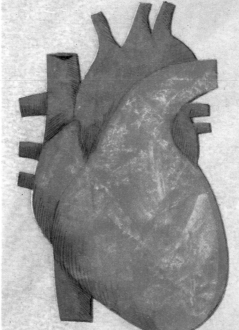

THE MESODERM

THE HEART
Since the fetus must draw sustenance from the mother's bloodstream early in development, the heart and circulatory system become the first functioning system in the body. By the fourth week the system is operational, though rudimentary. Like almost every other muscle, the heart is formed from mesodermal cells. Its mature form is achieved by the eighth week, although the development of individual cells *(opposite, left)* is not nearly complete *(far right).*

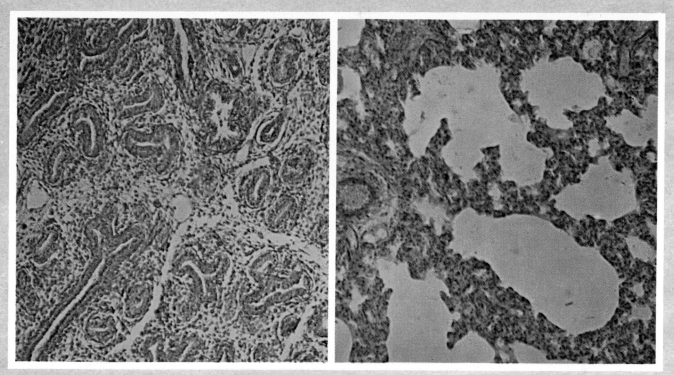

The lighter areas of lung tissue in a 12-week fetus *(left)* become enlarged after birth *(right),* when respiration fills the lungs with air.

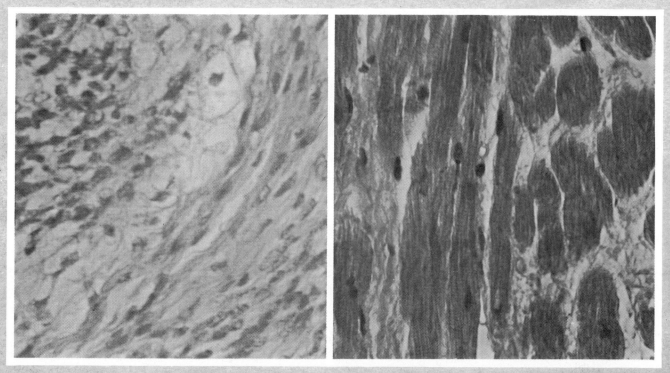

In the third month *(left),* the heart cells are poorly defined, and are noticeably narrower than those of a mature heart muscle *(right).*

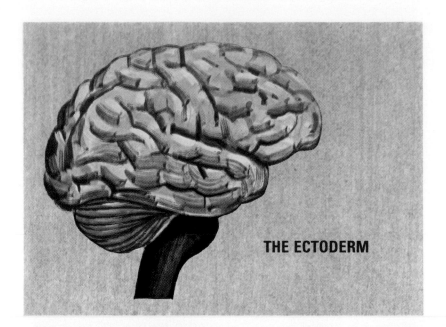

THE ECTODERM

Forming the Network of Nerves

The nervous system, the body's complex communications network, starts to develop during the third week. Its progenitor is a section of ectoderm called the neural plate *(bottom left)*. The entire system evolves from this plate: massive structures like the brain *(left)* as well as the delicate fibers of motor neurons *(right)*. The full complement of nerve cells—perhaps 100 billion or more in humans—is present by the time of birth. From that time on, no new nerve cells will be added; existing cells will enlarge to keep pace with normal body growth.

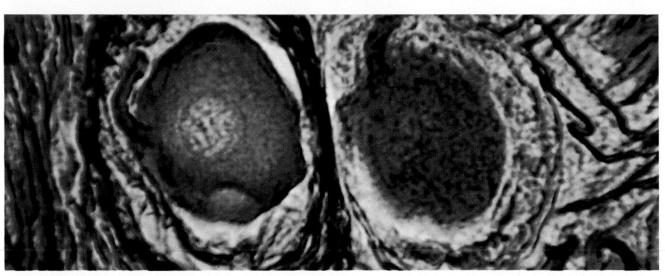

CELLS OF THE SENSES

Two sensory neurons, which were formed in the neural crest *(3, below),* appear above in their mature state. The cells are unipolar: They have only one fiber attached to the cell body. In the photomicrograph above, the fibers extend to the left of each cell. Outside the cell body the fiber divides. One extension goes to the skin or other sensory area to pick up stimuli; the other transmits the stimuli to the spinal cord.

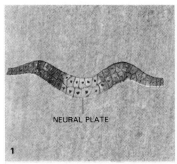

1

NEURAL PLATE

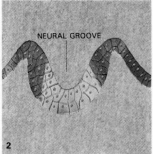

2

NEURAL GROOVE

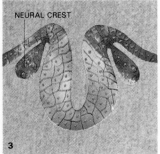

3

NEURAL CREST

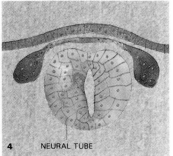

4

NEURAL TUBE

RISE OF THE NERVOUS SYSTEM

The development of the neural plate, illustrated in cross section about 150 times actual size, shows how cell movement molds a complex structure from a single layer of cells. First the plate thickens and bulges downward (1). The bulge enlarges (2 and 3) until the edges of the plate, along with the cells at the tips of the folds, fuse (4), forming the neural tube and two rows of cells. The tube *(yellow)* forms the brain and spinal cord, including motor neurons *(opposite).* The rust-colored layer gives rise to sensory cells *(above),* and the top layer *(pink)* will become skin.

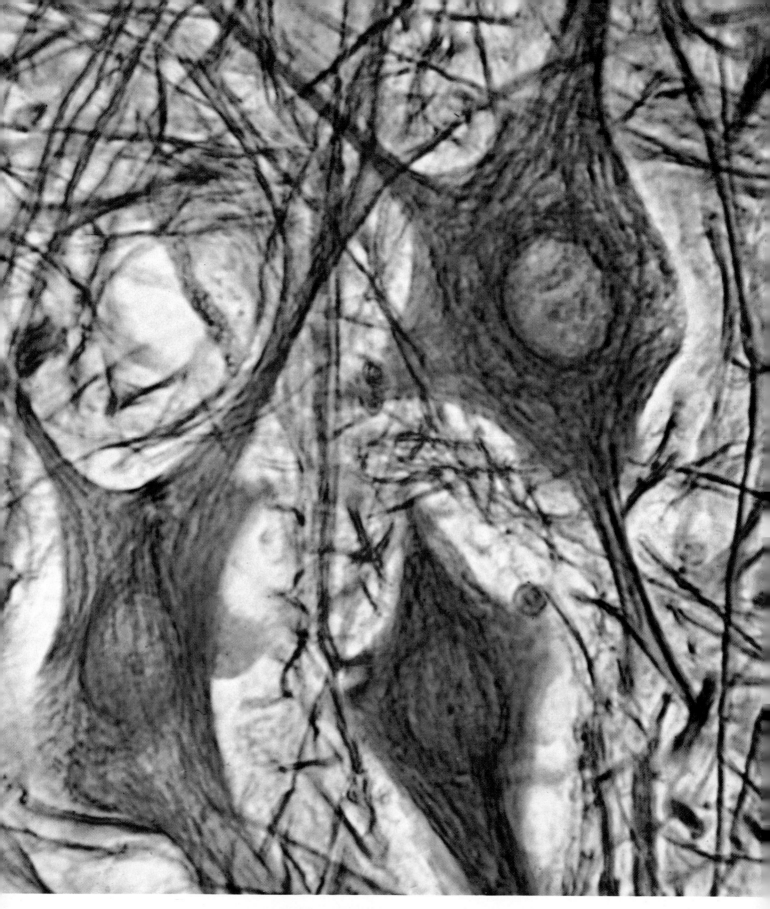

THE WEB OF WORKER CELLS
Three motor neurons, products of the neural tube, stand out against their conducting fibers in the spinal cord. Unlike the sensory neurons opposite, which receive impulses from only one site, the motor neuron's many fibers pick up instructions from thousands of sources in the brain and spinal cord. A single output fiber carries the message to activate the muscles.

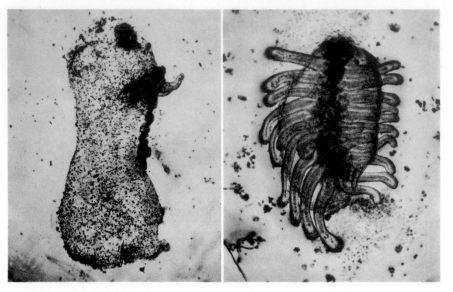

CELLS THAT HELP OTHER CELLS
Clear evidence of induction is provided in these photographs of skin taken from a chicken embryo. When French biologists Etienne Wolff and Philippe Sengel grew skin tissue in a culture without nerve cells, the resulting skin was bald *(far left)*. Another fragment of skin from the same embryo, kept alive in a culture of brain extract, sprouted feathers on schedule *(left)*.

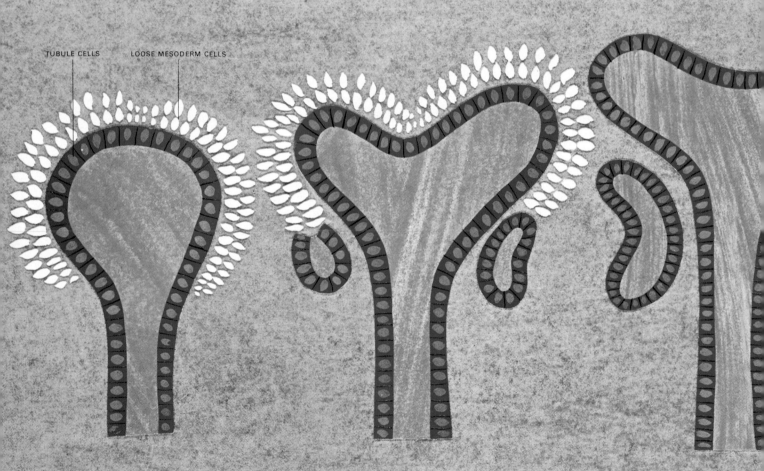

TUBULE CELLS   LOOSE MESODERM CELLS

INTERACTION BUILDS A KIDNEY
Kidney tubules, tiny tubes which extract wastes from the bloodstream and pass them to the bladder, begin to form in the sixth week as two types of mesodermal cells begin to interact.

BRANCHING BEGINS
By the seventh week the loose mesoderm cells around the immature tubule cause it to branch out. Simultaneously the tubule cells influence the loose cells to form two spherical masses.

REACHING FOR UNITY
During differentiation both the tubule and its two associated groups of cells have enlarged. Interaction continues to operate, stimulating the three bodies to grow toward one another.

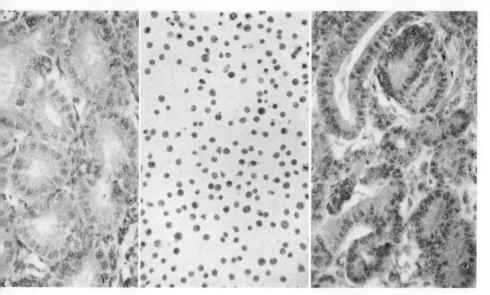

A KIDNEY RESTORED
To demonstrate that certain cells retain the ability to interact even when the structure they have formed is destroyed, biologist Aron A. Moscona experimented with nearly mature kidney tissue from a chick embryo. The tissue *(left)* was broken into a disorganized group of cells *(center),* which soon regrouped, forming a new tissue remarkably like the original *(right).*

The Importance of Control

Development, which is initiated by changes in the structure or location of individual cells or cell groups, soon comes under the control of more sophisticated processes in which cells must interact with one another. Following a genetically preset schedule, a cell or group of cells releases substances that cause neighboring cells to embark on a new course of development, a process called induction. In the embryonic chick, for example, skin cells will not differentiate into feather cells until nerve cells are also present *(opposite, above).* In the human fetus, two relatively unspecialized types of cell unite to form kidney tubules—but only in the presence of each other *(left).*

Cellular interaction not only induces individual cells to differentiate, but also prompts groups of cells to arrange themselves into functioning organs *(above).* These interactions are a fundamental part of orderly development, for nerves, muscles, bones and blood do not function in isolation. Each must be ready at the right time and in the right place for the growing organism to survive.

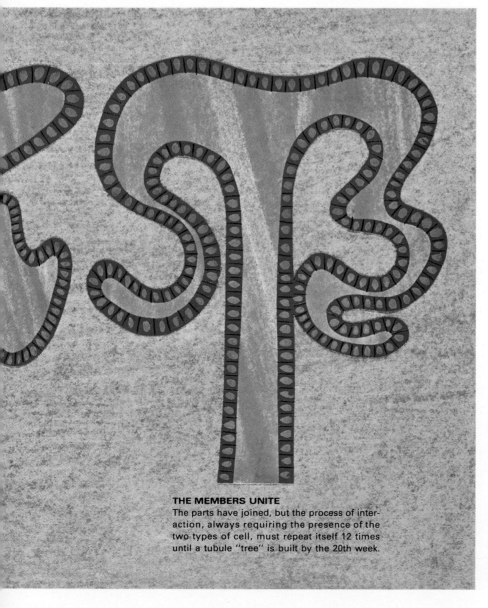

THE MEMBERS UNITE
The parts have joined, but the process of interaction, always requiring the presence of the two types of cell, must repeat itself 12 times until a tubule "tree" is built by the 20th week.

A CHANGE IN SHAPE
The metamorphosis of the Southern bullfrog provides a spectacular example of the role of cell death. For three to six months after hatching, the tadpole grows but retains its fishlike shape. After attaining full growth its tail cells begin to die off. The tail shrinks steadily until, 15 months after hatching, the tadpole has become a frog. For the remainder of its life, the frog continues to grow but its shape does not alter.

Death to Form the Living

The mass production of new cells is so obviously important to growth that it tends to obscure an equally significant process. Surprisingly, destruction rather than production of cells is the determining factor in shaping some parts of the embryo.

Cell death is most crucial in major reorganizations of form such as the metamorphosis of a tadpole into a frog *(opposite)*, or the transformation of a stubby chunk of tissue into a highly organized limb *(right)*. But it is as important in human embryos, whose hands and feet first appear as solid lumps; the sculpting of the fingers and toes requires the death of many thousands of cells.

One way in which such "sacrifices" are accomplished has been discovered. In a metamorphosing tadpole, each tail cell contains a sac of enzymes called a lysosome. At a genetically determined time, the sac's membrane ruptures and releases the enzymes, which then digest the contents of the cell. It may be that the same mechanism operates in the human embryo. What happens to dead cells is unknown, although it is possible that scavenger cells reprocess their chemicals for use elsewhere in the body.

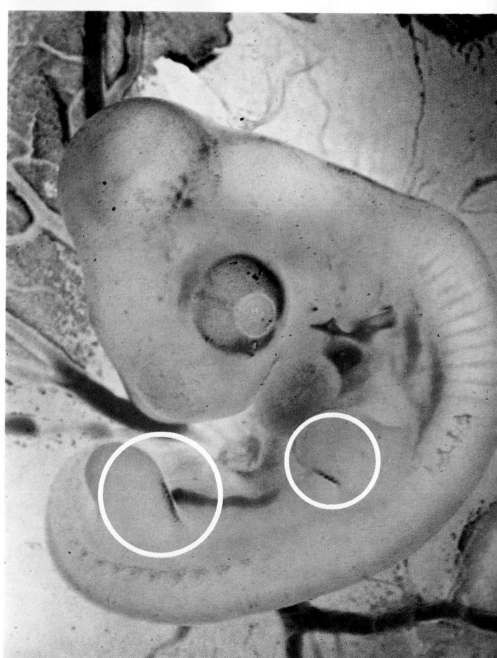

SCULPTING WINGS AND FEET
Using a dye that stains only dead cells, scientists can easily spot areas of degeneration in the wing and foot buds of a four-day-old chick embryo *(above)*. The degeneration aids in shaping the wings and feet of the newborn chick *(top)*. Even when particular cells scheduled for destruction are transplanted to another part of the embryo, they die at their appointed time.

Chromosomes: The Ultimate Secret

Every process of growth, from multiplication to cell death, is ultimately controlled by the genes, which lie in stringlike chromosomes and "instruct" the cell in its duties. But what controls the genes? Cells that assume different forms and functions must be receiving different instructions. The processes that activate one gene while inhibiting others are still unexplained, but biologists are turning up clues.

The first clue came from researchers studying the midge *Chironomus tentans*. They found that the chromosomes taken from a particular organ were puffed out at one point *(opposite and below)*. They concluded that the puffs must consist of activated genes. Molecules of deoxyribonucleic acid (DNA), which constitute the genes'

coded instructions, were at that moment supervising the manufacture of ribonucleic acid (RNA), the messenger which conveys the instructions to the body of the cell. Later experiments have shown that in some cases a particular hormone acts on a receptor protein, which in turn activates specific genes. For example, when a *Chironomus* is injected with a hormone that induces molting, chromosome puffs form within 30 minutes, incidentally indicating the genes that control molting. More experiments will be needed before man achieves a complete understanding of these secrets of development. When that happens, however, he may be able to exercise far more precise control over the growth of domesticated plants and animals—and even over himself.

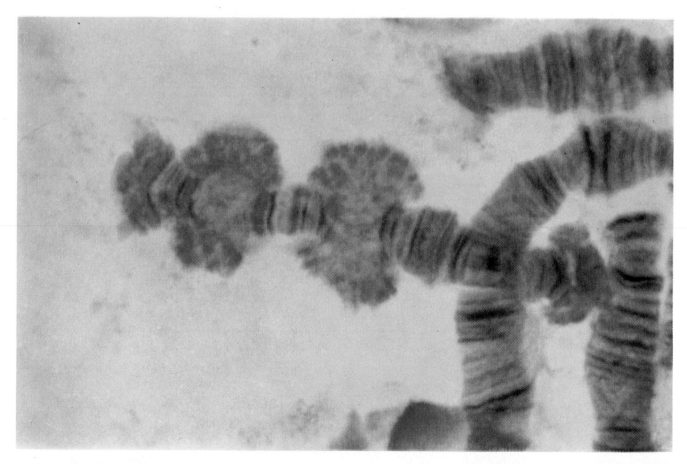

TWISTED THREADS OF LIFE
Giant chromosomes from a salivary-gland cell of a *Chironomus tentans* show concentrations of DNA stained brown, and puffed-up areas where certain genes of this particular chromosome

have been "activated" to direct some specific function of the cell. The green areas indicate the presence of a protein, whose function, though believed to be important, is not known.

A PUFF OF A DIFFERENT COLOR
In another *Chironomus* chromosome, a stain colors DNA blue *(opposite)*, and reveals the presence of RNA *(purple)* in the puff. Presumably this RNA, duplicating the DNA's code, will carry instructions to the outer portion of the cell to direct the cell's various chemical activities.

3
The Next
Seven Months

BY THE NINTH WEEK of uterine life, development has progressed so far that the growing individual is no longer called an embryo, but a fetus. The fetus has a recognizably human head, arms and legs, and all of its vital organs have been outlined and formed. Its heart is beating and the nervous system has begun to function in a primitive fashion. The cartilage of its emerging skeleton has begun to turn to bone. Much more growing remains to be done, and much refinement of structure is yet to be accomplished. But the emphasis has shifted radically. From here on, the development of function becomes the most important part of the growth process. The seven months still separating the fetus from birth are mainly months of practice, in which the fetus's body learns to use all the intricate, delicate equipment it has been building as it grows.

The answer to the question "Will the baby be a boy or a girl?" will usually remain concealed until birth. If the physician suspects a congenital defect in the baby, he can perform a test called amniocentesis, in which a sample of the amniotic fluid is removed for examination. Because this fluid contains a few of the baby's cells, he can then also determine the infant's sex. From the very beginning, differences exist between the cells of males and females. But for most prospective parents, sex is a subject of unscientific conjecture. According to superstition the arrival of a boy is heralded by good disposition on the part of the mother during pregnancy, a girl's presence by a moody mother. But such reasoning is no more valid than the ancient Hindu theory that the mother's right breast and eye enlarge if she is carrying a boy.

Although the infant's sex is determined at the moment of fertilization, the reproductive system does not begin to develop until the second month. Once it does, however, progress is so rapid that the differences between the sexes are unmistakable by the time the embryo has become a fetus. The gonads, or sex glands, develop in the sixth or seventh week, appearing on either side of the abdominal cavity as paired blocks of tissue, with the same structure in both sexes. By the ninth week they have differentiated into testes or ovaries. The formation of these primary sex organs sets the stage for the development of the rest of the structures that make up the reproductive system.

By the end of the second month, the embryo has manufactured two pairs of tubes, all four roughly parallel with one another. One set is known as the Wolffian ducts, after Kaspar Friedrich Wolff, and the other as the Müllerian ducts, after Johannes Müller, a German biologist. If the baby is a boy, the newly formed testes stimulate the Wolffian ducts to develop further into several structures which include the *vas deferens*, the route along which the sperm will be carried. As these ducts develop, the Müllerian ducts fade away to stubs. If the baby is a girl, the Müllerian ducts grow into the Fallopian tubes, the uterus and the upper part of

A PIONEER WORK IN OBSTETRICS
This page from a medieval Latin manuscript is based on the work of Soranos, the eminent Second Century Greek gynecologist who promoted the idea that it was safe for babies to be delivered feet first. He also taught midwives how to handle babies who were in unusual positions in the womb, thus saving countless mothers and children from injury and death.

the vagina, and the Wolffian ducts fade away. These internal structures lead to the development of the external sex organs.

The most powerful influence on the formation of the reproductive system seems to be the hormones manufactured by the testes. This conclusion is suggested by examination of defective human fetuses: When the testes fail to form properly, the rest of the reproductive system develops along female lines. And it has been confirmed by several ingenious experiments. In one extraordinarily delicate operation, A. Jost of the Collège de France in Paris managed to remove the testes from the fetuses of male rabbits immediately after their formation, and at the same time to keep the tiny creatures alive. Thereafter, the fetuses followed a completely feminine course of development. On the other hand, when Jost removed the ovaries from the fetuses of female rabbits, their development continued unaltered.

By the fourth month, the entire reproductive system has been formed, and the fetus has begun to show that it is active and alive. The salivary glands have started working; peristalsis, the wavelike contractions that will in the future move food through the intestine, has begun; the kidneys now function, discharging waste into the amniotic fluid. The four-month fetus will curl its fingers when its palm is tickled, curl its toes when the soles of its feet are tickled, and can even grip things with fingers and thumb. But it still could not survive outside the womb.

The mobile fetus

Within its warm and protected world, however, the fetus has a marvelous ease of movement. Suspended in the fluid that fills the amniotic sac, the fetus is virtually weightless. Still tiny—no more than eight to 10 inches (20 to 25 cm) long—and weak, it can nevertheless perform many feats that will be far beyond its capacity for months after birth. Unlike the four-month baby, the four-month fetus can bend sharply from the hips and waist; it can twist its body; it can shift from one side to the other; it can roll over completely; it can even turn somersaults.

The fetus's practice movements make themselves known to the mother as little kicks and starts, shoves and gentle pangs. The mother may even be awakened at night by the vigor of its movements. She cannot feel the beat of the fetus's heart, but the doctor can detect it. If she is carrying more than one fetus, the doctor may have clues to this fact.

The chances of having twins are complicated to compute. Fraternal twins are more common than identical twins. The reason is simple: Identical twins come from a single fertilized egg that divides into two and produces two distinct individuals with the same genetic endowment. However, this is a rare occurrence. More often two eggs are released from the ovaries at the same time, and each egg is then fertilized by a different sperm, with the result that fraternal twins are produced.

A number of factors have been discovered that increase the likelihood that a woman will bear fraternal twins. Age is a determinant, and prior childbearing also seems to increase the possibility of having twins. An American girl from 15 to 19 who has never had a baby before has one chance in 200 of giving birth to twins. For a woman 35 to 39 who has already borne a number of children, the likelihood rises to as much as one chance in 50. In recent years, as large numbers of American women have postponed childbearing, there has been an increasing proportion of twins born to women experiencing their first birth between the ages of 25 and 30. Why this is so is unknown, though perhaps age is responsible. There is also some suspicion that women who have used oral contraceptives for a number of years are more likely to have twins.

The impact of age

Science has not yet been able to determine why age should raise the likelihood that a woman will bear twins. It has been suggested that in older women hormonal changes may develop that make the cycles of ovulation less regular and predictable. During one month, an older woman may not ovulate at all, while during the next, two ova may be released into the Fallopian tubes. Such hormonal changes may also be induced by the drugs used to treat infertility. Women taking such drugs are prone to multiple births.

Genetic characteristics, both familial and racial, may play a part in producing multiple births. Twinning sometimes seems to run in females of the same family, being passed on from mother to daughter.

One other fact is known with certainty about twins. They are more likely than other children to be born prematurely. On the average, twins arrive three weeks early and often weigh less than five pounds. But birth weight alone, or even the estimated duration of the mother's pregnancy, is not by itself a reliable guide for determining whether a baby, twin or singleton, is premature. Instead, the baby's overall development at birth is assessed. A number of factors such as the thickness of the baby's breast tissue, the speed of reflexes, general alertness and condition of the skin on the palms of the hands and the soles of the feet give more reliable information than any single factor can.

The usefulness of this kind of evaluation is demonstrated in the case of twins. Even when carried to term they are usually smaller than single babies, because two have been occupying space more suitable for one. Yet this does not necessarily diminish their fitness. Full-term twins under about five and a half pounds (2,500 g) have a chance of survival superior to that of full-term single infants of the same weight, who are classified "small for gestational age." These singletons used to be classified as

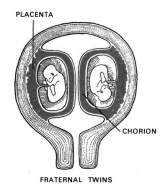

FRATERNAL TWINS the more common of the two types of human twinning, are produced by fertilization of two different ova which arrive in the Fallopian tubes at approximately the same time. Genetically different, they are contained within separate chorionic sacs in the womb and are sustained by separate placentas.

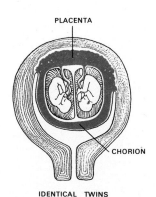

IDENTICAL TWINS result when the embryonic material growing from a single fertilized ovum separates into two distinct masses. The twins are genetic copies of each other and thus must be of the same sex. In most cases, they share one placenta, though they have separate umbilical cords. Siamese twins are born when separation is incomplete.

premature. But in fact they have more severe problems than simply being born too soon. Some of them apparently suffer from an inability to grow normally. In other cases the mother's excessive smoking or alcohol intake has inhibited development. The true premature baby can continue growing normally after birth, but the baby who is small for its gestational age may be permanently hampered in its development.

Birth before term can be ascribed to a number of causes, which may be linked to the mother's health or, more specifically, to the uterine environment. Thus a chronic disease or an acute infection in the mother may cause premature delivery. It may also occur if the placenta separates from the uterine wall, or if the membranes around the fetus tear. Any of these conditions or accidents can bring on labor, and once labor begins, little can be done to stop it. In many cases, the baby is then doomed.

Rescue by incubator

Prematurity is the most common cause of infant mortality in the United States, accounting for about 50 per cent of all newborn deaths. In only rare instances is premature delivery beneficial. If a sonogram—a picture produced by ultrasonic waves—shows that a fetus is pathologically small for its gestational age, the physician may induce labor as much as six weeks early. Even though premature birth entails risks, such a baby fares better than it would if carried to full term. Fortunately, the modern incubator greatly reduces the hazards of early birth. Essentially, the incubator is an artificial womb: Its warm, moist, sterile atmosphere duplicates as much as possible the protection of the uterus. One of the spectacular saves in history occurred in 1938. On January 14 of that year Jacqueline Benson was born at St. Anne's Hospital in Chicago, weighing only 10 ounces (284 g)—a mere five eighths of a pound (0.284 kg). After four and a half months in an incubator she was able to leave the hospital; she went on to grow to normal womanhood.

The smallest American-born baby known to have survived, Jacqueline was probably born in the sixth month of her mother's pregnancy. And the six-month baby, even when it weighs considerably more than she did, has practically no chance of survival. It has to contend with the circulatory and respiratory difficulties that are created by incompletely developed body structures and an immature nervous system.

By the sixth month many organs are almost completely developed. The nostrils have opened, eyebrows have begun to appear, and the ears are so fully developed that fetuses in the womb can be startled by loud noises. Although the mother cannot hear the beat of her fetus's heart, the fetus may hear the beat of hers. If it does, this soothing rhythm is part of its experience of life from the moment the hearing sense begins to function. It may even play a role in development and growth.

An interesting experiment was conducted by Lee Salk with the cooperation of officials at Elmhurst Hospital in New York City. Dr. Salk installed two loud-speaker systems in the nursery where newborn infants are kept for four days. Through these speakers he broadcast for 24 hours a day the beat of the normal human heart, 72 times a minute, at a moderate volume. When the babies exposed to the heartbeats were compared with a control group who were not, some extraordinary differences were recorded. Sixty-nine per cent of the babies who heard the heartbeat gained weight during their four days in the nursery, while 67 per cent of those in the control group did not. Most of them, in fact, lost an average of 0.71 ounce (20 g). Moreover, the heartbeat babies cried less, and breathed more deeply and regularly than the others, a fact to which Dr. Salk attributed their gain in weight. They put their energy into growing instead of dissipating it in tears and yells. It is probably no accident that mothers—whether right- or left-handed—tend to hold their infants on the left side of the body rather than the right. In this position, the baby can more easily hear its mother's heartbeat.

The strongest muscle

Approximately 38 weeks after fertilization and 40 weeks after the first day of the mother's last menstrual period, the fetus is ready for birth. The elastic walls of the uterus have stretched to capacity. Now the contractions begin that will push the fetus out. These rhythmic movements, which make themselves known as labor pains, have an enormous force behind them. The uterus is the largest and most powerful muscle of the human body, stronger by far than a boxer's biceps. Even at the very beginning of labor, the contractions put 25 to 30 pounds (11 to 14 kg) of pressure on the contents of the womb.

The first necessity in labor is to force open the cervix, the neck of the womb, so that the fetus can enter the birth canal. This takes much longer than either of the next two stages of birth, which are the actual expulsion of the fetus, followed by delivery of the placenta. Throughout the mother's pregnancy, the cervix has been virtually closed. It must open to a diameter of about four inches (10 cm) if the fetus's head is to be able to pass through. The uterine contractions of the first stage of labor put so much pressure on the cervix that finally it dilates sufficiently.

Although the birth canal, like the uterus, can stretch, the fetus's head always forces it. During birth the head is pressed somewhat out of shape, but this produces no damage. The fetus's skull bones have not yet knit together and are separated by sutures; although they are pushed together as the fetus traverses the narrow birth canal, they are never crushed. The head regains its normal shape a few days after birth. It takes longer for the skull bones to knit together; the soft spot at the top

BRAIN DEVELOPMENT in the fetus is far enough along by the fourth month *(left)* that three major regions of the brain—the medulla, cerebellum and cerebrum—are clearly separate. By the sixth month *(middle)* a dentlike fissure appears on the surface of the cerebrum which will mark the border between the centers of sensation and voluntary muscular control. As the cerebrum expands, its surface, or cortex—the seat of higher mental processes—folds into many other fissures, thereby greatly increasing its area with a minimal increase in total brain volume.

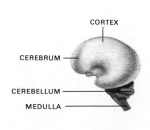

CORTEX
CEREBRUM
CEREBELLUM
MEDULLA

FOUR MONTHS

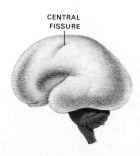

CENTRAL FISSURE

SIXTH MONTH

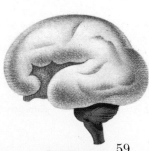

SEVENTH MONTH

of a baby's head may not disappear until the child is more than a year old.

Until the moment of birth the mother has done everything for her fetus. She has provided it with food, protection, warmth and a nest in which to develop. She has even breathed for it. In the placenta, oxygen from her bloodstream has been transferred to the fetus's bloodstream and carbon dioxide has been removed. But if the baby does not breathe air once he is born, nine months of growth will have been to no avail. Moreover, he must take his first breath fairly quickly. We do not yet know precisely how long an infant can survive outside the womb without breathing. If the mother dies before delivery, it is possible for the fetus to remain alive as long as 20 minutes. But this figure is somewhat misleading, for until the umbilical cord is cut, the placenta may still contain some oxygen. An adult will suffocate after only a few minutes without air. This is probably the limit for an infant's survival after birth, too.

What impels the baby to take that vital first breath? Until recently the shock of birth seemed the only explanation. Everyone gasps on stepping into a cold shower or plunging into the icy ocean for a swim. It is possible that the newborn experiences birth in much the same way. Ejected forcibly from the warm world of the womb into the cold, he gasps. And in that first gasp and cry of protest he helps assure his survival. The attending physician's traditional slap on the baby's bottom provides another kind of shock, and is used when the shock of birth does not force the first breath. Other factors are also at work. As anyone knows who has watched a litter of kittens or puppies being born, a newborn will sometimes lie still, unbreathing, for quite a while, and then suddenly "come to" with a sharp intake of breath. Shock cannot explain this response. It is likely that the breathing muscles are triggered by chemical changes within the body and changes of pressure in the chest cavity.

The process of breathing

In the brain there are chemoreceptors sensitive to carbon dioxide. One theory holds that their sensitivity increases sharply at birth to the point where they are activated by the carbon dioxide in the baby's blood and prompt the control center to initiate the breathing process.

According to Stanley James of Babies Hospital in New York City, pressure changes may also play a major part in causing the infant to take his first breath. While the fetus is still in the womb, its lungs are crumpled up and deflated, although they contain some fluid. When the fetus passes through the birth canal, its chest cavity is subjected to considerable pressure. This forces some of the fluid out through the nostrils and mouth. Immediately after birth, when the constriction has been removed, the chest expands the way a sponge does after being squeezed, and air rushes into the lungs to fill the vacuum. The baby's first sound

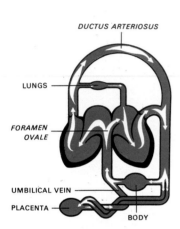

FETAL CIRCULATION is structurally quite different from postnatal circulation, because life-giving oxygen is delivered by the placenta, rather than the lungs. Most of the blood is diverted from the lungs by a special vessel, the *ductus arteriosus,* and a temporary hole between the right and left chambers of the heart, the *foramen ovale.*

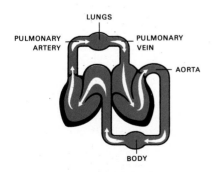

POSTNATAL CIRCULATION begins when the umbilical cord is clamped and the baby takes its first breath. The pulmonary arteries expand at this moment. As blood rushes into the lungs, muscles in the wall of the *ductus arteriosus* contract and close off the vessel. Pressure rises in the left chamber of the heart and the *foramen ovale* shuts permanently.

may not be the traditional cry, but a cough that expels more fluid.

The first independent breath may take as much as 10 times the inhalation force required of an adult. After the first labored inhalation, the baby breathes more easily. As much as 40 per cent of the air inhaled remains in the lungs so less force is required to expand them in subsequent breaths. The exchange of oxygen and carbon dioxide between air and blood occurs in tiny pockets of the lungs, the alveoli. With each breath they expand, then deflate slightly. A substance called pulmonary surfactant reduces surface tension within the alveoli so that less pressure is needed to expand them. Preterm babies sometimes have breathing difficulties because their lungs are deficient in pulmonary surfactant.

Closing a valve

The circulatory system must also change dramatically if the baby is to survive. While the fetus is in the womb and its lungs are idle, relatively little blood flows through their capillaries. The major route of circulation runs directly through the heart. Blood enters the upper right chamber, the right atrium, then passes to the upper left chamber, the left atrium, through an opening called the *foramen ovale*. When the blood reaches the left atrium, it is pumped into the lower left chamber, the left ventricle; then it goes into the aorta to begin its circulatory path. To keep blood from seeping back from the left atrium to the right, a flap descends over the *foramen ovale* after the blood has left the right atrium.

After birth, the circulation route is completely different. Now all the blood must be sent to the lungs for purification and oxygenation. The venous blood, containing the waste products of metabolism, enters the right atrium, is squeezed into the right ventricle, and from there is sent via the pulmonary artery to the lungs. From the lungs, the oxygenated blood is returned to the left atrium, pumped into the left ventricle, and sent out through the aorta to begin circulating through the body.

Only 10 per cent of the fetus's blood is sent to the lungs; 55 per cent returns to the placenta for oxygenation and 35 per cent circulates through the blood vessels. The small amount of blood passing through the lungs comes from the right side of the heart. While most of the blood in the right atrium passes over to the left, some of it squeezes into the right ventricle; part of it is pumped to the lungs. But more is present than the 10 per cent that the lungs can handle. To assure that the lungs do not get more than their share, the embryo builds a shunt, the *ductus arteriosus*. The *ductus*, which begins to form in about the fifth week of uterine life, leads from the pulmonary artery to the aorta; through it the right ventricle pumps all the blood not sent to the lungs.

The changeover from fetal to normal circulation thus requires an enormous change not only in the functioning of the heart but also in its structure. The *foramen ovale* must be permanently sealed to keep the venous and arterial blood from mixing. For the same reason, the *ductus arteriosus* must constrict. Both processes begin with the first breath. The flap that seals the *foramen ovale* comes down permanently and in time adheres to the muscular wall separating the right atrium from the left. The *ductus arteriosus*, kept open before birth by a hormone-like substance called prostoglandin, now constricts; in 24 hours it has shut down. By the time the baby is two months old, it has become a fibrous cord. If these events do not occur and the venous and arterial bloodstreams mix, the body may not receive enough oxygen. Surgery can now repair nature's lapses by sealing off the *foramen ovale* or the *ductus*. The pioneer in this field was Dr. Robert E. Gross of Children's Hospital Medical Center, Boston. On August 26, 1938, Dr. Gross cut the open *ductus arteriosus* in the body of seven-year-old Lorraine Sweeney and tied off both its ends, making her circulation normal. Surgery may eventually be replaced by drug therapy for the preterm baby whose *ductus* is still kept open. A new drug, indomethacin, blocks the action of prostaglandin, allowing the *ductus* to close within a few weeks after birth.

The baby's first breath and the changes in his heart and circulatory system are the climax to nine months of growth in the womb. Not until he reaches puberty will comparably dramatic changes occur.

Early Scenes in a Human Life

The metamorphosis of a cell into a human being has occurred billions of times, but until recent years it was a mysterious and unrecorded process. To capture it as completely as possible, Swedish photographer Lennart Nilsson began photographing the stages of prenatal growth in Stockholm hospitals, where embryos and fetuses were removed for various medical reasons. The pictures on the following pages are part of his remarkable record. They show life before birth in a form that is as fascinating as pictures of the far side of the moon. They depict, as one gynecologist put it, "living tissue in the living state." The circulation of blood, the first fetal movements and many other developmental matters are seen more clearly than was ever possible before. Nilsson's study provides science with a superb record of a process hitherto inferred from circumstantial evidence.

THE BEGINNING OF FORM
Floating in a fluid-filled sac called the amnion, the 10-week-old fetus is a recognizable, if rudimentary, human. It measures about two inches (5 cm) from crown to rump. The fringed tissue seen at the right is the placenta, through which, via the arteries and vein of the umbilical cord, the fetus receives the oxygen and food products it requires from the mother and discards its wastes.

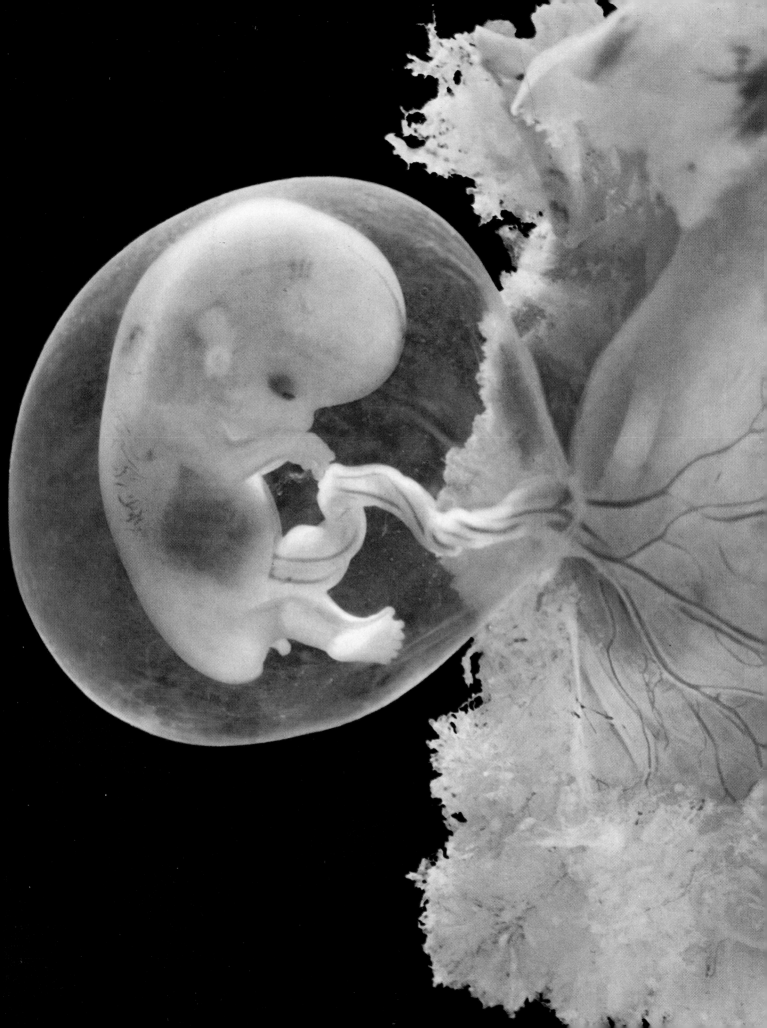

FOUR WEEKS OLD, the embryo *(left)* nestles inside a mass of feathery tissue called the chorion, which in turn is implanted in the uterus, cocklebur-fashion. The embryo draws nutrients from its mother through outgrowths, called villi, which help form the placenta.

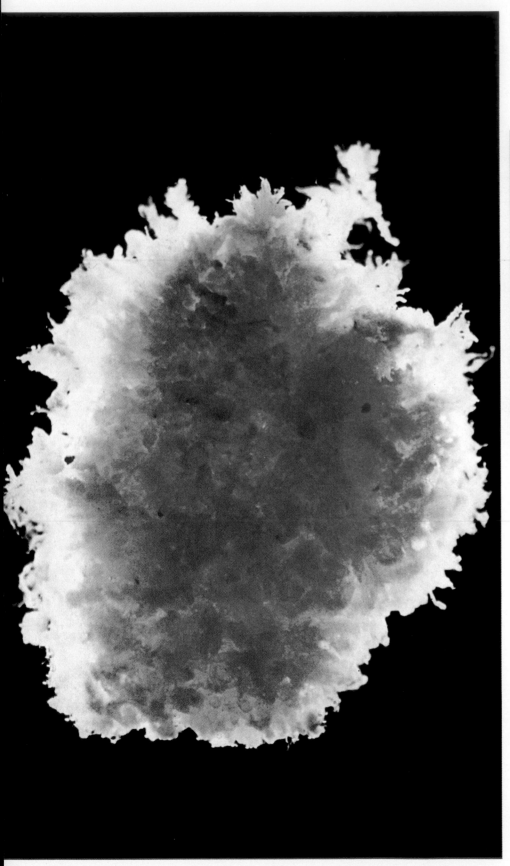

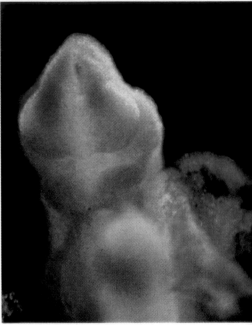

A SERIES OF BULGES, at 26 days, marks the areas of head and heart. The swellings at the top will become the forebrain; the smaller ones beneath them that look like cheeks are actually the lower jaw. The depression between these two sets of bulges will become the mouth. At the very top, a tiny hole is the end of a tube that forms the brain and spinal cord. Below the head, on the right, is another bulge containing the heart, where the first heartbeats have begun.

EYES, EARS AND LIMBS have appeared *(opposite)* by the sixth week, the latter as arm and leg "buds." The eye looks like a dark-rimmed circle; just in front of it is a bulge, part of which will form the nose. The series of little folds that look like a mouth are actually the beginnings of the outer ear. These features, which now seem out of place, will take their correct position when the embryo acquires a neck and begins to uncurl. The embryo is about an inch (2.54 cm) from crown to rump.

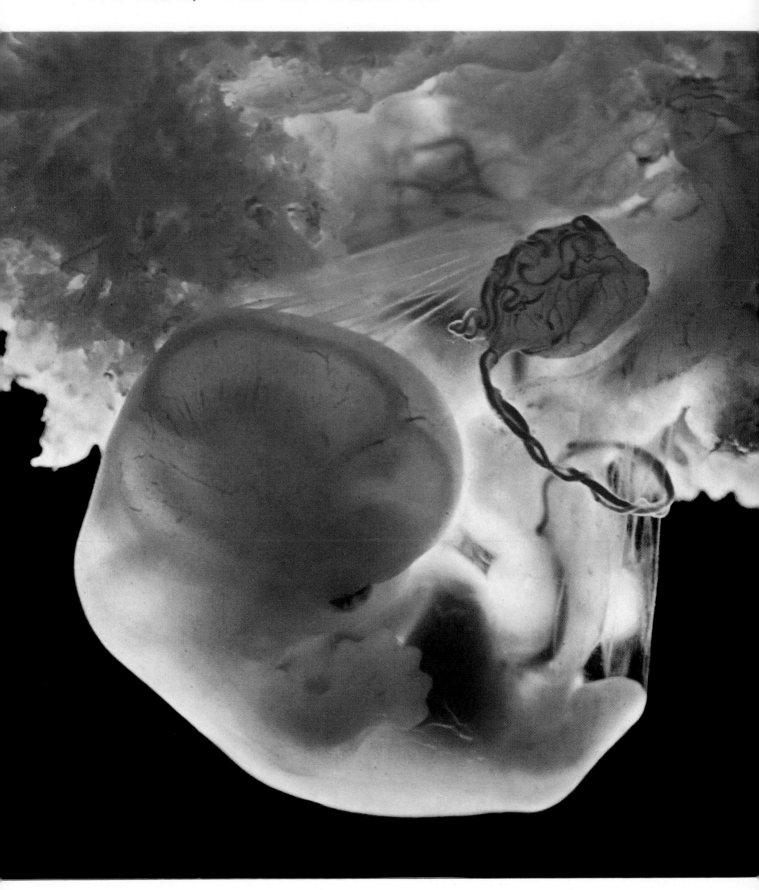

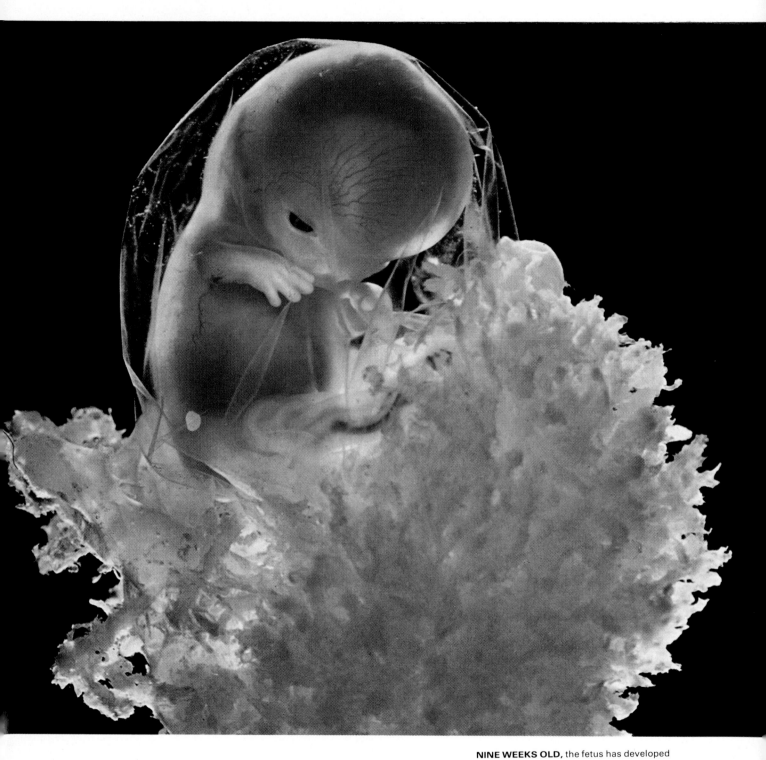

NINE WEEKS OLD, the fetus has developed well-formed fingers; its eye is assuming an oval shape. The fetus now measures about 1¼ inches (3.17 cm) from crown to rump. The kidneys have begun functioning at this stage, adding fetal urine to amniotic fluid.

THE YOLK SAC, prominent in this picture of an embryo at six weeks *(opposite),* produces red blood cells in the first two months of growth, but soon loses this function. It is rarely present at birth. Beneath the head, the arm can be seen with its developing hand.

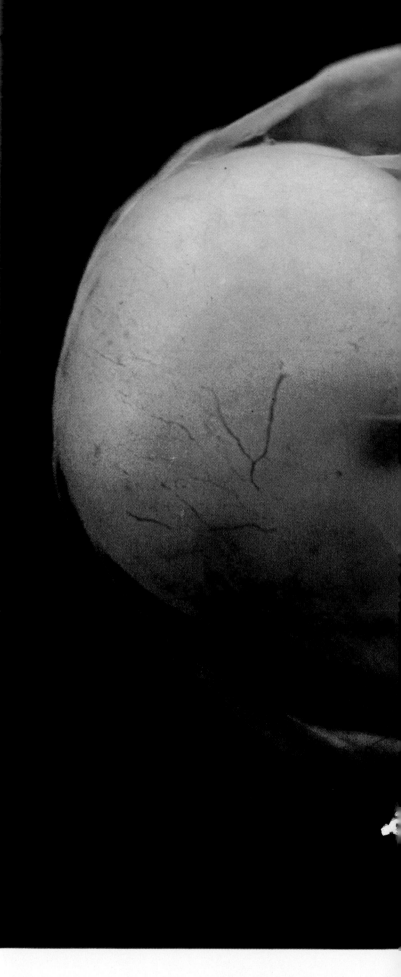

AN EYELID FORMS
. . . AND CLOSES

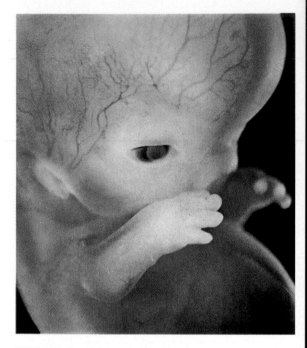

THE FACE of an eight-week-old embryo
(above) reveals an eyelid forming over the lens,
and the iris beginning to develop pigment.
In the ninth week, the upper and lower lids
meet, fuse, and do not reopen until the seventh
month. The ear can be seen at the left.

EARLY IN THE THIRD MONTH the sex of the
fetus becomes distinguishable. Around the
ninth week a female's ovaries differentiate and
a male's testes begin to secrete testosterone,
which stimulates the formation of the penis and
scrotum. In the twelfth week a female's external
genitalia take shape. The fetus may double in
length during the course of the month: The one
shown here measures about 2½ inches (6.35 cm)
from crown of the head to the rump.

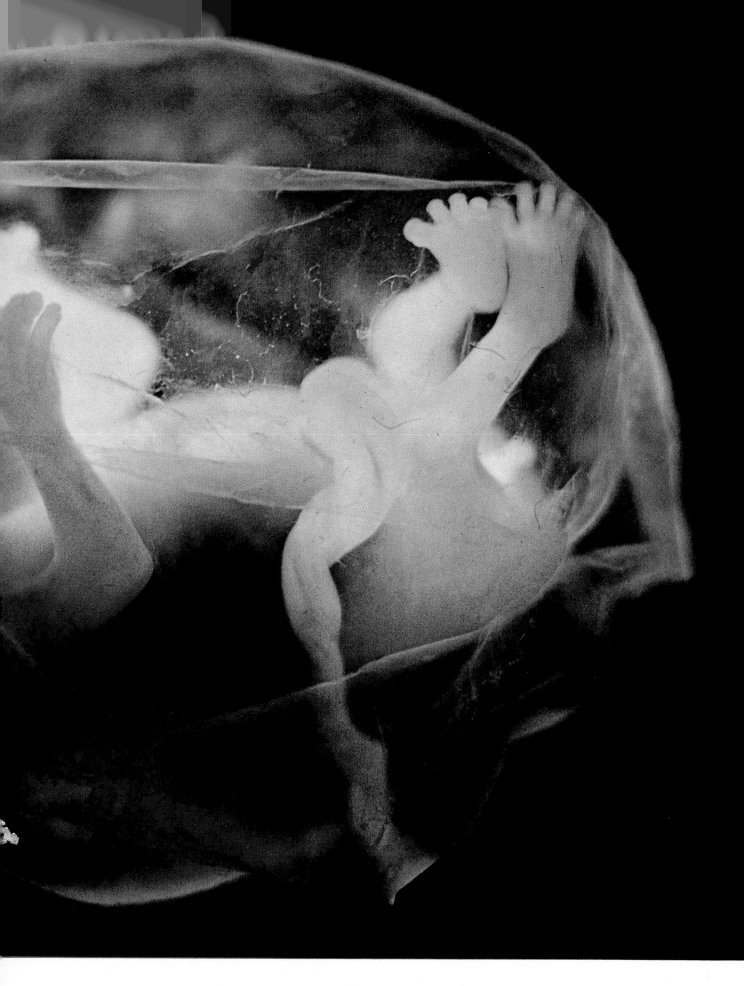

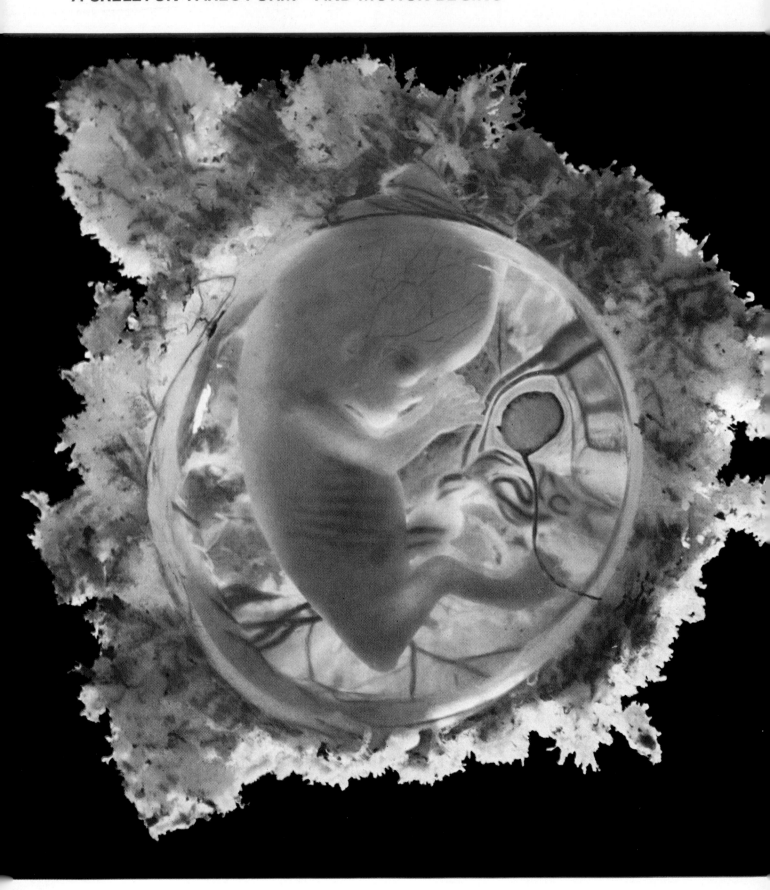

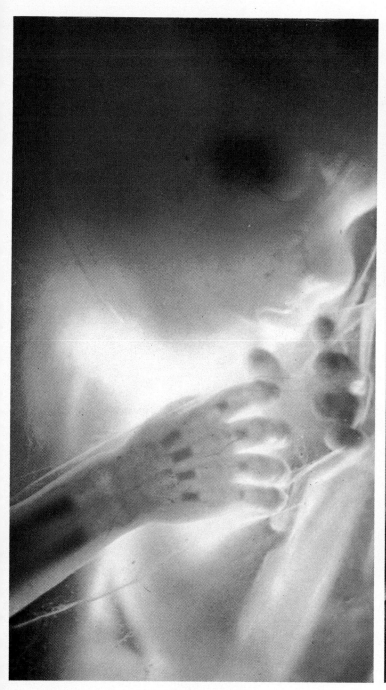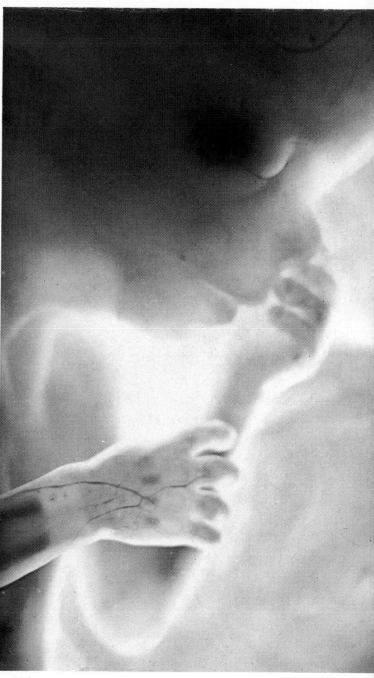

THE FIRST MOVEMENTS are reflex gestures, shown above in two pictures taken only seconds apart. Here, 12 weeks old, the fetus raises its hand to its mouth and makes mouth movements suggestive of sucking. It also contracts the other hand. The substitution of bone for cartilage in the long bones of the arms and legs is now well under way.

THE RIB CAGE of an 11-week fetus *(opposite)* can be seen in the chest region just below the elbows. The ribs and spinal column develop from cartilage cells, which begin to be replaced by bone cells at about the ninth week. Each rib grows out of a vertebra, but eventually a flexible joint will develop between the two.

FIFTH TO SIXTH MONTH: ACTIVITIES MULTIPLY

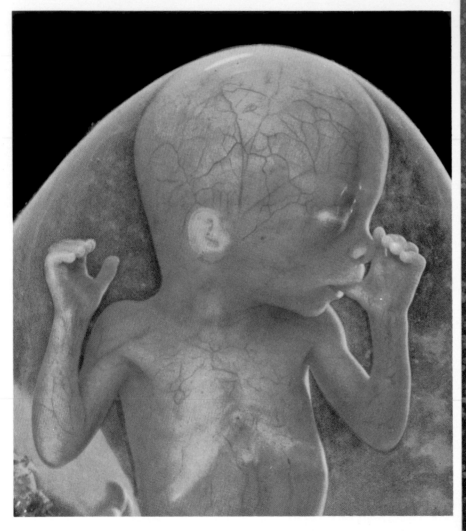

SUCKING ITS THUMB at 4½ months *(above),* the fetus foreshadows the motions of nursing. Some babies are born with thumb calluses from too much sucking in the womb. The fetus's movements intensify and are felt by the mother as "quickenings"; a series of rhythmic jolts means the fetus is hiccuping. Nearly six inches (15 cm) from crown to rump, it has almost fully developed ears and eyes. The blood vessels show through its translucent skin.

FLOATING IN ITS SAC, the five-month fetus has settled into a favorite "lie," or resting position (each fetus picks its own). The umbilical cord is kept from getting kinked by the pressure of blood flowing through it.

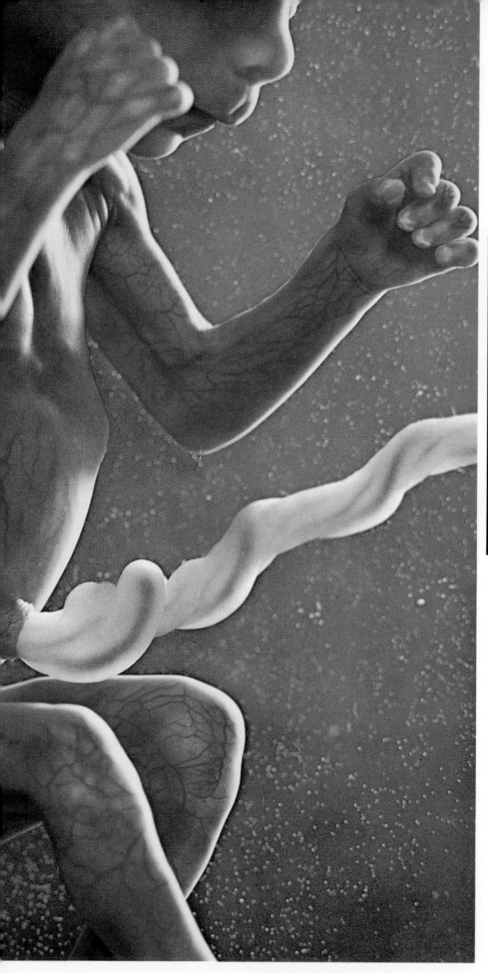

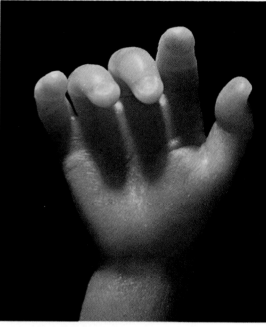

CURLING ITS FINGERS, a six-month-old fetus reveals emerging fingernails; by birth they will have grown long enough to need trimming. The fingerprints, which will forever mark it as unique, also begin to appear. The skin on its hands and feet has begun to thicken, in preparation for the wear and tear of postnatal life. At this stage the fetus's grip is strong enough to hang on to anything within its reach. In fact for reasons that embryologists do not fully understand, a fetus's grip in its sixth month is stronger than it is after birth. The waxy appearance of the hand comes from a protective film secreted by the skin.

IN THE LAST TWO MONTHS

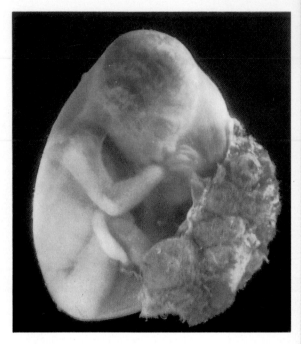

SEVEN MONTHS OLD, the fetus has acquired certain immunities and accumulated fat for warmth in preparation for the outer world. By now its digestive and respiratory systems have also become remarkably efficient. Born at this stage of development, however, a baby can survive only with careful tending.

A NEWBORN BABY emits a cry of life upon being thrust into the world. The umbilical cord, the vital supply line between baby and placenta for almost nine months, has been cut and closed off with a surgical clamp. As he draws his first breath, the baby's lungs take over the placenta's function of supplying the body with oxygen and carrying away carbon dioxide.

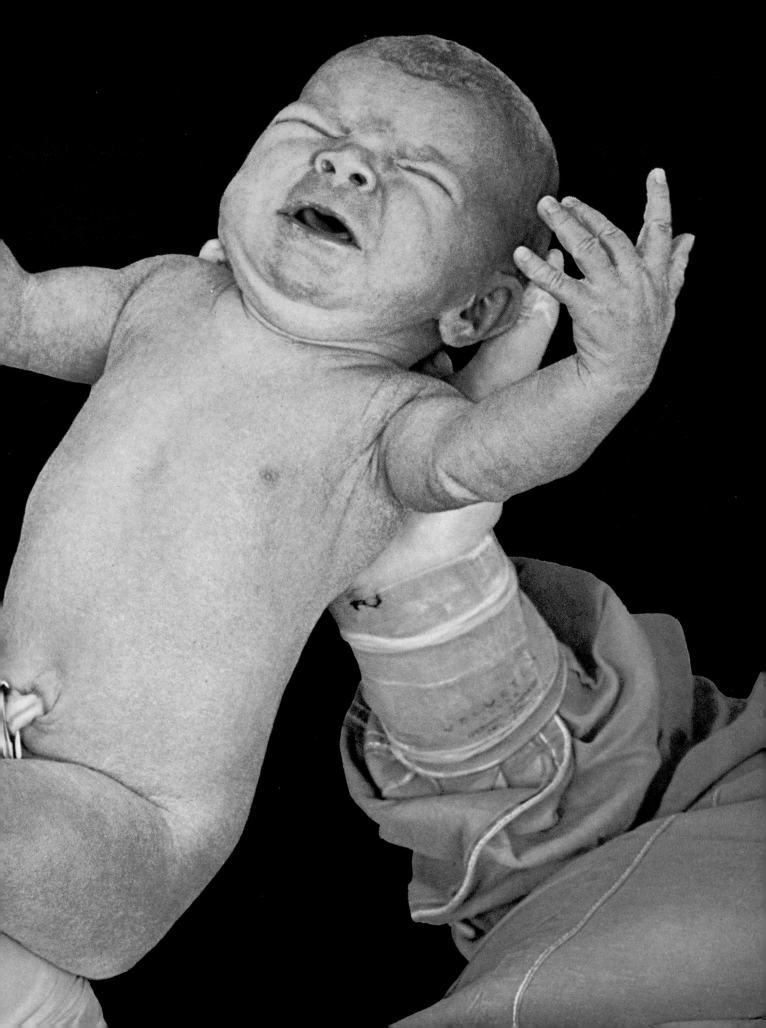

4
Some Yardsticks
of Growth

ON APRIL 11, 1759, a French gentleman, Philibert Gueneau de Montbeillard, became the father of a son. De Montbeillard was a talented amateur scientist who had contributed to the immense encyclopedia of natural history compiled by his friend, Count Buffon. In the interests of science he measured the baby's length at birth, and for the next 18 years he continued this practice, checking his son's height every six months or so. From these measurements he derived a table showing the height the boy had gained during each six-month interval—showing, in other words, the youngster's rate of growth, from infancy to adulthood.

The table indicated that this rate was not uniform from year to year. Each year the boy was taller than he had been the year before, but he grew less during his second year than during his first, and still less during the third than during the second. From his fourth to his eighth year he continued to grow at about the same rate. Then his speed of growth dropped again. At 11½, however, he began to shoot up, and for the next three and a half years he grew more each year. At 15, his growth curve slacked off for the last time. From then on he continued to grow less every year.

When de Montbeillard showed these figures to Buffon, the great naturalist decided to include them in a supplement to his encyclopedia. De Montbeillard's table was to become famous as the first longitudinal study of growth—the first examination of a child's pattern of growth over a period of time.

More than 100 years elapsed before any other scientist got around to following up the lead that de Montbeillard had provided. Thereafter a host of longitudinal growth studies proved that his observations were sound. Science now knows that all children grow in much the same way: rapidly at first, then more slowly, but very quickly indeed when puberty arrives. The same studies have shown that this general pattern leaves room for considerable individual variation: in the child's overall speed of growth, in the ages at which he grows most rapidly, and in the trajectory he follows to reach his destined height. These investigations have given rise to new methods of measuring growth and assaying a child's progress toward maturity. They have also shown that the child who is ahead of or behind his contemporaries, physically or mentally, will not necessarily remain in that position. And finally they have revealed that in many areas of the world children are growing larger and maturing earlier than they did a century ago.

The first scientifically based, large-scale longitudinal studies of growth in the United States were undertaken by the anthropologist Franz Boas. One of the towering figures in the field, Boas got into it by an indirect route. After studying physics and mathematics in his native Germany, he became interested in geography. In 1883, at the age of 25, he set off

INFANT TO YOUNG LADY
The snapshot history of one child records human growth from infancy to adolescence. Grace Osgood was eight weeks old in the first picture; the others were taken at yearly intervals. At six *(second row, second from right)* she no longer looks like a baby, and at 13 *(bottom row, second from left),* at the peak of the adolescent growth spurt, she is suddenly a young lady.

for Greenland to study its landforms. He never got there. Stopping off on Baffin Island, he became fascinated by the local Eskimos. A year with them convinced him that his real vocation was the study of man.

Tradition has it that Boas' academic career in the United States had an equally unorthodox beginning. In 1888, a year after he had emigrated, he was on his way to a meeting of the American Association for the Advancement of Science. On the train he fell into conversation with G. Stanley Hall, a psychologist who had just been named President of Clark University in Worcester, Massachusetts. Hall was so impressed with his traveling companion that before the trip was over he had offered the young man a position as head of the anthropology department at Clark. There, in 1891, Boas began his pioneering study of growth.

Measurements that mislead

Scientific growth studies were not entirely unknown when Boas began his research, but until then the subject had been investigated almost exclusively through so-called cross-sectional studies: one-time measurements of large numbers of children at different ages. Cross-sectional studies are inexpensive and can be carried out quickly and easily, and they are an excellent means of establishing standards of height and weight at various ages against which to measure the individual child. However, as Boas recognized, they have a serious limitation. Because they deal only with averages, they offer no information at all about the growth pattern of any individual child. They show where he stands in relation to his contemporaries, but they do not show how far along he is in his own program of development. They can even lead to serious scientific error.

While Boas was still at work on his study, another investigator, Dr. William Townsend Porter, reported on a cross-sectional study of St. Louis school children. This indicated that youngsters who were advanced in their schoolwork were taller and heavier than children of the same age who were in lower grades. From these figures, Porter made a prediction: Because he assumed that all children grow at the same rate, he declared that those who were taller and brighter as children would invariably be taller and brighter when they became adults.

Although Boas' longitudinal study lasted only a year, it provided enough clues to convince him that Porter was wrong. Boas' sample was made up of 100 Worcester school children—50 boys and 50 girls, ranging in age from five to 16 years old. At both the beginning and the end of the experimental year, he and his assistant took a number of measurements on each child: height, both standing and sitting; weight; length and breadth of head; length of forearm and breadth of hand. In analyzing the data, Boas took account of each youngster's height in relation to

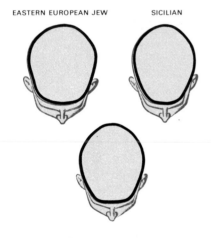

EASTERN EUROPEAN JEW   SICILIAN

CHILDREN OF IMMIGRANTS

A STUDY OF SKULL PATTERNS led to the discovery in 1912 that environment plays a role in shaping human heads. Previously, it had been assumed that the shapes of heads stayed extremely constant within races and ethnic groups. Then the pioneering anthropologist Franz Boas measured the heads of 18,000 immigrants and first-generation children of immigrants. The study showed that American-born children *(bottom)* of Eastern European Jews *(upper left)* had longer heads than their round-headed parents, and the heads of the children of long-headed Sicilians *(upper right)* became shorter.

the average for his age and sex. From all these statistics he was able to extract a number of conclusions. The children's speed of growth, he found, depended on their ages: The younger grew more slowly than those who had reached adolescence. Age was not the only factor. Each child seemed to have his own internal clock, regulating his journey to adulthood at its own speed. Among the younger children, the shorter ones grew more slowly, but among the adolescents, the pattern was reversed. The shorter ones grew more rapidly; in addition, they continued growing for a longer period of time.

Boas' most important discovery, and one which has been confirmed by every subsequent study, was that speed of growth is not decisive in fixing a child's final height. True, some slow-growing children never become tall. But others, simply by continuing to grow for a longer time, may end as adults of above-average height. And what is true of height is true of all other aspects of development. Every child grows at his own individual speed, some maturing early, others late. As Boas himself phrased it, in a paper published in the 1930s, "In some individuals the whole physiological development . . . proceeds rapidly and energetically and the whole development period is short; in others it is sluggish and occupies a much longer period."

Since this is the case, a child's chronological age cannot describe his progress very meaningfully, especially during puberty, when growth is rapid and so much change is going on. The statement that a boy is 14 does not tell whether he is in the middle of adolescence, has already passed it, or has not yet reached it. Because it says nothing at all about his level of maturity, it offers very little guidance to physicians, educators or parents—the people most intimately concerned with the youngster's growth. What they need to know is the point he has reached in his own development. His developmental age, as it is called, is far more important to them than his age in years.

Measuring by remembrance

The concept of developmental age was first put forth by Charles Ward Crampton, a New York physician and a collaborator of Boas. Crampton suggested that the appearance of pubic hair in boys and the onset of menstruation (the menarche) in girls be used as the base points of measurement. Developmental age would then be determined by counting backward or forward from this time. But it soon became evident that this information would not suffice. The accuracy of the method depended entirely on the accuracy of the child's memory, and although girls are likely to remember when they began to menstruate, boys are apt to be quite vague in their recollections of the date that pubic hair first appeared. To meet this objection, other criteria were gradually added:

the appearance of pubic hair in girls and of axillary (armpit) hair in both sexes; the development of the sex organs; the emergence of the breasts in girls, and of facial hair and the Adam's apple in boys. The degree of development of all these characteristics can be rated on a sliding scale, and by combining the ratings the physician can measure developmental age in the adolescent period.

This approach, based as it was on the outward signs of puberty, had a drawback: It was not satisfactory as a way of measuring developmental age during childhood. By offering a look backward from puberty, it could lead to inferences on where the child had been at various times in his earlier years. But it provided no way of measuring his developmental age in childhood or of determining his speed of growth.

Clues from X-rays

During the early years of the century, two investigators working independently found a method of assaying growth that works on children of any age. Using the then-new technique of X-ray photography, they discovered that the ossification of the hand and wrist bones varies considerably among children of the same age. All 29 bones in this area begin as bits of cartilage; gradually, in regular and predictable stages, they harden into bone. Once the sequence of these changes was carefully mapped, assigning a developmental age to any growing child became a relatively simple matter. An X-ray of the youngster's wrist, showing how far ossification had progressed, could be compared with a set of standard charts. The method is very useful, because neither the order of events nor the nature of the changes that occur is affected by the child's health or by any of the myriad of other processes that normally go on in his body, apart from diseases of the hand bones themselves.

Today, two other structures may also be X-rayed to find developmental age: the bones of the knee, and the teeth. For the period of infancy—between six months and two years—the milk teeth can be used, since they emerge and fall out in a fairly regular order; between six and 13 years, the equally regular appearance of the permanent teeth provides an index of growth. Assessment of dental development through X-rays will eventually allow scientists to chart every stage of growth from birth on.

Except for the teeth, which appear to develop on their own timetable, all these measurements agree quite closely among themselves in providing a determination of a child's developmental age. They also provide scientific confirmation of a fact suggested by everyday observation: Girls move toward maturity more rapidly than boys. X-rays of both hand and knee show that girls are on the average about 20 per cent ahead of boys at any age up to physical maturity. Even the teeth reflect a difference.

Though both sexes acquire their milk teeth at about the same age, permanent teeth appear earlier in girls—the molars by about two months and the canines by as much as 11.

In fact, girls seem to start out in life with certain advantages over boys. Until the age of five months, girls lead in the ability to perform the movements that are prerequisite for creeping, sitting and walking, and even after that age they generally remain ahead in fine movements and gross motor coordination, such as tying bows or skipping. They usually learn to control their bladders earlier. In theory, this feminine advantage should result from a more rapid development of the brain, paralleling the faster skeletal development of girls. But no evidence of brain differences between the sexes has yet emerged, although the studies conducted by Jesse L. Conel at Harvard University threw light on the developmental processes in the cerebral cortex, the region of the brain that governs perception, thought and voluntary muscle control.

By mapping the patterns of growth in the cortex during the first two years of life, Conel was able to show why the skills of both sexes emerge in the order that they do. By the time a baby is born, he has already developed all of the neurons, or nerve cells, he will ever have. After birth there is an increase in the size of the cells and in the number and complexity of the axons and dendrites, the long, branching fibers that carry impulses from one cortex cell to another, enabling the cells to function together. These postnatal increases, Conel has found, occur first in the areas of the cortex that control movement, then in the sensory areas, beginning with those that govern the sense of touch. The vision and hearing areas develop somewhat later. However, these later-developing areas are already functional at birth. Experiments have shown that even a week-old baby can perceive simple differences in shapes, showing more interest in a pattern of concentric circles than in a triangle. The ability to perceive more complex patterns—and this includes people—develops later: It takes several months for even a wise child to know his own mother or father.

The development of coordination

Conel also found sequential priorities in growth even within particular areas of the cortex. For example, the motor cells that control the muscles of the upper arms develop interconnections before those that control the hands. (Any parent knows that a baby can flail its arms about long before it can control its fingers sufficiently to pick something up.) In 1970 John Dobbing and Jean Sands, working at the University of Manchester, pinpointed one of the mechanisms underlying a baby's motor development. They measured changes in the amount of DNA the brain contains at different times, ranging from a gestational age of 10 weeks

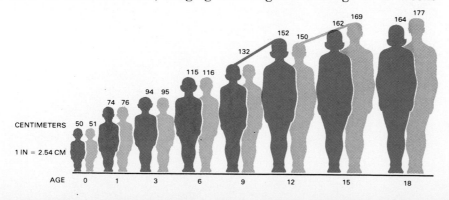

CENTIMETERS 50 51 74 76 94 95 115 116 132 152 150 162 169 164 177

1 IN = 2.54 CM

AGE 0 1 3 6 9 12 15 18

THE RACE FOR MATURITY between the sexes is seen in this chart comparing ages and approximate heights (reported in centimeters based on the U.S. National Center for Health Statistics' 50th percentiles) of growing boys and girls. Both sexes grow nearly evenly until an early adolescent growth spurt makes girls uncomfortably taller than boys. The boys gain the lead when a delayed and larger spurt carries them toward a final five-inch (13 cm) margin.

81

up to a year after birth, and discovered that the brain of a three-month-old baby undergoes a growth spurt. It apparently results from the production of new glial cells, which manufacture a substance called myelin. Myelin insulates the nerve fibers and allows clear passage of electrical impulses essential to full motor development and coordination.

As the parts of the cortex continue to mature, all of the baby's responses to stimuli and all of his movements become more precise. By the time he is one and a half, he can learn to walk and feed himself, though sloppily. At two he can control his bowels and can begin to control his bladder. By this age, too, most children have begun to speak.

All these responses can be delayed by serious illness or by severe deprivation. But in a normal child, none of them can really be stopped. On the other hand, none of them can emerge before the brain has matured to an appropriate degree; throughout the growing years the child's behavior is heavily dependent on the development of his nervous system. For this reason specialists in development warn parents against attempting to impose behavior patterns, such as toilet training, on a child before his nervous system is mature enough to cope with them.

The adolescent spurt

It is at the beginning of adolescence, the years of greatest growth, that developmental differences between girls and boys become most evident. Girls generally reach puberty ahead of boys: They embark on the adolescent growth spurt at an average age of 11, as against 13 for boys. Although the intensity and duration of this spurt vary widely from one youngster to another, it usually lasts for two to two and a half years in both sexes. The growth and transformation that occur in this short period of time are enormous, second in magnitude only to those that take place in the womb.

Though the growth spurt begins earlier in girls, it is during this period that boys outstrip them in development. In childhood, boys and girls of the same age are practically the same height. But the boy's spurt is markedly greater. While it is going on, the average boy grows approximately eight inches (20.3 cm) taller and adds 45 pounds (20.4 kg) to his weight; at its peak, about 14, he is growing at the rate of four inches (10 cm) a year. Girls gain about six and a quarter inches (15.88 cm) in height and 35 pounds (15.9 kg) in weight during the spurt. Their peak comes sooner, at about 12, when their rate of growth averages three and a quarter inches (8.26 cm) a year. The more powerful acceleration in boys is an important reason that men are, on the average, taller than women, but an even more important reason may be that the growth spurt comes later in boys, who can thus continue growing for a longer time.

Every muscular and skeletal dimension of the body seems to take part in the adolescent spurt. The growth of the heart, stomach and other visceral organs speeds up. The head, whose increase in size has been almost imperceptible since the child was eight, steps up its pace of growth slightly. Even the eyeballs expand in front-to-back measurement. Sometimes this increase is disproportionate, and leads to nearsightedness.

The contours of the face, which have been altering gradually throughout childhood, show particularly marked changes. The whole profile becomes more angular, the forehead more prominent, the chin more pointed, the nose longer. These changes, which are associated with the growth of facial bone, are accompanied by subtle changes in muscle size and in the distribution of fatty tissue under the skin, making the adolescent's facial configuration so different from that of a child.

In both sexes, strength increases, although the increase is proportionately much greater in boys than in girls. Before puberty, most girls can hold their own in tussles with boys of the same age. But this changes after the growth spurt. Males double their muscle mass in adolescence, and the average adolescent boy can exert more than 120 pounds (54.4 kg) of thrust with one arm, as against 70 pounds (31.7 kg) for girls.

Growth may continue, although slowly, for many years after adolescence. Some people are still growing—though almost imperceptibly —in their forties. For all practical purposes, however, growth ceases in the teens. In general, boys reach 98 per cent of their final height by the time they are 17¾, girls by the time they are 16½.

A pattern of differentials

These statistical and descriptive summaries of the adolescent spurt, like most summaries, oversimplify what is in fact a rather complicated process. Detailed studies have shown that the various parts of the body grow at different rates, as do various dimensions of each part. Moreover, each part, each dimension reaches its maximum rate of growth at a different time. The feet speed up first, reaching their peak growth rate only about three months after the spurt has started. In another six months it is the turn of the calf and the thigh. Four months later the hips and chest begin broadening at an accelerated rate, followed by the shoulders. In both sexes, the length of the trunk and the depth of the chest reach peak growth speed last of all.

Measurements of all growth factors—from degree of bone ossification to overall body proportions—provide something more than a simple description of the child's level of development at any given time; they can predict his future as well. For example, in 1954 a 10-year-old girl applied for admission to the Royal Ballet School in England. Although she gave evidence of considerable talent as a dancer, the director was quite hesitant about accepting her application. She was small for her age, and he feared her height as an adult would be less than five foot two (157 cm), the minimum for ballerinas in most professional companies. But the youngster was eager and persuasive, and the director finally agreed to consult a growth expert who might be able to forecast her final height. The expert compared such telltale factors as the rate of ossification of her wrist bones with the data he had laboriously collected for hundreds of children over a period of 15 years. From the comparison, he concluded that the girl had more growing ahead of her than the average child of her age, and that she would be about five foot three (160 cm) when she reached maturity. On the basis of this prediction, the girl was admitted to the school. She grew to five foot four (163 cm), and after graduation became a member of the corps de ballet of a major dance company.

The internal regulator

The concept of developmental age and the discovery of ways to determine it have added considerably to knowledge of the growth process. For example, science now knows that the internal clock which regulates each child's speed of growth is capable of making many adjustments for interference from environmental obstacles. Illness or poor diet may slow the clock temporarily, so that the child grows at a reduced rate for a while. However, if the interference does not last too long, the clock will eventually speed up, and the child may grow at double or even triple his normal rate until he makes up the lost time.

Differences in individual rates of growth can create social and psychological difficulties. The child who is ahead in physical development at an early stage of his life will have few such problems. This youngster is likely to remain ahead of his contemporaries throughout the growing years, despite temporary setbacks. Not so the child, especially the boy, who develops slowly and late. Late-arriving maturity is a lesser problem for girls and may even prove advantageous in certain activities. In gymnastics, for instance, a small build combined with agility is an important advantage for female competitors. Though a boy may eventually grow taller than another who matures early, he may meanwhile be made miserable in any number of ways.

In a society that tends to group children almost exclusively on the basis of their chronological age, the late maturer is constantly at a disadvantage. Not only is he smaller and lighter; he is, on the average, a little behind in the development of strength, endurance and motor skills, and may therefore do less well in athletics and other activities. As a result he may be put in a class with children a year or more younger than he is. Being "held back" may produce emotional problems that further affect his ability to learn. Trapped in a vicious circle, he may keep dropping behind, so that even when he finally catches up in

PRECOCIOUS INTELLECTS, 17th Century French mathematician Blaise Pascal and German poet and playwright Wolfgang Goethe, are commemorated on these stamps. Both displayed astounding creative development at an early age. Pascal *(top),* without any books or teacher, taught himself geometry before the age of 12. Goethe *(bottom)* wrote his first play when he was 10.

size, he may be unable to catch up emotionally and intellectually.

Actually, a child's rate of development—physical or intellectual—is a totally inadequate clue to his final achievement. The life histories of any number of successful people make it clear that slow growth is not always an unmixed curse. Two of the greatest men of the 20th Century —Albert Einstein and Winston Churchill—were considered backward as children. Einstein was so late in learning to talk that his parents feared he was subnormal. He also appears to have been slow in overall physical development. As a man he was of medium height, with broad shoulders and a well-developed musculature. As a child he was small, slender and notably unathletic. He considered himself a weakling, and disliked such physical activities as running, jumping and playing games. Churchill, who was born prematurely at seven months, was always shorter than other boys his age. His father, his governess and most of his teachers were convinced he was dull and untalented. Sent to school when he was seven, he hated it from the beginning, was always at the bottom of his class and was "kept back" several times.

Although late intellectual flowering may simply reflect slow growth, precocious mental ability in young people often reflects something more than rapid growth. A favorable environment and parental encouragement may stimulate a youngster's intellectual development, but they are not enough to explain the feats that child prodigies have been known to achieve. The 19th Century British philosopher John Stuart Mill was the son of a brilliant man who was himself a philosopher of note. But the word "brilliant" does not begin to describe young John. He learned Greek at three, wrote a history of Rome when he was six and a half, was deep in the study of solid geometry when he was nine, and at 12 frequently debated philosophy as an equal with his father. Mozart, one of the greatest names in music, was himself the son of a musician. Both he and his sister were subjected to enormous pressure by their ambitious father. But these facts cannot account for the composer's early signs of genius. At three, Mozart could memorize musical passages simply by listening to them once. Before he was seven he was touring the courts of Europe, giving recitals on the violin and the clavier. Minuets he wrote when he was six are standard learning pieces for many beginning piano students, and he wrote his Fourteenth Symphony, which is still in the repertoire of most orchestras, when he was only 15 years old.

Brain, environment and intelligence

Precocity like this may in part reflect rapid growth, but it must also have something to do with particular characteristics of the brain, which result from some peculiarly favorable combination of heredity and environment. The nature of these characteristics is not known, although it is generally agreed that intelligence is related to the number and nature of the interconnections among the cells of the brain, and to the action of the various chemical substances it secretes. The development of intelligence, precocious or otherwise, is much influenced by the child's environment. Indeed, environmental changes are presumably responsible for an apparent rise in the general level of intelligence—at least as measured by I.Q. tests—among American children. The rise seems to have been going on since about 1916, when the tests were first put into common use. Some of the changes that have undoubtedly gone into producing it are better living conditions, including better nutrition; improved means of communication; improved methods of education; improved intelligence tests; even improved skill among children in taking the tests. However, the rise may also stem from another factor: a long-term—or in statistician's jargon, "secular"—trend, a decade-to-decade, generation-to-generation tendency of people to mature earlier and faster, and to grow bigger, taller and heavier.

The long-range trend

The oldest statistical evidence of such a trend dates back to the early 19th Century. For more than 200 years the Norwegian Government has kept records of the heights of all the young men who have served in that country's army. These records show no appreciable average increase in height for the first 90 years. But about 1830 the figures began to rise, and they have been rising consistently ever since. By 1875, the average Norwegian soldier was half an inch (1.3 cm) taller than his forebear of a half century before, and by 1935 he was an inch and a half (3.8 cm) taller still.

Many countries in the world have been affected by the secular trend. It has been observed in Japan and in Argentina, in Estonia and in the United States. The changes associated with the secular-trend increase show themselves very early. Since the middle of the 19th Century, babies in many parts of the world have been increasing in size and weight at birth. Older children have also been growing bigger. Between 1880 and 1950, for example, the average height of American and Western European children between the ages of five and seven increased more than half an inch (1.3 cm) every 10 years, for a total of more than four inches (10 cm); the average height of adolescents increased by seven inches (18 cm). Records at Marlborough College in England indicate that between 1873 and 1943 the average height of its 16-year-old students increased more than half an inch (1.3 cm) every 10 years.

Adults have increased in height less spectacularly than adolescents: about four inches (10 cm) in America and Western Europe from the mid-19th Century to the 1960s. However, while children are growing faster, they also stop growing sooner. Early in the century, most men reached their final height at around 26 years; since then the age has dropped to 18 or 19.

The young ladies of Manchester

Just as growth now ends earlier, so adolescence and its growth spurt now begin earlier. It is known that girls have been reaching the menarche at a younger age since the early part of the 19th Century. Records from the industrial city of Manchester, England, show that in 1820 girls from the lower social and economic classes attained menarche at an average age of 15.7. "Educated ladies"—who benefited from adequate nutrition as well as a ladylike education—reached it at 14.6 years. A 1963 report gave the figure as a little over 13 years for the first group and a little under 13 for the second. Records kept since 1900 show that the age of menarche has been dropping in the United States, too. In many other countries girls have been reaching puberty earlier than their mothers did. All told, the average age of menarche has dropped three to four years since 1850. There is much recent evidence that the trend toward early menarche is now leveling off at around age 12½.

Over the course of centuries there have been ups and downs in average heights and the onset of maturity. Traditions and historical documents of both the ancient world and medieval Europe indicate that in those periods puberty occurred at about age 14. The Jewish ritual that invests a boy with adult responsibility—the bar mitzvah—traditionally takes place when he is 13. Shakespeare's Juliet was 14, and all through the Middle Ages marriage at that age or even younger was common. More recently, the secular trend has at times slowed down or even reversed itself in situations where living conditions worsened. In battle-torn countries of World War II, children were shorter and lighter for their age, and babies were similarly undersized. In a number of developing countries adult heights have shown no increase during periods where increases did occur in more advanced countries. In fact, adult height has actually decreased during the last quarter century in India. This is probably due to a combination of inadequate nutrition and frequent bouts with infectious diseases that weaken growing children and divert nutrients from the growth process toward fighting infections. The result is that children are prevented from reaching their full genetic potential for physical stature.

But the explanation that improvements in nutrition and disease control are responsible for the secular trend does not seem to account for all the facts. During World War II, when the countries around it were suffering a severe decline in living standards, neutral Switzerland enjoyed prosperity and a normal standard of living. Yet the babies born there just after the war were smaller and lighter than normal, just as in the neighboring countries where the war had been fought.

Several other explanations for the secular trend have also been advanced—none of which, however, is really satisfactory. It has, for example, been attributed to a long-term rise in the world's temperature. Few scientists take this proposal very seriously. Studies of animals, indeed, suggest that a hot, moist climate may actually retard growth. Certain animals in cold climates average larger than closely related species in warmer areas. The existence of more mobile populations, resulting in intermarriage between genetically diversified people, has also been advanced as a reason for the trend. This may indeed be a factor that would explain part of the increase, but science does not yet have sufficiently detailed knowledge of the genetics of height to be able to endorse the suggestion completely.

The long-term effects of the secular increase are far from clear. Physically bigger does not necessarily mean better. Furthermore, cultural taboos and traditions have not altered to accommodate the earlier achievement of maturity, and people who are in a physical sense adults are still expected to play a childish role. The result is a troublesome social prolongation of adolescence long after it has ceased to be a physical reality.

Searching for the Secrets of Development

The mechanisms that form the basis for the seemingly limitless differences among individuals in growth, size, shape, health and behavior are the subject of long-term appraisal at two institutions, the Fels Research Institute of the Wright State University School of Medicine in Yellow Springs, Ohio, and the University of Montreal Research Center for Growth and Development. The Fels Institute is the seat of a great variety of research projects, among them its well-known longitudinal study of growth, the oldest study of its kind in the world. Since 1929 the pioneering institute has compiled information on more than 800 individuals, many of whom were still participating in the study a half century later, along with their children and grandchildren. The University of Montreal's newer longitudinal study, launched in the late 1960s, includes innovative investigations of dental development and psychological growth.

A DECEPTIVE COMPARISON
Jennifer Stover, a second-generation participant in the Fels Research Institute's longitudinal study, tries some informal—and unreliable—measuring with Asha Morgan as they arrive for a regular evaluation. Though Jennifer now tops her friend by several centimeters, X-rays of their hands and wrists, together with other information, may foretell that Asha will end up the taller of the pair.

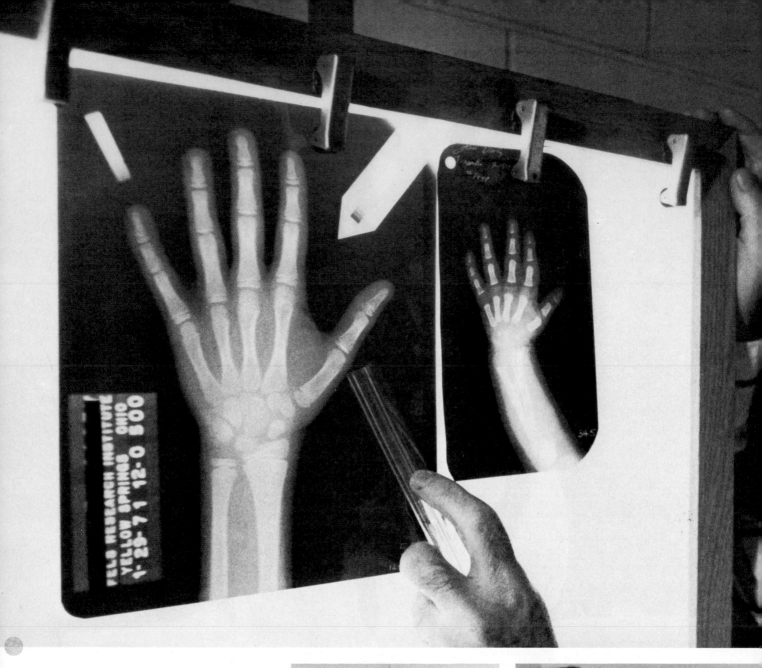

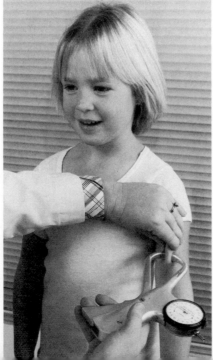

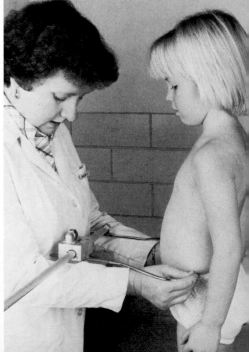

A MEASURE FOR FAT
A skinfold caliper's dial registers the thickness of the skin and subcutaneous fat overlying Diane Pavey's bicep muscle. Skinfold readings are taken at six other spots as well. A comparison of her skinfold size with her weight indicates whether she is overweight, underweight or normal.

At Fels, Plotting Physical Growth

Essential to the study of growth is anthropometry—the scientific techniques that quantify the changes the body undergoes throughout life. Participants in the Fels study, like six-year-old Diane Pavey *(below)*, are measured twice a year until they are physically mature, and less regularly thereafter. About two dozen measurements are taken, including the standing height and the length of the body while lying down (they are seldom the same), weight, and the circumferences of abdomen, legs, arms and chest. X-rays are made of the knee, hand and wrist, and head.

Data gathered at Fels over the years have been combined with information from other growth studies in the United States to help chart norms for stature, weight and head circumference of different age groups and sexes. These charts are used by doctors across the country to assess the development of their patients.

Fels scientists are also examining their data to determine the relationships among various aspects of growth. They have discovered, for instance, that up to the age of 14 obese children tend to be taller and more advanced in skeletal and sexual maturation than their lighter peers. Why this is so is an intriguing puzzle yet to be solved.

FROM CARTILAGE TO BONE
Dr. Alex F. Roche, director of the Fels longitudinal study, compares the dark areas of cartilage in the fingers of a three-month-old *(right)* with the clearly defined, bony epiphyses between the long bones of a 12-year-old's fingers. The degree to which the epiphyses have hardened and fused with the long bones can be used to estimate the biological age of a child.

A CLUE TO BRAIN GROWTH
The maximum head circumference reflects the growth of the brain, which proceeds at a fast rate in early childhood. Diane Pavey's brain, and thus the circumference of her head, are now 400 per cent greater than at birth and have reached about 95 per cent of their ultimate size.

IN CHILDISH PROPORTION
A digital caliper measures the span between the iliac crests, or outermost points on Diane's pelvic bone. The ratio between her hip and shoulder widths will remain the same as a boy's for another three years or so, and then her hips will start to outstrip her shoulders in growth.

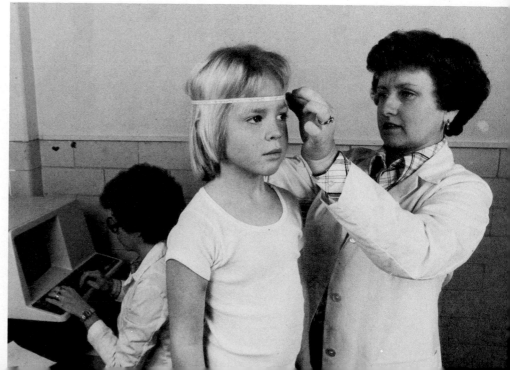

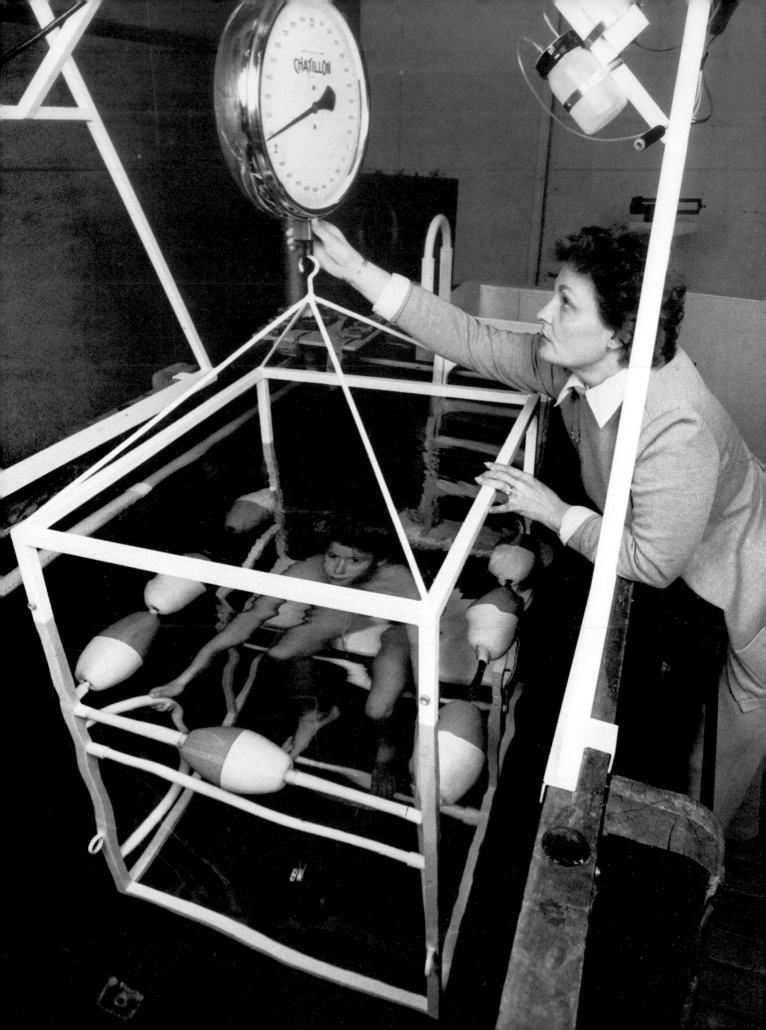

Probing the Body's Make-Up

In the 1970s an investigation of body composition was launched as part of the Fels longitudinal study. The immediate aim of the Fels scientists is to quantify the relative percentages of fat and muscle in the body of an individual. Ultimately, they hope to determine what impact heredity has on body composition.

The study is focused on body fat, since obesity is a serious health problem that increases the risk of diabetes, heart disease and hypertension. For this program, Fels has collaborated with Webb Associates, a private laboratory that uses sophisticated equipment for measuring the body's weight, volume and the volume of the lungs with great accuracy. The measurements are entered into a mathematical formula that yields the density of the body. This figure is compared to the density of fat, which is lower than the density of muscle, to arrive at an estimate of total body fat.

Fels scientists are also testing the hypothesis that a person with an unusually large number of fat cells is more likely to become obese, since he has a greater storage capacity. From a small sample of fat removed from the buttocks, the size of the individual's fat cells is measured and their total number in the body estimated. Although final results of the body-composition study are years away, preliminary findings indicate that the adolescent growth spurt cannot be counted on to pare away "baby fat." A child who is fat at six stands a very good chance of becoming a fat adult.

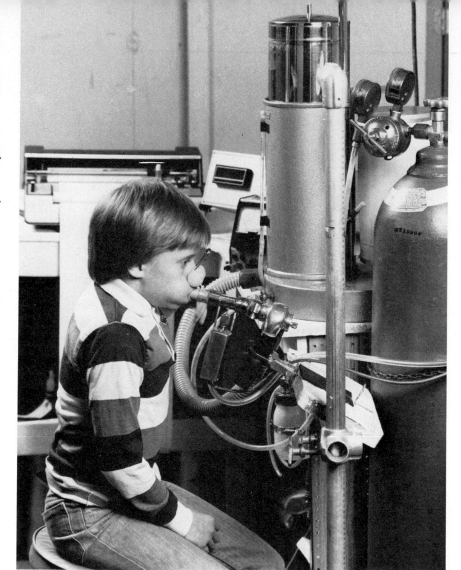

OXYGEN IN, NITROGEN OUT
After exhaling as much air as possible, Daniel breathes into a respirometer filled with pure oxygen. Since exhaled air contains a known proportion of nitrogen, the volume of air remaining in his lungs can be calculated by measuring the amount of nitrogen in the respirometer.

WEIGHING IN WATER
In order to have his weight in water measured for a body-density calculation, 10-year-old Daniel Barnett sits on a scale suspended in a tank four feet deep, exhales fully and ducks his head below the surface. The buoyant effect of the residual air in his lungs will be taken into account.

VOLUME FROM AIR DISPLACEMENT
Daniel peers out of a closed tank that measures body volume. When a set quantity of air is injected, his bulk causes air pressure to increase more than if the tank were empty. The amount of air the body displaces, and hence the body's volume, can be derived from the pressure change.

Tracking the
Genes of Disease

In 1976 Fels researchers launched a genetic study of five large Ohio families that include members with severe high blood pressure. Evidence suggests that hypertension runs in families, and Fels researchers aim to pinpoint the role heredity plays in its development. A lengthy physical examination at Wright State University's School of Medicine established for each of the 600-odd subjects measures of blood pressure, blood chemistry, certain hormone and enzyme levels, and information about personality factors, diet, work and other environmental factors. The subjects' blood pressure and their cardiovascular function were monitored during stress tests, such as mental arithmetic and isometric exercise. From the cumulative data the Fels Institute scientists hope to identify major genes that regulate blood pressure and to spot early symptoms of hypertension so that this disease can be headed off with prompt treatment.

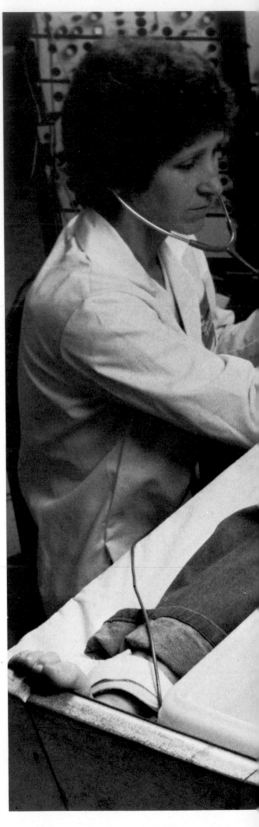

THE EFFECTS OF TENSION
In a stress test, Wendy squeezes a dynamometer at one third her maximum grip for three minutes. The physiological effects of this isometric exercise vary according to age, but hypertensive people routinely have a more marked rise in their blood pressure and blood flow.

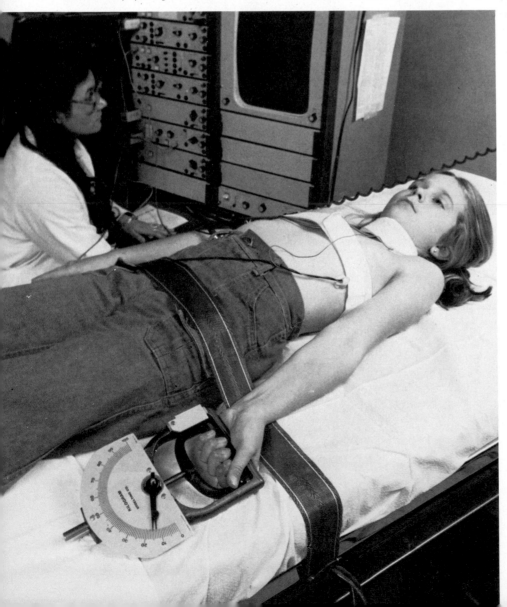

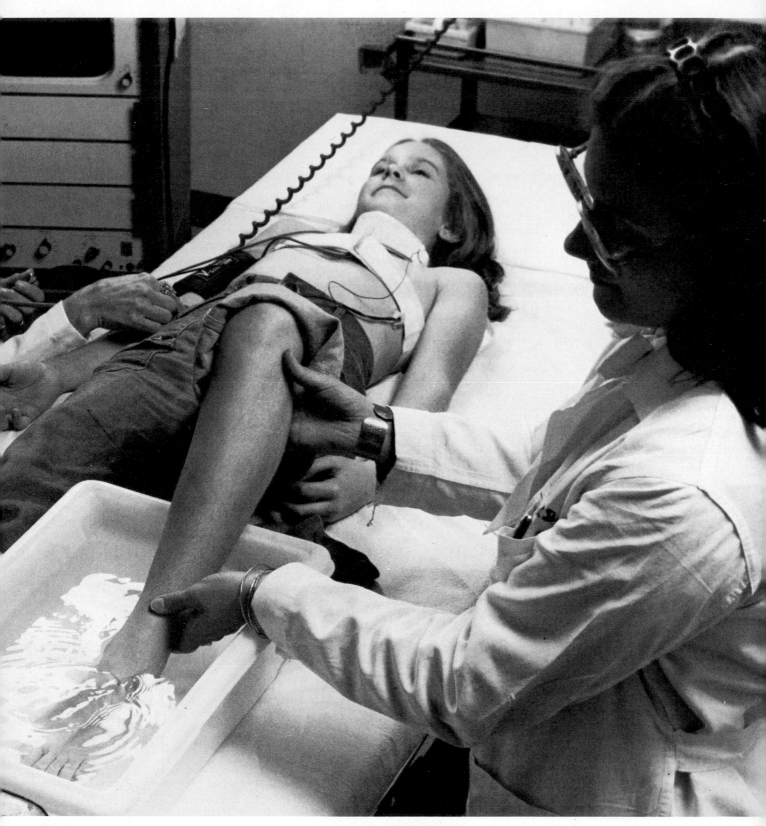

WIRED FOR SOUND
As nine-year-old Wendy's foot is immersed in ice water (4° C.), three electrocardiograph terminals record the reaction of her heart to cold. One microphone picks up the sounds of her heart, while two other microphones on her neck and right ankle detect her pulse. These simultaneous readings reveal to scientists the speed with which blood travels through her body.

A RECORD IN PLASTER

Bite casts like the one Dr. Demirjian holds monitor year-to-year changes in jaw structure and reveal misalignments of upper and lower teeth. Malocclusions usually result from the inherited shape of the jaws; environmental factors such as thumb-sucking can also cause a faulty bite.

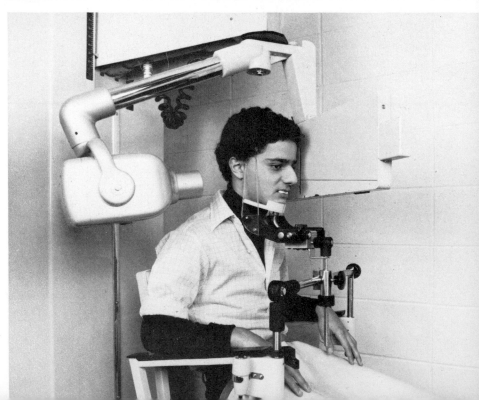

REDUCING RADIATION RISKS

The arm of a panoramic dental X-ray machine *(right)* travels in an arc around Ari Demirjian's mouth and produces an image of all his teeth on a single piece of film. The exposure to radiation that accompanies the use of this equipment is only one tenth that of conventional machines.

At Montreal, Another Dimension of Development

The 200 boys and girls participating in the longitudinal study at the University of Montreal Research Center for Growth and Development, like the children at Fels (*pages 90-91*), are meticulously measured and X-rayed for indications of somatic and skeletal development. To these indexes of growth, Montreal's director, Dr. Arto Demirjian, has added the category of dental development.

The development of both deciduous, or baby, teeth and permanent teeth begins with a soft bud buried in the jaw. In the Montreal study, yearly X-rays track eight stages as the teeth enlarge, change shape and calcify. The first stage is the calcification of the cusps—the outermost points on the biting surface of the tooth—and the last is the maturing of the root tip. The actual cutting of a tooth is not among the eight stages, but Dr. Demirjian is working out a means of predicting the time of emergence from the stage of root development.

In addition to X-rays, plaster casts of the teeth and jaws provide a three-dimensional growth record. A child's overall dental maturity is scored on a scale of 0 to 100, when all but the wisdom teeth have completed growth. Girls typically have a higher score than boys, just as X-rays of the skeleton show them to be more advanced. For every individual, however, dental development operates according to its own timetable and is not correlated with skeletal age or sexual development, both of which can be thrown off course by malnutrition or disease. Because the teeth are less vulnerable to such influences, dental age may prove a reliable gauge of physiological age, to which sexual and skeletal maturity can be compared.

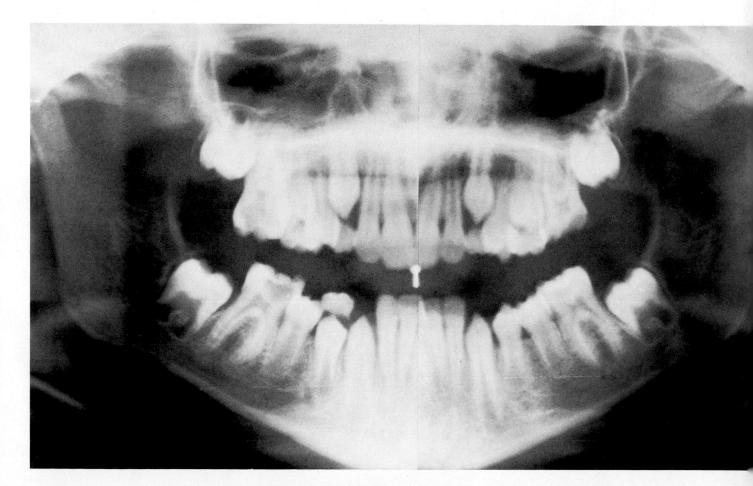

A WRAP-AROUND IMAGE
A panoramic X-ray captures the dynamic movement of a nine-year-old's teeth. A permanent canine, fifth from the right in the lower jaw, has already emerged, while its mate above has yet to dislodge the small deciduous tooth and break through the gum's surface. Such X-rays also increase the chances of accurately diagnosing jaw fractures, tumors and other disorders.

Movement Toward Muscle Control

Practice alone does not make perfect in controlling the body's movements. Motor development depends on the intricate interplay of muscle growth, the nervous system's maturation, and experience as well. This aspect of development proceeds in steps: Sure control of the large muscles of the limbs and trunk precedes dexterity of the hands. Montreal researcher Giselle Talbot-Donnelly is seeking to determine what levels of motor skills are typical of Canadian children at different ages.

At each visit the children in this study, who range from three months to six years, are given a battery of tests appropriate to their age level.

Parents are also asked what their children are able to accomplish by themselves in their everyday activities, such as dressing and undressing. Their gross-motor, or large-muscle, coordination and balance are demonstrated in such exercises as walking heel to toe. In snipping with scissors or constructing a block tower, a child's control over the small muscles of the hand and the coordination of hand and eye are demonstrated.

Past experience is also a major contributor to achievement in childhood: Through trial and error a child learns the architectural fact that the most stable tower has its blocks placed squarely one on top of the other.

EYE AND HAND TOGETHER
Four-year-old Frédéric Bourgeois *(above)* concentrates on keeping his scissors between parallel lines as he cuts a piece of paper in half. In a second test of eye-hand coordination, children are asked to cut along a single line. Their performance is then assessed according to age.

AN UNCERTAIN BALANCE
As Giselle Talbot-Donnelly times him with a stopwatch, Frédéric waves his arms and curls his foot to maintain a one-legged stance *(left)*. Such movements are necessary for four-year-olds, since the cerebellum, the center of the brain controlling balance, is still developing.

The Growth of Language

The University of Montreal's study of language development assesses a child's cognitive abilities as well as his verbal skills. Adeptness in language is closely connected with memory and perception.

When a child extracts information from his sensory experiences, he creates a series of perceptual units in which to categorize it. At the same time, he is discovering that these units have labels—words—attached to them. A simple test for children 18 and 24 months old asks them to identify pictures of familiar objects, such as a car or a dog. When a child responds with the right name, he shows that he not only knows a word but also understands, for example, what a dog is, whether it is a dachshund or a great Dane or another breed.

By the time a normal child is four or so, he has mastered the essentials of grammar, whatever his native language is, and can generate an endless variety of novel sentences to communicate his thoughts. His analytical powers have also grown, and tests for older children concentrate on their ability to comprehend and talk about more abstract concepts such as big and little, hot and cold.

Poor hearing or other sensory impairments can affect a child's test performance, or he may be intellectually slow and unable to formulate abstract ideas. Although language screening tests cannot be used alone to diagnose disorders, they do flag problems that will have to be investigated.

A MEANINGFUL GESTURE
Caroline Bibeau pretends to eat when she is asked "What do you do when you're hungry?" Many three-year-olds act out their answer to the question, but within a year most of them will respond with words alone, gesturing only when they are asked to show what they mean.

SIZING THINGS UP
With both a word—*petite*—and a gesture, Véronique Bibeau defines the dimensions of a mouse. Through four years of comparing objects and analyzing their differences, she has evolved the opposing abstract concepts of big and little and has learned to label them correctly.

A LOPSIDED GAME
Four-year-old Frédéric Laurendeau assumes the role of fishmonger in a game with his little sister Sophie. His skill in language enables him to embellish his role with details he has observed in real life, while the more passive Sophie is limited to a few words as she accepts her purchases.

FINDING THE FEATURES

Like the great majority of two-year-olds, Antoine Véronneau is able to point to his mouth and other principal features of his body. If a child of this age cannot, there is a strong probability that something is amiss in his development.

AN UPSIDE-DOWN FACE

Three-year-old Caroline Bibeau adds ears and other features to a hairy felt head. Though she has turned it upside down and has apparently perceived the hair as a beard, the features are correctly oriented in relation to one another.

THE MISSING PART

Five-year-old Véronique Bibeau shows her "tadpole man," a trunkless figure with limbs that spring from the head. But her grasp of the human form is now sophisticated enough so that she can draw all its other major parts.

Perception: Order from Chaos

From birth a child is flooded with sensory input—sounds, objects that are sometimes stationary and sometimes moving, and a vast spectrum of colors, shapes and textures. Perception evolves in identifiable stages as the brain and sensory organs develop; the child learns to extract information from countless impressions and organize it into coherent patterns.

To establish the level of perceptual development typical of Canadian children at different ages, Montreal's researchers have drawn upon screening tests used in older growth studies and have created new evaluation techniques. One part of the study determines progress in comprehending the form and distinguishing features of the human body. Children are also asked to build a three-block bridge, a seemingly simple task that nevertheless requires an understanding of the spatial relationships among objects. The tests are an important diagnostic tool that can alert parents to learning problems.

Many Canadian hospitals give perceptual screening tests to young patients along with motor and language tests. If a child's overall score is low, he is sent to specialists for diagnosis.

Caroline Bibeau works on a puzzle testing her ability to recognize geometric shapes. The time it takes her to complete it is recorded.

5
The Tempestuous Years

THE SPURT IN PHYSICAL GROWTH that takes place during adolescence is the most obvious aspect of that transitional period but not the most important. The alterations in appearance that accompany adolescence are merely external evidence of internal processes producing greater changes in the body than it has experienced since birth. The adult is not simply bigger and stronger than the child—he is a different person.

In particular, he is a person who has achieved sexual maturity and fallen heir to all the possibilities and problems this status implies. The physical modifications of adolescence, apart from those which are simply increases in size, are nearly all related in one way or another to this single, central fact. So, too, are many of the psychological changes. Because he is physically a different person, the adolescent must behave differently. But while the physical developments take place automatically, the changes in behavior do not. Most of them must be learned, and the learning process in contemporary Western society is protracted, difficult and often painful for the adolescent—and for his family.

Scientifically, one of the most intriguing puzzles of adolescence is why it happens when it does. We know that it is set off by different hormones secreted by the endocrine system into the bloodstream, and the action of these hormones has already been fairly well traced. But what causes the change? Why should the endocrine glands, which for 10 or 12 years have operated in a fixed, self-regulating pattern, shift to a new one?

The best evidence at present suggests that the whole process begins in the nervous system, in the small mass at the top of the brain stem that is called the hypothalamus. This tiny cluster of nerve cells plays a part out of all proportion to its size in the body's economy. It is the control center for a host of vital functions: It regulates the heartbeat, the rate of breathing, body temperature, and the cycle of wakefulness and sleep. In addition, the hypothalamus appears to act as a kind of biological timer. It turns on the hormonal processes that produce the adolescent growth spurt and sexual maturity; at the proper moment, it turns them off. This it does through its effect on the body's "master" gland, the pituitary, which lies immediately beneath it and which regulates the activity of other endocrine glands.

This description of the hypothalamus's role is based on some experiments conducted on rats. In one, the British physiologist Geoffrey Wingfield Harris and a Swedish colleague, Dora Jacobsohn, removed the pituitary gland from an adult rat and as a substitute grafted on the pituitary of a newborn rat. At once, the new gland started to release the hormones appropriate to an adult. Clearly the infant gland has received a message of some sort from the adult body, which impelled it to this unusual premature activity.

Yet another experiment, also carried out by a binational team, indi-

ENTERING MANHOOD
Puberty is marked in many cultures by traditional ceremonies; among Jews it is the religious ceremony of bar mitzvah. Wearing prayer shawl and cap, Carl Jay Bodek *(opposite)* stands with his father and the rabbi in the synagogue, on the sabbath closest to his 13th birthday, and prepares to read the daily passage from the sacred Torah for the first time in his life.

cated that the message came from the hypothalamus. Dr. B. T. Donovan of London and Dr. J. J. van der Werff ten Bosch of Leiden, Holland, were able to bring laboratory rats to premature puberty simply by damaging a portion of the animals' hypothalamuses. In all other respects, the experimental rats seemed normal: Although they were much too small to have reached puberty, they were the proper size for their actual ages.

What the hypothalamus "knows"

These experiments have been interpreted to mean that the hypothalamus regulates the pituitary gland by reacting to some of the body's other hormones. During childhood, it is apparently very sensitive to the small quantity of sex hormones present in the bloodstream even before birth. Responding to their presence, the hypothalamus prevents the pituitary from releasing its gonadotrophic hormones, which would stimulate the sex glands to step up their hormone production.

Science has not yet discovered how the hypothalamus "knows" when the time for puberty has arrived. The process is thought to be connected with the general level of growth and development that the organism has achieved. Whatever the explanation, the hypothalamus at a certain time apparently becomes less sensitive to the sex hormones and ends its inhibition of the pituitary. Then the pituitary is free to release gonadotrophins. These, in turn, prod the sex glands into stepping up their own output and sexual maturation begins. These interlinked processes continue until the sex hormones in the bloodstream reach a level that can stimulate the hypothalamus, which thereupon calls a halt to further sexual changes. Thus the level of sexual development is stabilized.

Since damage to the hypothalamus can bring on premature puberty in rats, it seems likely that tumors or other abnormalities in this tiny region could bring young children to sexual maturity long before the adolescent growth spurt would normally occur. Examples of this condition have been reported in medical history for centuries. In 1658, a German physician, J. A. von Mandelslo, described the case of a girl who had begun menstruating at the age of three and gave birth to a son when she was six. The most celebrated case in recent times occurred in April 1939, when a ragged Indian woman from the foothills of the Andes brought her small daughter, Lina, to the hospital at Pisco, Peru. The mother was convinced that her child's bulging belly was a sign of possession by evil spirits. The examining physician, Geraldo Lozado, at first believed that the child was suffering from a tumor. Both were wrong. Lina was actually eight months pregnant, and in May, Dr. Lozado delivered the 70-pound (31.8 kg) child of a healthy six-and-a-half-pound (2.95 kg) boy. Lina's exact age at the time is not clear. According to her birth certificate, made out in the primitive village in which she had been born, she was four years and eight months old. But her developmental age, based on X-rays of her teeth and bones, indicated she was about six.

Fortunately, cases of sexual precocity are rare. In a study made during the 1940s by a British physician, Hugh Jolly, only 69 instances were discovered in the United Kingdom. More than two thirds of these were girls —a disproportion no one has yet been able to explain.

Premature sexual development does not necessarily lead to premature sexual activity, though it does produce at least some dislocation in a child's emotions and behavior, as a maturing endocrine system leaps ahead of the brain in development. Sexual precosity also seems to affect physical growth. Children of this type are generally taller than their contemporaries and, therefore, usually prefer to play with older girls and boys, who are closer to them in developmental age. Ultimately, however, most of them end up shorter than children who develop according to a normal timetable.

In ordinary children, all the changes associated with puberty occur during the adolescent growth spurt in a relatively coordinated and harmonious fashion. Usually, the outward evidences of emerging maturity begin to show themselves at about the same time that the spurt commences. Boys begin to look like men: Their shoulders widen, their hips become proportionately narrower, and their legs and arms lengthen and become more muscular. Girls show female signs of maturity: Their breasts develop, their hips widen, and deposits of fat beneath the skin produce rounded contours.

Broad hips, broad shoulders

The differential in hip and shoulder growth between boys and girls reflects specialization on a cellular level. The cartilage cells of the pelvic area are highly responsive to estrogen, a female sex hormone. The large amount of estrogen that a girl produces at puberty results in a great growth spurt in the hips. Boys have much lower estrogen levels, and correspondingly less hip growth. Conversely, shoulder cartilage cells are responsive to male hormones, especially testosterone, so greater shoulder growth ordinarily occurs in males.

These alterations in structure at puberty serve functions that are obvious in some cases, less so in others. Women's broader hips aid in carrying and bearing children, and their fatty deposits provide reserves they can draw on to nourish unborn or infant children when food is in short supply. The function of a man's broad shoulders and heavy musculature is perhaps twofold. In primitive times, they made him a more adept hunter and increased his ability to ward off predatory enemies. And if, like other primates, our male ancestors fought each other over females, strength was a great sexual advantage.

A PUBERTY CEREMONY for girls of an Apache Indian tribe is symbolically depicted in this old painting on doeskin. Each girl being initiated shares a blanket with an old woman "guardian," who is sworn to protect the girl for life. Medicine men in headdresses dance around the fire, which represents cleansing. The stars stand for good will.

The secondary sex characteristics evolved over millions of years because they were useful. They have survived, it appears, partly because they are still useful in attracting the opposite sex. Though standards of beauty vary enormously from one culture to another, a man's broad shoulders or a woman's ample hips can nevertheless evoke interest in members of the opposite sex almost anywhere in the world. In humans, as in other species, the secondary sex characteristics appear to act as automatic releasers of the mating impulse. (There is some evidence that children as well as grown-ups possess physical releasers. The rounded faces of infants—baby chicks as well as baby boys and girls—may serve to stimulate protective behavior in adults. Because babies are cute, people want to cuddle and nurture them.)

Preparation for biological maturity

The primary sexual changes which prepare the body for reproduction take place at about the same time as the secondary ones. In boys the testes become larger, and inside them the tubules which manufacture sperm come to maturity. The prostate gland develops, and begins to secrete the seminal fluid. The growth and development of these reproductive organs trigger the appearance of two other secondary sex characteristics. These, more than any others, are the ones that announce to the world that the boy has become a man: the deepened voice and the bearded face. In fact, the boy then is in a sense already a man, since these changes usually occur after sexual maturity has been achieved. They are produced by testosterone, the hormone secreted by the testes. As it moves through the bloodstream, it stimulates the growth of facial hair and also stimulates growth in the cartilage of the larynx, thus changing the pitch of the voice.

In girls the growth and development of breasts, uterus and ovaries come first. Shortly after the peak of the growth spurt, the menarche follows. This announcement of maturity is sometimes deceptive. Uterus and ovaries do not always develop synchronously, and it sometimes happens that the uterus begins its monthly cycle before the ovaries release mature eggs. Generally, however, no more that a year elapses between the menarche and the attainment of fertility.

All these dramatic physical occurrences are bound to affect the feelings of adolescents about themselves and others. The adolescent years are a period of search and questioning. A British physican specializing in the problems of adolescence, Doris Odlum, listed these as questions the introspective adolescent asks:

" 'What sort of person am I?'

'Are my thoughts and feelings similar to those of other people or am I quite different?'

'Am I better or worse than other people?'

'Would people want me if they knew what I was really like or would they reject me?'

'What sort of people are my parents?'

'How do they compare with other children's parents?'

'What do I think about my friends?'

'What sort of person do I wish to be?' "

A thousand similar questions are also voiced, relating not only to the adolescent's immediate environment but also to the world in general and the meaning of life itself.

In comparing himself with his contemporaries, the adolescent often focuses on externals. Good looks, however defined, are valued virtually everywhere, so he often measures his worth as a person and his chances of success by the degree to which he meets his society's standards of attractiveness. If he feels inadequate on this score he worries. A physician who examined a group of American adolescents over an eight-year period discovered that a third of the boys and nearly half the girls were concerned about their appearance. Boys fretted because they were short or fat or did not have athletic frames or because they had bad skin—or simply *felt* ugly. Girls worried because they were too tall or fat or generally homely, or because their breasts were small or their figures unformed. Not surprisingly, the late maturers were the most self-critical. They were, after all, at an obvious disadvantage when they compared themselves to others of the same age.

The late maturer

This disadvantage seems to be more acute among boys than among girls. Late-maturing boys' dissatisfactions with themselves are reflected both in the opinions of their classmates and in their own responses to psychological tests. Questionnaires circulated among adolescents reveal that late-maturing boys are more often described as show-offs than those who are early maturers. They are also considered more restless, bossier, less grown-up, less good-looking. Tests of the late maturers indicate that they are more likely to feel rejected, rebellious and aggressive. At the same time they are much more dependent, with a greater need for psychological support from friends and family. In other words, they tend to be both angry and afraid, a combination that makes for conflict between the boys and their environment as well as within the boys themselves.

The slow-growing boy's problems are rendered even more acute because his special difficulties are heaped on top of others which affect both boys and girls in the early years of adolescence. Social custom in our society ignores an elementary biological fact: Until quite late in the teens, girls outpace boys in development. They reach puberty at a younger age, and they experience psychological changes before their male contemporaries. Surveys of junior high school students show that girls are at least two years ahead of their male classmates in physical development. Many have reached puberty by the time they enter junior high, while many boys have not yet reached puberty when they enter senior high. As a result, during these crucial years boys and girls alike have little opportunity to know members of the opposite sex who are on the same level of development as themselves. At the same time, young teenagers experience social pressure to date. The ones who yield to this pressure may not have had sufficient time to learn the meaning of friendship with members of the same sex—a development that the late anthropologist Margaret Mead found disturbing. She believed that the capacity to form and keep close friendships with one's own sex can best be developed in childhood and that it is closely related to the ability to achieve mature love relationships in later life.

Are the tensions and anxieties of adolescence dictated by nature or imposed by society? The answer seems to be that they are imposed by society in advanced countries, because society's timetables are not synchronized with man's natural growth timetable.

Of all animals, man is the slowest to reach physical maturity. A cat can have kittens at 12 months, a lioness can produce cubs at about 28 months. Even the great apes, closest to man in their body structure and in intelligence, reach puberty between six and 10 years. Man's delayed maturity cannot have been simply a biological accident. Evolutionists think it is correlated with the development of the remarkably complex endocrine and nervous systems that are the matrix of human behavior.

Nearly all human behavior is learned rather than inherited. Man is much less a creature of instinct than any other animal. Indeed, the capacity to learn, to substitute flexible thinking for the rigidities of instinct, is a basic measure of intelligence in man or any other species. But learning is a time-consuming business. Hence man's protracted childhood is a necessity to give him time to acquire the mass of information and skills without which he could not survive as an adult, even on a primitive level.

Society and adolescence

In primitive societies, the years of childhood offer all the learning time an individual needs to fit into his culture. As a result, sexual maturity and social maturity are reached almost simultaneously. The in-between period is at most two or three years.

In modern industrialized societies, the situation is very different. These complex cultures demand complex skills and complex behavior habits which cannot possibly be acquired in a baker's dozen of years. The

DIFFERENT APPROACHES by the sexes to the same problem are evident even in the preadolescent years. In a series of tests at the University of California, children 11 to 13 years old were given a variety of toys and told to create an "exciting scene." Girls almost always selected and arranged their toys to emphasize inner space, such as the enclosed family scene below. Boys stressed outer space, with elaborate rockets and towers.

time lapse between sexual and social maturity is therefore long and drawn out. In most Western countries, few people achieve economic independence before their late teens, and those who go on to higher education must wait until their twenties. The intervening years are a no man's land. The adolescent is no longer physically dependent, as he was in childhood, but he is still dependent psychologically and economically. He is increasingly held responsible for his actions, yet still controlled and supported by his parents. Generally he is physically ready for an adult sexual relationship long before he is considered ready, economically or psychologically, for marriage.

"The lesson of not caring"

The contrast between adolescence in primitive and in modern societies is pointed up in classic studies of two primitive cultures that were conducted by Margaret Mead at the beginning of her long and distinguished career as an anthropologist. During the 1920s she spent six months among the people of Tau, a tiny island in the Samoan group, and a similar period among the Manus, an equally primitive people of New Guinea. The two cultures differed from each other in almost every respect save one: In neither was adolescence a time of stress and conflict. In both places, boys became men and girls became women without any of the anxieties and emotional problems that are considered inevitable in modern cultures.

The Samoans showed a nonchalant approach to the world. "No one plays for very high stakes, no one pays very heavy prices, no one suffers for his convictions or fights to the death for special ends," Mead wrote in her book, *Coming of Age in Samoa*. "No implacable gods, swift to anger and strong to punish, disturb the even tenor of their days. No one is hurried along in life or punished harshly for slowness of development." Everyone did his job, at his own level of proficiency. Words like "intensity," "ambition" and "competition" had virtually no meaning at all to the people of Tau. Samoa, said Mead, "is kind to those who have learned the lesson of not caring, and hard upon those individuals who have failed to learn it."

In the Samoan culture all the events of life, from birth through death, were simply taken in stride. The child was not shielded from any of them. Sex and procreation, growth and development, were all accepted without fuss, and the Samoan youngster slid from childhood into puberty almost imperceptibly. No one was concerned about a girl's first menstruation, and she herself took it completely for granted. Nor did it alter her social position in any way. By the time she reached the menarche she had already graduated from her childhood task of taking care of her younger brothers and sisters. She still had some years before she would take on woman's work: weaving, bark-stripping, fishing, light farming.

A couple of years after she arrived at puberty, the Samoan girl was admitted to the group of older girls and became her culture's version of a debutante. She spent her days primarily in sleeping and her nights in dancing and making love. In time, she chose from among her many lovers the young man whom she liked best, married him and settled down. For a Samoan girl, adolescence was the happiest period of her life.

"No word for love"

The Manus islander that Mead studied in the 1920s was a radically different person from the Samoan. "The whole of life, his most intimate relation to people, his conception of places, his evaluation for his guarding spirits, all fall under the head of *kawas*, 'exchange,' " wrote Mead in *Growing Up in New Guinea*. "He has no other word for friend. Friends are people with whom one trades, or who help one in trade. Pregnancy, birth, betrothal, marriage, death, are thought of in terms of shell money, pigs and oil."

Manus men and women, antagonistic and hostile to one another, viewed every natural function of the body with shame and disgust. "The Manus language has no word for love, no word for affection or caress." Parents arranged marriages when their offspring were still children. A girl whose father had not been able to buy her a husband by the time she reached puberty became an object of pity in the community. When she achieved menarche, the Manus girl's family marked the fact with an elaborate public ceremony, which touched off a whole round of party-giving and exchanges of property and food between her family and the family of her betrothed. But the girl herself played little part in all these festivities. For five days and nights she sat in a special room, without washing and hardly moving, guarded at night by other village girls. Then came more feasts, more ceremonies, canoe parades, exchanges of beadwork and food, and a series of boastful, pretentious speeches—by the chiefs, by the girl's father and by the father of her betrothed.

Several years would elapse between these bleak celebrations and the girl's marriage. During this period, her standing in the community was in no way changed; her work and her relationships with others remained the same. The only difference was that she had reached puberty—and must keep all evidence of this shameful event concealed. "Forbidden to go abroad in the dark night, she lies awake and listens to the hour-long colloquies between mortals and spirits," wrote Mead. "Except for the unusual intrusion of a brief and penalty-ridden sex affair, these years are not years of storm and stress, nor are they years of placid unfolding of the personality. . . . In Manus, a girl has no need to seek a husband; he has been found. She may not seek a lover; she is denied the outlet of close friendship with other girls. She simply waits, growing taller and more womanly in figure, and in spite of herself, wiser in the ways of her world."

By Western standards, the Manus way of life that Mead saw was stultifying in the extreme. The concepts of freedom and choice were as foreign to the Manus islanders as were the words for love or friend. But if Manus life was grim, it was at least secure. There, as among the more permissive Samoans, the adolescent knew at every moment what the future held in store. The pattern of his life was fixed by tradition, and he was spared the pain and conflict of having to make choices or decisions independently.

The adolescent in more modern societies, coping with the lengthening gap between physical and social maturity, must at the same time discover who he is, what he wants, what he believes to be "good" and "bad." Among the Samoans or Manus he would not have needed to ask such questions. The values of these societies, whether pleasant or unpleasant by modern standards, were simple and consistent, and he absorbed them without thinking. By contrast, modern cultures—particularly American society—present the adolescent with a bewildering variety of options: in religious affiliation, political belief, vocational possibilities, hobbies and leisure-time pursuits. The search for values and goals, difficult even for an adult, is doubly difficult for the adolescent. Often he cannot decide which way to turn. Shall he go back to the protected world of childhood dependence and submission to authority? Or should he take a chance and move forward to independence and adult responsibility?

Rebellion and protection

Because the answers he puzzles out for himself are often confused and equivocal, his behavior is likely to swing from one extreme to another. Often he rebels most vociferously against orders from the adult world when what he really wants is to be protected by it. Often, too, his parents and his culture are not much help. They prod him to grow up and to be independent, but they cannot give him the economic means of achieving this goal. They may encourage him to date at an early age, but they caution him against sex. They permit him to drive a car when he is 16 and consider him old enough to fight for his country only two years later. But only since 1971 has he been accorded the right to vote in elections at age 18 and given a voice in determining how his society shall be governed.

Because the adult world itself is so frequently unsure of just what it wants from youth, it may hesitate to assume the authority that is in fact its prerogative. From World War I until the middle 1950s American parents became increasingly permissive in dealing with their children. This change in educational philosophy had the most profound influence on the younger generation. Lacking guidance from those who were older and more experienced, children turned to each other, creating a subculture with its own distinctive clothing and behavior, its own heroes and villains, its own language, music and beliefs. Instead of coming increasingly to feel a part of the broader society, adolescents became more and more alienated from it. This trend has continued, exacerbated by a revulsion on the part of many young people against war and social injustice, foisted upon them—they feel—by their elders.

Making the passage from childhood to adulthood a less painful and disaffecting experience is a difficult proposition. Modern society, unless it changes radically, is geared to maintaining rather than reducing the stresses of adolescence. Technologically advanced societies demand a highly trained population, yet that very training, often extending into the mid- or late twenties, postpones social maturity. And for others who want to enter the work force at an earlier age there may be no jobs available. But a return to the simpler and more static world of the past, let alone the worlds of Samoa or New Guinea that Margaret Mead knew, is of course impossible. Though awareness of the adolescent's problems may point the way to alleviating them, a measure of tension, anxiety and even pain while growing up seems to be part of the price exacted for civilization and freedom.

Ordered Designs and Patterns

The growth of every creature on earth is precisely regulated in accordance with exact patterns. These patterns dictate that every human being, for example, shall have fingerprints, and that all flamingos shall have long legs. So precise are these patterns that the offspring they produce are often exquisite examples of form and symmetry. This regulation governs not only size and shape, but also the timetable by which a given animal will develop. Even so, adequate allowance is made for individuality. No two human fingerprints are ever exactly the same; no two chickens have identical sets of feathers, and no two oysters ever have identical shells. Within each species further individuality comes about as a result of each individual adaptation to environment. The muscles of a man who does heavy work will increase in size more than those of a sedentary man, no matter what the muscular man's original growth pattern may have called for.

REGULATED BUT RANDOM
The ridges on a human thumb *(opposite)* help fit the human hand for its basic function: grasping objects. The pattern of ridges is determined by the growth of papillae, minute elevations beneath the skin that contain capillaries and sometimes nerve endings. A random element in the growth of these papillae produces a pattern that is never exactly the same from one individual to another.

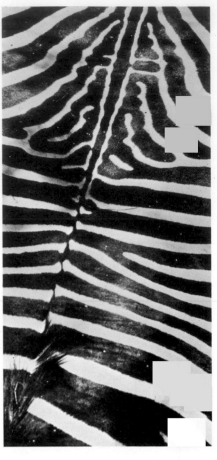

STRIPES FOR CAMOUFLAGE
The showy black and white stripes of the zebra's coat would seem to make it highly visible. But in fact they blend with the zebra's environment and help it to elude the eyes of predators.

AN AERODYNAMIC DESIGN
The tip of a crane feather *(left)* reveals the loose structure common to bird plumes. Their design reduces friction and air turbulence during flight and provides warmth at other times.

Form to Fit Function

The patterns of growth by which individual animals have adjusted to their environment have produced designs that are often striking. Just how these different patterns came into being is obscured in the antiquity of evolution. However they came about, patterns such as those shown here serve specific functions. A bird's feathers are designed to prevent air friction; the zebra's hide offers protective camouflage; the teeth of a skate are steadily replaced by new ones to keep up with its growth; coral skeletons build on one another for strength.

But nowhere is this adaptation for specialized function more evident than in the insect world, whose numbers are estimated to exceed five million species. For example, the water-dwelling whirligig beetle has one pair of eyes for seeing things in the air and a second set for underwater viewing. The tiger beetle is equipped with a pair of barbed spurs on its back, with which it anchors itself against the wall of its underground burrow in case its prey is big enough to pull it out of the ground. All such structural characteristics are the result of growth patterns that determine the final appearance of living organisms.

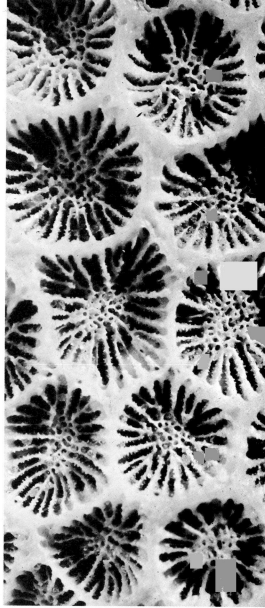

HOMES OF CORAL POLYPS
Looking like a cluster of fluted cupcake holders, the skeletal remains of individual coral polyps are nested together. For protection against the surf, each polyp encircles itself in a skeleton.

AN ARSENAL OF TEETH
Rows of replacement teeth bristle from the jaw of a skate. The skate continually sheds its old teeth as it grows, replacing the ones it loses with the next older ones growing in the row behind.

Polarity in Growth

In nearly all organisms, from the single-celled paramecium to the most complex mammal, the first and most important expression of the growth pattern is polarity—the basic indication of the direction in which a creature develops. In most organisms, this direction is established in the egg and becomes apparent the first time the egg divides. This cleavage establishes a line—generally a longitudinal, or head-to-tail. axis around which the entire creature is organized. Some organisms, such as the starfish, may exhibit radial symmetry, a pattern suited to their needs. In higher animals, the head-to-tail axis forms a line around which the creature's symmetrical structures develop, though all of these creatures include asymmetrical structures as well. Some very simple animals, such as the amoeba and certain sponges, exhibit an asymmetrical structure.

118

A SYMMETRICAL SERPENT

This skeleton of a four-foot-long (1.2 m) Gaboon viper *(below)* is one of the most elaborate examples of bilateral symmetry along the head-to-tail, or longitudinal, axis. Its 160 paired, movable ribs extend from the creature's central spinal column to form an exactly balanced pattern.

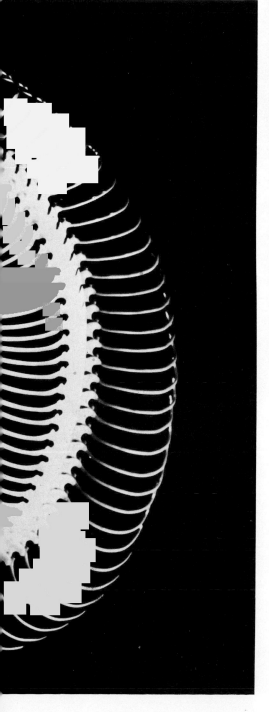

RAYS FROM A CENTER

Radial symmetry is best represented in the external structure of the starfish *(above)*. Being a relatively inactive creature, the starfish must gather its food from its immediate environment. Sense organs in the arms enable the starfish to search out nourishment in every direction.

ASYMMETRY WITHIN SYMMETRY

Man's external form is bilateral: The left side is an almost perfect mirror image of the right. Internally, however, there is much asymmetry, as this Da Vinci sketch *(left)* shows. Heart and stomach, for example, are on the left, liver on the right. The intestines lie in asymmetrical coils.

Lifeless Forms on Living Bodies

A man's fingernails, a ram's horns and a snail's shell share an important characteristic: All are produced by a type of growth called accretion. In human beings accretionary growth is predominantly displayed in toenails, hair and bone. In these structures, living cells cast off nonliving matter which accumulates outside the cells. The fingernail, for instance, grows from the epidermis, which secretes a soft, lifeless substance called keratin. This matter forces previously secreted keratin out from under the cuticle and forward, where it hardens and dries into a solid plate. Accretionary growth often produces the spiral shapes that many organisms exhibit in their horns or shells. These spirals are created because more matter is produced on one side than the other, since there is an uneven secretion at the growth base. If, for example, the secretionary rate is greater at the front of a horn than at the back, a rearward spiral will develop. This pattern, typical of horned animals such as sheep and goats, is also found in the shells of many mollusks.

A ROLLED-UP CONE
Spiral accretion is perhaps most perfectly represented by the nautilus shell *(right)*. The accretion rate on the animal's upper and outer edges exceeds that on its inner surface. In addition, as the nautilus grows, its secreting base enlarges and fashions bigger and bigger whorls.

BIDIRECTIONAL GROWTH
A ram's horn *(above)* spirals in two planes. Its base is triangular, and no two of the three sides secrete at the same rate. Thus the pushing force is outward as well as backward. The corrugated pattern reflects periodic growth, each ring representing a specific period of growth.

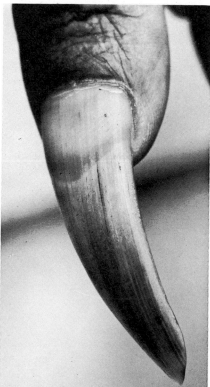

ACCRETION IN MAN
A professional trademark, this long, tapering thumbnail *(left)* identifies its Taiwanese bearer as a fortuneteller. When human fingernails or toenails are permitted to grow long, they form accretionary spirals of the same type as those found in the ram's horn and the nautilus shell.

THE REGENERATION CYCLE
This series of pictures shows the progressive stages in the regeneration of a lobster's claw —a process that takes about three years. The animal above lost its left claw near the base *(arrow)* a few weeks earlier. The wound has now healed and a half-inch-long appendage has grown out—the delicate bud of a new claw that will eventually replace the missing limb.

EARLY MONTHS OF GROWTH
Membranous, translucent tissue that will ultimately be a functioning claw grows downward, as seen in the center of this close-up. The bud, about an inch long, still has no shell covering it.

HEALED BUT NOT WHOLE
In regeneration, man is far less capable than the lobster, as shown in this 17th Century print of two badly crippled veterans. Pointing out that the soldiers are permanently crippled, the sign above observes sardonically that the two men are now less useful than one whole man.

A Renewal Pattern

All organisms to some extent have the ability to replace destroyed, defective or damaged tissue with new growths. This capacity, a pattern of growth called regeneration, varies widely from species to species, and in man and other complex animals it is severely limited. The human potential for regeneration does not go much beyond the healing of wounds, the production of new blood cells, the replacement of tissue in broken bones and in some internal organs. In contrast, such lowly animals as lobsters, crabs and salamanders can replace entire limbs, and flatworms or hydras can grow entire new bodies from a small fragment.

The inability of humans to match the regenerative power of lower organisms has long been a biological puzzle. Particularly bewildering was the observation that the salamander, which has limbs very nearly as complicated as a person's, can regenerate all four legs completely if necessary.

When a salamander loses a leg, the cells around the wound regress to an unspecialized state. Then, like the cells of an embryo, they divide rapidly and differentiate into the types of tissues needed to build a new limb.

What allows the salamander to recapitulate embryonic events? The answer may lie in the difference between the nervous systems of lower and higher animals. The salamander has a large peripheral nervous system; in humans, nervous tissue is concentrated in the brain. The volume of nerves in a person's arm, for instance, may be below a critical amount needed for complete regeneration. Research in the 1970s points to electrical currents produced by the nerves as the force sparking regeneration.

SIZE BUT NOT STRENGTH
At eight months, the regenerating claw is now about two inches long. It has begun growing its protective shell and in a few months will split along the white stripe running down the center to form its characteristic pincers. The greatest amount of the limb's structure is established during the first year. During the last two years of growth it merely gets bigger and stronger.

THE YEAR-OLD CLAW
Within a few days the pincers of this already well-defined claw will separate and it will become fully functional. Lobsters, like crabs, are also capable of regenerating smaller limbs.

Fully regenerated, the claw is smaller than the last one, and always will be. Each time a limb is lost, regenerating power diminishes.

Hypertrophy: Response to Strain

When illness, surgery or exercise places prolonged, abnormal strains upon certain portions of the body, the tissues affected respond by toughening or increasing in size—a pattern known as hypertrophy, or compensatory growth. When a man's kidney is removed, for instance, the other kidney will grow much larger, enabling it to handle a double work load.

Similarly, hard physical labor requires that an extra supply of oxygen be conveyed to the muscles, a need that the heart meets by enlarging to increase its blood-pumping capacity. The most obvious example of hypertrophy in man is in the area of muscle development. The powerful arms and chest of the oarsman and the bulging legs of the dancer are testimony to years of intense physical activity.

Little is known of the mechanics of compensatory growth, but it differs from other growth patterns in two important ways: During the period of development, new cells are not added; instead, existing cells enlarge. Compensatory hypertrophy does not involve the genes and thus cannot be passed on to the next generation.

ON THE MARK
Olympic contenders *(opposite)* spring forward at the start of a track race. Their muscles, developed for speed and strength by years of training, would revert to normal or even become flabby—a condition of atrophy—if these athletes were to adopt a sedentary way of life.

SOMETIMES GOOD, SOMETIMES NOT
Habitual hard labor has produced the bulging muscles of these workers straining to lift a heavy load. Hypertrophy is a useful condition in this case, or in an athlete's heart that has grown bigger and stronger to meet the extra physical needs. But in the case of a heart enlarged by disease, as often happens with high blood pressure, hypertrophy is very undesirable.

Proportional Patterns

The head of a newborn baby, like the legs of a newly foaled colt, seems out of proportion with the rest of its body. However, as in all creatures, the proportions of the baby and the colt will change from infant to adult. The baby's head and the colt's legs grow much more slowly than their other parts. These changes in proportion show that the various parts of the body have different rates of growth. Growth rates also differ from one species to another.

It has been postulated that alterations in growth rates have played a part in the evolutionary process. This concept originated with a British biologist, the late Sir D'Arcy Went-worth Thompson, who compared the physical characteristics of many related species. Through these comparisons, Thompson showed, for example, that two related kinds of fishes could have evolved structural differences merely through shifts in the relative growth rates of different parts—a faster-growing fin in one, a faster-growing head in the other *(below)*.

These variations, clearly visible in related species, are also quite obvious within the same species. Even a cursory examination of any group of human faces will reveal the enormous diversity resulting from slight differences in the growth rates of people's eyes, noses and mouths.

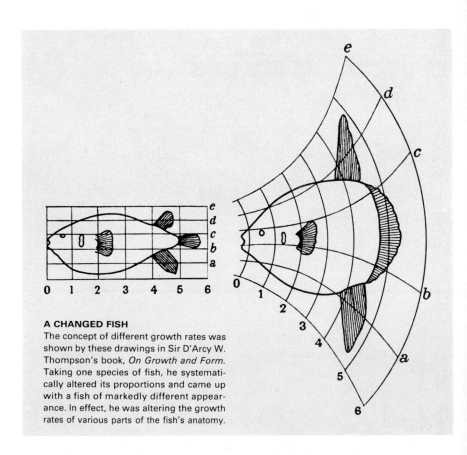

A CHANGED FISH
The concept of different growth rates was shown by these drawings in Sir D'Arcy W. Thompson's book, *On Growth and Form.* Taking one species of fish, he systematically altered its proportions and came up with a fish of markedly different appearance. In effect, he was altering the growth rates of various parts of the fish's anatomy.

A LEGGY COLT
The foal standing by its mother *(right)* is an example of differential growth rates. The foal's body must do much more growing than the legs to attain the proportions of its mother.

Structured Relationships

If an ant were as big as a horse, could it move mountains? No. A giant ant would be a structural failure. Its legs would cave in under it. The weight of a supersized ant would increase as the cube of its height, but the strength of its legs, which depends on their cross-sectional area, would only increase as the square of the height. Thus an ant of only 10 times average size would be 1,000 times heavier—but its legs would only be 100 times stronger.

In growth, the proportions of any organism must be shaped to suit its individual and environmental needs.

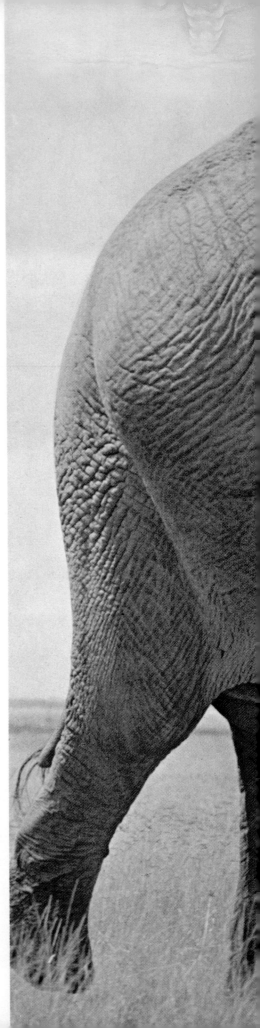

EXTREMES IN STRUCTURE
Five flamingos *(above),* each weighing about seven pounds (3.2 kg), are supported on legs half an inch wide. The elephant at right, weighing 14,000 pounds (6,350 kg), needs four thick columns, each 14 inches (36 cm) in diameter, for sufficient underpinning. If flamingos grew to an elephant's weight, their legs would be only six inches (15 cm) wide—and would collapse.

6
Genes, Hormones and Environment

IN THE PROCESS OF GROWTH, the genes, hormones and environment work neither in isolation nor in sequence. Instead, they work upon one another, backward as well as forward, to control the order and timing of development. Genes and environment interact from the moment life begins. In the embryo, growth and development result from an interplay between the inherited material of the genes and their cellular environment. The interaction between genes and hormones is equally intricate and still only partially understood. The most common view has been that the genes alone determine all the structures and functions associated with such characteristics as sex. In this view, genes cause hormones to be secreted. The hormones then act upon various tissues and serve as intermediaries to carry out the genes' instructions.

Investigations suggest that this interpretation is too simple, for hormones can also act directly upon genes. In one experiment, the bodies of roosters were made to behave like those of hens. Hens' livers, stimulated by the action of the female sex hormone estrogen, normally produce a protein that shows up in egg yolk. The livers of roosters do not. Yet when roosters are injected with estrogen, their livers begin to make this substance. The hormone apparently does this by activating a gene in the liver cells that would not otherwise have been called into play.

Despite the constant interaction of the three determinants, some growth factors can be examined independently of others. Some traits are known to be genetically determined, and to be very little influenced either by the environment or by the action of the hormones. Blood type and eye color are examples. These are passed on from parent to child in accordance with the simple laws described in 1866 by the Austrian monk Gregor Johann Mendel, whose plant-breeding experiments first established the science of genetics. Characteristics like these are known to be influenced by a relatively small number of genes. But other traits involve large numbers of genes; in addition, most are known to be strongly influenced by environment as well as inheritance. For these reasons, they are more difficult to study. Fortunately, however, identical twins provide a way of examining them. Because they arise from the splitting of a single fertilized egg, identical twins are born with identical genes. If the geneticist can prove that identical twins share a specific characteristic more frequently than do fraternal twins or ordinary brothers and sisters, he can conclude that the trait is at least partly genetic in its origin. Height, build, intelligence and the rate of growth appear to be among these traits. On the average, identical twins reach menarche within two months of each other, while fraternal twins often attain it a year apart.

In addition to the age at which puberty is attained, the general pattern of a child's growth also seems to be controlled primarily by genetic factors. Ordinarily, the growth curves of siblings bear only a general resem-

PITUITARY EXPERIMENT
The dwarfed rat opposite weighs less than a quarter as much as its companion, a normal animal of the same age. Its stunted growth was caused by removal of its pituitary, the "master" endocrine gland. Attached to the underside of the brain, the pituitary secretes at least eight hormones. One stimulates growth directly, others through endocrine glands elsewhere in the body.

blance to one another. But this is not true of identical twins, whose growth curves are almost always similar and often nearly exactly the same. The bodies of the twins, in other words, appear to be responding virtually identically to the messages of their identical genes.

During their stay in the uterus, identical twins may grow somewhat differently from each other because of their different positions in the uterus. Dr. R. S. Wilson of the Twin Research Study in Louisville has shown that identical twins sharing a placenta may receive unequal amounts of nutrients because of interconnection of their blood vessels. At birth, identical twins differ slightly more than nonidentical twins in length and weight. But by one year old the identicals differ only by about 0.4 inch (1 cm) on the average, where nonidenticals have grown much farther apart.

Hormones: chemical messengers of growth

Why do specific genes become active at specific times? The answer does not seem to lie in the genes alone, for the hormones also play a part.

The first of these substances to be recognized was secretin, discovered in 1902 by William Bayliss and Ernest Starling, who later named them hormones (from the Greek *hormon*, "to stir up").

Since that time dozens of hormones have been discovered. Most of them are produced by the endocrine, or ductless, glands, which discharge their secretions directly into the bloodstream or into body fluids. Because hormones regulate metabolic processes and since growth depends upon metabolism, all hormones contribute to growth, at least to some extent. But certain hormones have the specific function of promoting growth, or they trigger the great turning points in human development. Any study of human growth must therefore focus upon these hormones and upon the glands which produce them: the pituitary, the thyroid, the adrenals and the gonads, or sex glands.

Ultimate control of all growth glands rests with a part of the brain, the hypothalamus. At the University of London Institute of Psychiatry in the 1940s, Geoffrey Wingfield Harris showed that the hypothalamus controls the nearby pituitary gland. He suggested that the nerve cells secreted hormones that in turn released or inhibited pituitary hormones.

In the following decade Harris' idea was bolstered by experimental evidence from Roger Guillemin in the United States and Andrew Schally in Canada. They found that when ground-up animal hypothalamus was added to pituitary tissue or glands in the laboratory, hormone output was stepped up or cut back. But the task of isolating and identifying the hypothalamic hormones was long and exacting. Researchers had to process more than a million pig and sheep hypothalamuses before, in 1968, they finally got one milligram of pure hypothalamic hormone. Guillemin and Schally shared a Nobel Prize in 1977 for isolating three such hormones. Two of them govern the pituitary's growth hormone, and the third controls the release of pituitary sex hormones. At least six hormones are secreted by the anterior lobe of the pituitary, which makes it second in command of all the other glands.

Our information on the pituitary has its beginning point with the hobby of a London surgeon of the 18th Century, John Hunter. Hunter's dominating interest was to assemble a systematic medical collection, the largest of its kind. As part of his collection, he wanted the body of a famous giant of the day—an Irishman called Charles Byrne, who claimed to be eight feet four inches (254 cm) tall. Learning that Hunter wanted his cadaver, the giant asked his friends to encase it in lead after his death and sink it at sea. The story goes that Hunter bribed the undertakers as they were just about to sink the body, bought it for £500, and added it to his collection. Alas, Hunter discovered that Byrne had been exaggerating somewhat. He was, in fact, a mere seven feet seven (231 cm), as his skeleton, still on view in London, shows.

In 1909—126 years after Byrne's death—the great American neurosurgeon Harvey Cushing, who had recently embarked on a study of the pituitary, examined the giant's skull. He discovered that Byrne had been the victim of a pituitary tumor: Deformation of bone in the area of the gland indicated that it had been considerably enlarged.

Earlier, at the end of the 19th Century, the French physiologist Pierre Marie had demonstrated a connection between pituitary tumors and acromegaly, the disease in which parts of the head, hands and feet begin growing again long after normal growth has stopped. Since that time, medicine had suspected that the pituitary played a part in growth disorders. Cushing's study confirmed these suspicions, but it still did not establish precisely how the pituitary influenced growth.

Rats, research and the pituitary

In the 1920s Herbert M. Evans of the University of California, one of the greatest modern endocrinologists, shifted the focus of research from the pituitary itself to the hormones it produces. Working with Joseph Long, Evans prepared an extract from the pituitaries of cattle and injected it into the body cavities of baby rats. His rats became giants, double the size and weight of normal adults. In 1944 came a major breakthrough when Evans and C. H. Li, working with cattle pituitaries, isolated growth hormone in a pure form, unadulterated by other pituitary hormones. By then, scientists had realized that the pituitary's control over growth and maturity was more complex than anyone had imagined.

Not all the many hormones the pituitary secretes are directly involved in growth, nor do all four hormones that most influence growth operate

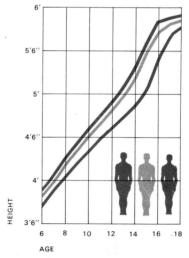

1 IN = 2.54 CM

TRIPLETS' GROWTH CURVES from six to 18 demonstrate the genetic control of growth. Two members of the triplet set are genetically identical *(light and dark brown)*, and their genes have resulted in very similar curves. The third triplet is nonidentical, or fraternal *(black)*. Since the triplets shared a similar environment, the dissimilar curve of the fraternal member must have resulted mainly from his different complement of genes.

133

directly. Although the pure growth hormone, called hGH in humans, does work directly to stimulate growth, the other three act indirectly by stimulating other glands. Thyrotrophic hormone speeds up the activity of the thyroid gland; adrenocorticotrophic hormone, or ACTH, affects the outer layers of the adrenals; and the two gonadotrophic hormones, FSH and LH, stimulate the gonads (the ovaries and testes).

The thyroid gland is a butterfly-shaped mass of tissue near the base of the neck. It secretes thyroxine, a hormone that is essential for the normal growth of most organs, and for proper metabolism at all stages of life. If a fetus's thyroid produces too little thyroxine, normal development will still take place since an ample supply produced by the mother's thyroid crosses the placenta to fill the fetus's needs. But from the moment of birth, both body and brain develop abnormally. This severe condition, called cretinism, can now be prevented. If a screening test, administered to all newborns in many states, reveals a problem, the baby is immediately started on a life-long treatment with synthetic thyroxine.

The hormones produced by the adrenal glands and the gonads work in a totally different way: Rather than acting to promote a steady increase in height and weight, they bring about abrupt changes in the overall pattern of growth. At puberty, when the final stage of growth begins, the adrenals and gonads become suddenly active. The pituitary begins to secrete large amounts of gonadotrophins. Under their influence, the testes and ovaries produce the hormones that bring the secondary sex characteristics to maturity. The boy becomes a man; the girl, a woman. At the same time, the adrenals begin to work as growth glands.

The adrenal: stimulus of the growth spurt

The adrenal glands, which are attached to the kidneys, produce three distinct groups of hormones. Two do not directly influence growth, but the third group, the androgens, collaborates with testosterone, an androgen produced in the testes, to stimulate the enormous spurt in growth that marks a boy's adolescence. Adrenal androgens are also active in the somewhat smaller growth spurt that girls experience.

What regulates the production of adrenal androgens is unknown. ACTH stimulates the adrenals to produce one of the other hormones—cortisol, the stress hormone. But at puberty, when levels of adrenal androgens rise, the pituitary produces no more ACTH than it does during childhood, ruling out that hormone as the control mechanism. Endocrinologists suspect that another hormone, so far unidentified, regulates androgen secretion. It has been tentatively named the adrenarche hormone, from the Greek word *arche*, which means beginning.

The testes begin producing hormones as early as the ninth week after fertilization, when they stimulate the formation of male genitalia. Geoffrey Harris' experiments with rats indicated that these hormones also affect the hypothalamus. A male rat cannot normally maintain the functioning of the ovary; if an ovary is transplanted from a female to a male, it will stop releasing eggs. Harris was able to alter this pattern. He castrated male rats within three days of their birth and later, when they had become adults, transplanted ovaries into them. Under these circumstances, the ovaries continued to function normally. From one point of view, Harris had simply created interesting—and somewhat horrifying—sexual freaks. From another, he had uncovered a hitherto unsuspected relationship between the hypothalamus and the male sex hormones.

The hypothalamus maintains normal ovarian function in a female rat. By castrating male rats, Harris removed their source of sex hormones. He drew this conclusion from his experiments: Within the first three days after birth, the hypothalamus of a male rat receives a message from the testes "telling" it that it is male, and the message is carried by the hormones. If the hypothalamus does not receive this message it will remain female. Normally, an organism's genetic make-up dictates that the sex of the hypothalamus and the rest of the body will be identical, but Harris has shown that this rule can be broken. By meddling with the hormones of his experimental animals, he negated the genes' instructions. Whether hormones cause a human fetus's hypothalamus to assume a male or female identity, as they do in a rat, is uncertain. Whatever the mechanism, the human fetus's identity is acquired long before birth.

The influence of environment upon growth seems simple compared to that of hormones. A child who has no food will not grow, no matter what messages his body receives from genes and hormones. And a child's illnesses, his psychological state, changes in the climate in which he lives—all these will affect his growth too, as surely as lack of food.

During a war or an economic depression an entire generation of children may exhibit slow or stunted growth because of the lack of food. Records were kept of children's growth in the German city of Stuttgart from 1911 to 1953. In the last years of World War II and the first few years after it, the average height of these children fell by more than an inch. Not until 1953 did the average height of Stuttgart children rise to meet the level of children measured in 1939.

Slowed down by starvation

Also in postwar Germany, Elsie Widdowson and R. A. McCance of Cambridge University conducted a controlled growth study of some 160 orphans. All of these children lagged 10 to 20 months behind normal levels of growth and maturity, simply because they were not getting enough to eat. Their diet provided only about 80 per cent of the calories needed for the satisfactory nourishment of a growing child. For a year,

A FAMOUS 18TH CENTURY GIANT, seven-foot seven-inch (231 cm) Charles Byrne toured England as a one-man sideshow. Later discovered to be the victim of a pituitary tumor, he attracted the attention of numerous surgeons, who connived to get his skeleton after he died. Though he was horrified at the idea, his bones in fact were preserved and are still on exhibit in London today.

Drs. Widdowson and McCance supplemented the children's diets with unlimited bread and other calorie-rich foods, such as jam, sugar, and semolina. As might be expected, the children shot up in height and gained rapidly in weight, to become normal in both respects.

Were the children permanently damaged during the years when near-starvation hampered their growth? Apparently not. Human beings have extraordinary recuperative powers. During a famine the human organism slows its growth rate and waits, as it were, for better times; it can make up the loss later if the famine does not last too long and is not too severe. Girls seem to resist malnutrition better than boys. Surveys in Guam, Hiroshima and elsewhere after World War II indicated a general retardation of growth, but all of them showed girls less retarded than boys. Similarly, the German girls studied by Drs. Widdowson and McCance returned to normal more quickly than the boys.

Other experiments conducted by Drs. Widdowson and McCance have thrown light upon the relation between emotional stress and growth. Most people would assume—and, as it turns out, assume rightly—that an unhappy child will not grow as fast as a happy one, all other things being equal. Normally, of course, "all other things" are very far from equal, and under normal circumstances the problem can hardly be attacked by science at all. But by using experimental and control groups (and partly by accident), Dr. Widdowson made observations that establish a clear connection between emotional states and growth.

The case of the cruel headmistress

Working with children in two orphanages—we can call them Orphanage A and Orphanage B—she chose a group of children from Orphanage A as experimental subjects. For six months she traced their growth on the orphanage diet, to establish their "normal" growth rate. Over the next six months, she supplemented their diet in the hope of producing a growth spurt. The children in Orphanage B, serving as control subjects, received no diet supplement at all. Theoretically, the two groups should have grown at about the same rate for the first six months; then the group in Orphanage A should have shot ahead. In fact, everything seemed to go wrong from the start. During the first six months, when both diets were unsupplemented, the children in Orphanage A gained more weight than the ones in Orphanage B. During the second six months, when the group in Orphanage A received diet supplements, they gained *less* weight than the group in Orphanage B.

The explanation, when it came, was simple enough. By coincidence, at the end of the first six-month period, a sternly disciplinarian headmistress had been transferred from Orphanage B to Orphanage A. She ruled the children rigidly at all times. What was worse, she chose meal-

GROWTH HORMONE, a chemical secreted by the pituitary gland, was discovered by the American biologist H. M. Evans during the 1920s and '30s. The result of one of his many experiments, shown here, dramatizes the hormone's potent effect. The dachshund at left was given injections of pituitary extract from birth. In eight months he became a waddling 40-pounder (18.1 kg)—nearly twice as large as his untreated brother.

136

times to administer public (and often unjustified) rebukes. Under her cruel charge, the growth rates of her tense, unhappy wards went down. And, unwittingly, she confirmed the researchers' conclusions in another way. She had eight favorite children, whom she took with her from Orphanage B to Orphanage A. Even in Orphanage B, these teacher's pets had gained more weight than the other children; in Orphanage A, where they received diet supplements, they gained weight faster than ever. This made quite clear the link between emotional state and the rate of growth. Or as Dr. Widdowson put it, in an apt quotation: "Better a dinner of herbs where love is, than a stalled ox and hatred therewith."

In dealing with such environmental factors as food and psychological stress, science has done little more than confirm popular opinion. Elsewhere, as in the influence of seasonal changes upon growth, science has come up with data for which it has no clear explanation, and which have no parallels in popular opinion. For example, on the average, growth in height proceeds faster in the spring than in other seasons. By contrast, gain in weight is fastest in the fall. In growing children and in adolescents, over half the annual gain in height occurs between the beginning of March and the end of August. The rate of gain in height in spring may be two to two and a half times greater than it is in autumn. On the other hand, two thirds of the annual gain in weight takes place between the beginning of September and the end of February. Weight may increase five times as much in the fall as it does in the spring. Some children actually lose weight in spring.

These figures, of course, are averages. Not every child shows such extreme differences, and it is interesting that well-nourished children seem to show them less than others. But the differences do exist, and they are generally substantial. We can improve our environments—that is, we can provide better food, eliminate disease, reduce psychological strains. But we cannot much improve genetic and hormonal growth factors. Scientific techniques are not yet sufficiently refined to isolate and work upon the genes responsible for growth.

The growing American

The case for hormone manipulation is somewhat brighter. Children have been cured of dwarfism by injections of the pituitary growth hormone. Children with defective thyroid glands grow normally if they receive regular doses of thyroxine early enough. But boys and girls with genetic or hormonal abnormalities are relatively rare, while environmental improvements could better the growth of whole populations.

Almost every year, new evidence is found of the dramatic effects of better environments upon growth. In 1965, Albert Damon of the Department of Anthropology at Harvard University reported the results of a 30-year study of some 200 men in the Boston area. Nearly all of them were born in the United States of Neapolitan parents, and all worked in the same factory. Those studied at the end of the research period averaged 2.1 inches (5.3 cm) taller than those who had been studied when the research began—a short-term increase in height. The hereditary backgrounds of nearly all these men were the same. What had changed was their diet, their medical care and their living conditions.

In the long run, improvements in environment can only permit individuals and populations to realize their potential. The fact is highlighted by another study, conducted by Harry Bakwin and Sylvia McLaughlin. Comparing the heights of Harvard freshmen of the 1930s with those of the late 1950s, they found significant differences between the growth trends of public-school and private-school graduates. Freshmen admitted to Harvard from public schools showed substantial height increases in the years covered by the study. Those from private schools did not. Why the difference? Drs. Bakwin and McLaughlin argue that the environments of public-school boys improved substantially between the 1930s and the 1950s, while those of private-school boys remained much the same. Better environments had enabled the public-school boys to reach their maximum potential height; the boys from private schools had always been reaching it.

The Body's Vital Chemicals

From conception to maturity, hormones play a vital role in growth. These chemical agents shape the growth of the child within the womb, stimulate the body's expansion from infancy to adolescence, bring about the transformation from adolescent into adult. In addition, hormones regularly prepare the bodies of women for the creation of a new organism. Some hormones act only on specific tissues. Others act throughout the body. Acting on the body at large, they also act on one another, regulating their output by a complex and sensitive feedback system. Hormones are secreted by the hypothalamus and the body's endocrine glands—the pituitary, thyroid, adrenals and gonads (opposite). During pregnancy, another, temporary source of hormones—the placenta—becomes operative. It serves as a sort of auxiliary endocrine gland, secreting substances that perform a vital role in the intricate physiology of mother and child.

SIX HORMONE FACTORIES
The glands most essential to growth are silhouetted within colored circles on the young runner opposite. The pituitary lies deep within the skull, the thyroid spreads across the front of the wind-pipe, the two adrenals cap the kidneys, the gonads are at the base of the torso. The pancreas, not shown here, plays no direct role in growth but influences it through the secretion of insulin.

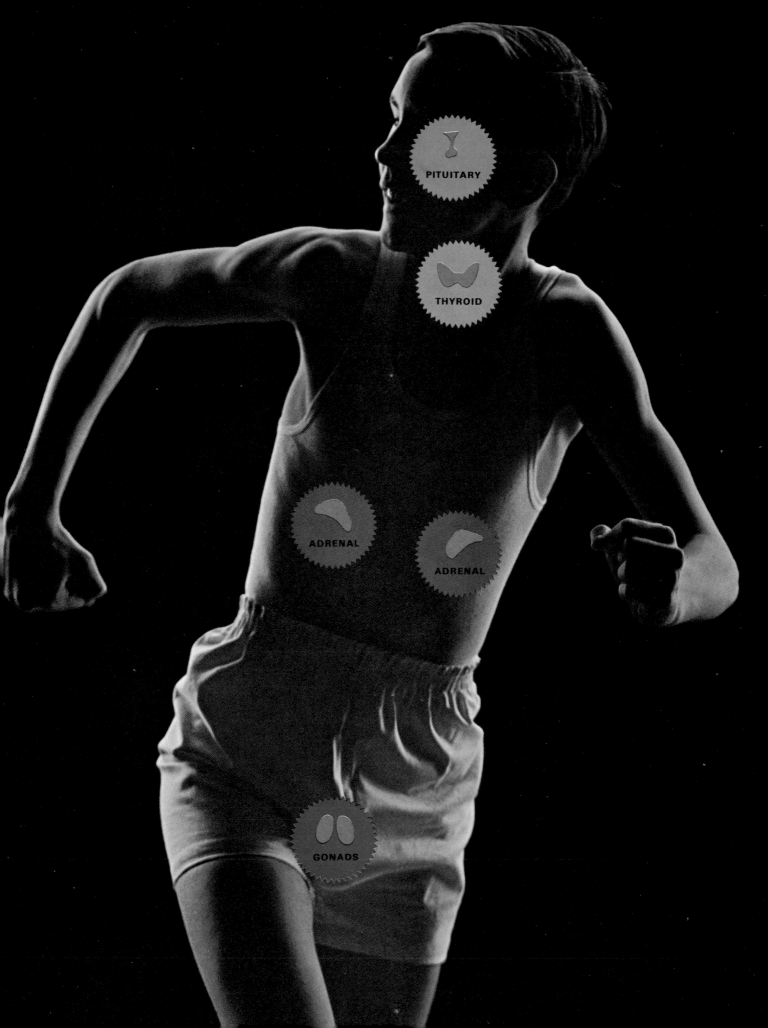

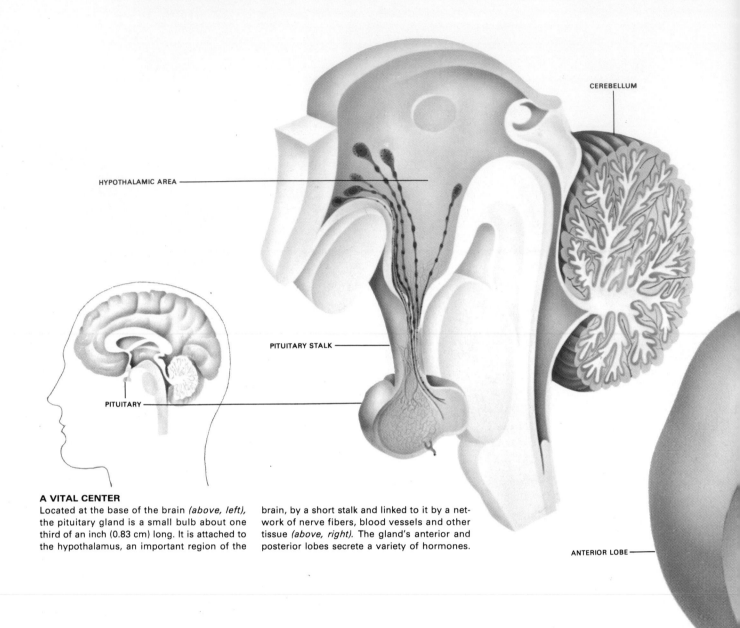

HYPOTHALAMIC AREA

CEREBELLUM

PITUITARY STALK

PITUITARY

A VITAL CENTER
Located at the base of the brain *(above, left),* the pituitary gland is a small bulb about one third of an inch (0.83 cm) long. It is attached to the hypothalamus, an important region of the brain, by a short stalk and linked to it by a network of nerve fibers, blood vessels and other tissue *(above, right).* The gland's anterior and posterior lobes secrete a variety of hormones.

ANTERIOR LOBE

Command Post of the Endocrines

Of all the glands in the body's endocrine system, the pituitary is predominant. Its anterior lobe serves as a compact field headquarters for all gland action aimed at growth. (The posterior lobe's hormones do not influence the growth process.) Most of the anterior-lobe secretions are "trophic," meaning nourishing, hormones. They are transported throughout the body by the bloodstream to their "target" glands, the thyroid, adrenals and gonads, where they stimulate hormone production. The pituitary gland not only issues orders; it also responds to the way those orders are carried out, boosting the output of trophic hormones when target glands lag, cutting back when their output is adequate *(page 142).* The pituitary also secretes growth hormone, a substance which promotes bone and muscle growth.

Often called the body's master gland, the pituitary has a master of its own, the hypothalamus. This mass of nerve tissue determines the timing of various growth stages, such as adolescence, by stimulating the pituitary to secrete more or less of its several products. What controls the hypothalamus is not yet known. There is some evidence that it contains a built-in physiological clock which "knows" when the time has arrived for a child to become an adult.

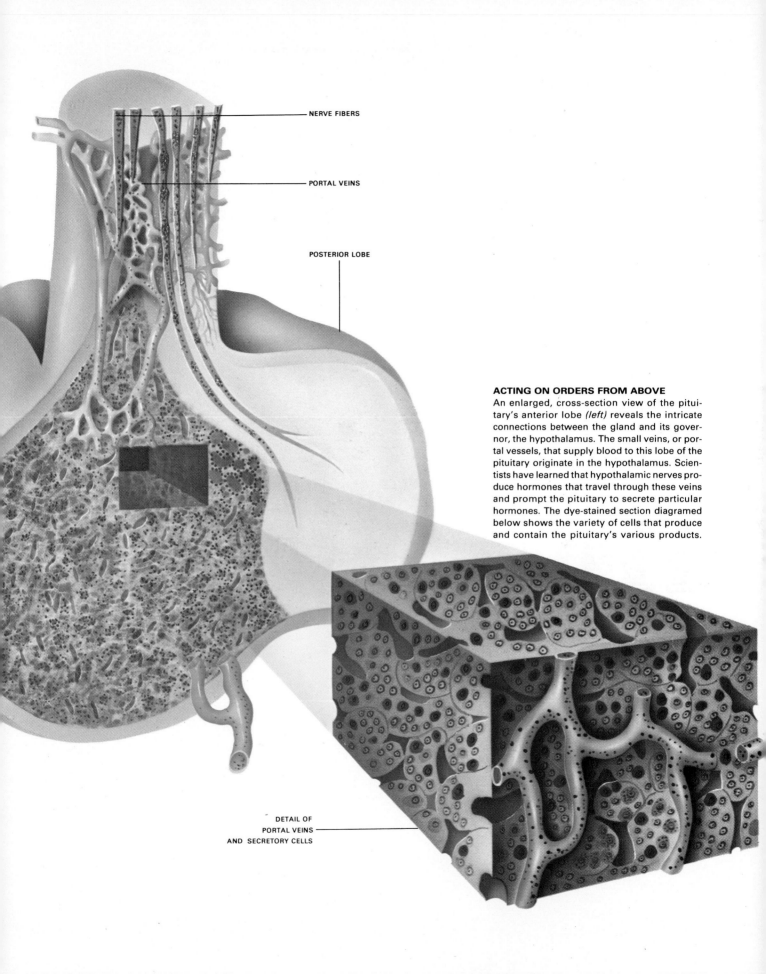

NERVE FIBERS

PORTAL VEINS

POSTERIOR LOBE

ACTING ON ORDERS FROM ABOVE

An enlarged, cross-section view of the pituitary's anterior lobe *(left)* reveals the intricate connections between the gland and its governor, the hypothalamus. The small veins, or portal vessels, that supply blood to this lobe of the pituitary originate in the hypothalamus. Scientists have learned that hypothalamic nerves produce hormones that travel through these veins and prompt the pituitary to secrete particular hormones. The dye-stained section diagramed below shows the variety of cells that produce and contain the pituitary's various products.

DETAIL OF
PORTAL VEINS
AND SECRETORY CELLS

141

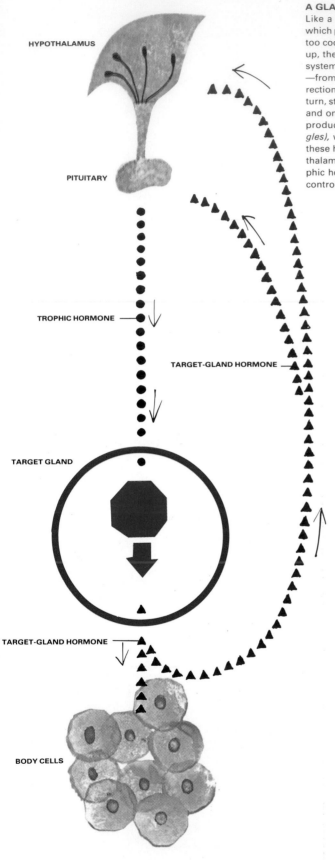

HYPOTHALAMUS

PITUITARY

TROPHIC HORMONE

TARGET-GLAND HORMONE

TARGET GLAND

TARGET-GLAND HORMONE

BODY CELLS

A GLANDULAR FEEDBACK SYSTEM

Like a furnace and its controlling thermostat, which produces more heat when the house gets too cool and less when the temperature warms up, the body's endocrines are a self-regulating system. Signals—trophic hormones *(black dots)* —from the pituitary are secreted under the direction of the hypothalamic thermostat. They, in turn, stimulate a target gland, circled in red here and on subsequent pages. The target steps up production of its own hormones *(black triangles)*, which act on body cells. Rising levels of these hormones feed back signals to the hypothalamus or the pituitary, and production of trophic hormones falls. The feedback mechanism controls production of these potent chemicals.

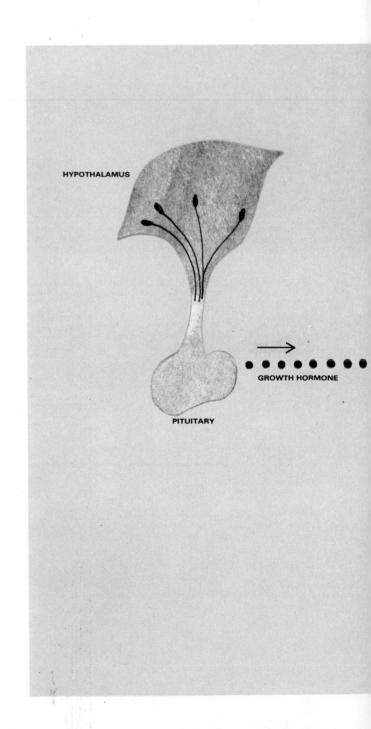

HYPOTHALAMUS

GROWTH HORMONE

PITUITARY

Hormone Action in Childhood

In the preadolescent years, growth is mainly a matter of building up a sturdy skeleton, laying down tissues and expanding the brain. Three hormones are chiefly responsible for stimulating this growth. Somatotropin, commonly known as growth hormone, or hGH, is one. Produced by the pituitary, somatotropin indirectly stimulates the growth of bone and muscle. It prompts the liver, and possibly other parts of the body as well, to synthesize somatomedin, a hormone that acts directly on bone and muscle tissue. A third growth-related hormone is thyroxine, secreted by the thyroid gland, which interacts with somatotropin to bring the growth hormone to its peak of efficiency. If for some reason thyroxine is missing, the somatotropin is only partly effective in stimulating the production of somatomedin, and the body's development is affected. Thyroxine, like the other two hormones, also influences other processes besides growth; it determines the rate at which the body metabolizes food and produces energy.

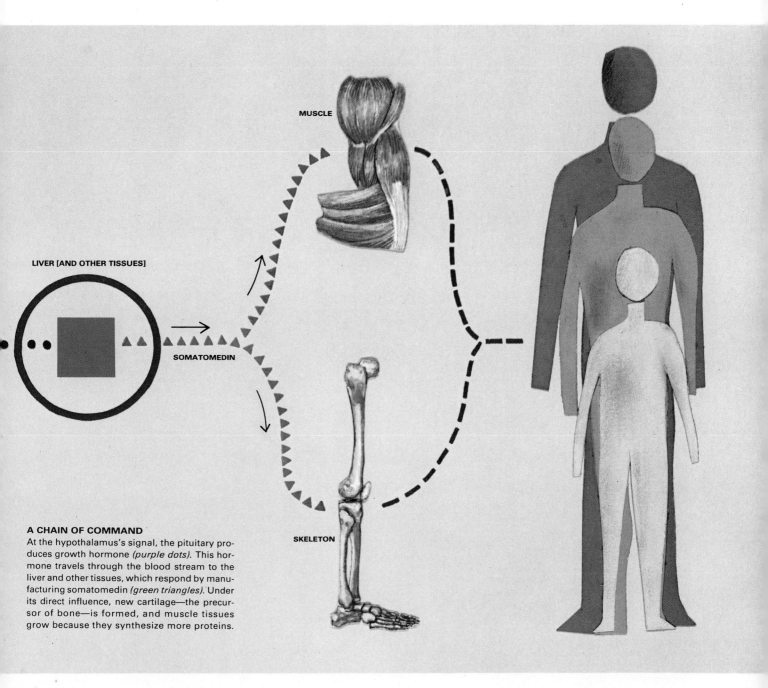

MUSCLE

LIVER [AND OTHER TISSUES]

SOMATOMEDIN

SKELETON

A CHAIN OF COMMAND
At the hypothalamus's signal, the pituitary produces growth hormone *(purple dots)*. This hormone travels through the blood stream to the liver and other tissues, which respond by manufacturing somatomedin *(green triangles)*. Under its direct influence, new cartilage—the precursor of bone—is formed, and muscle tissues grow because they synthesize more proteins.

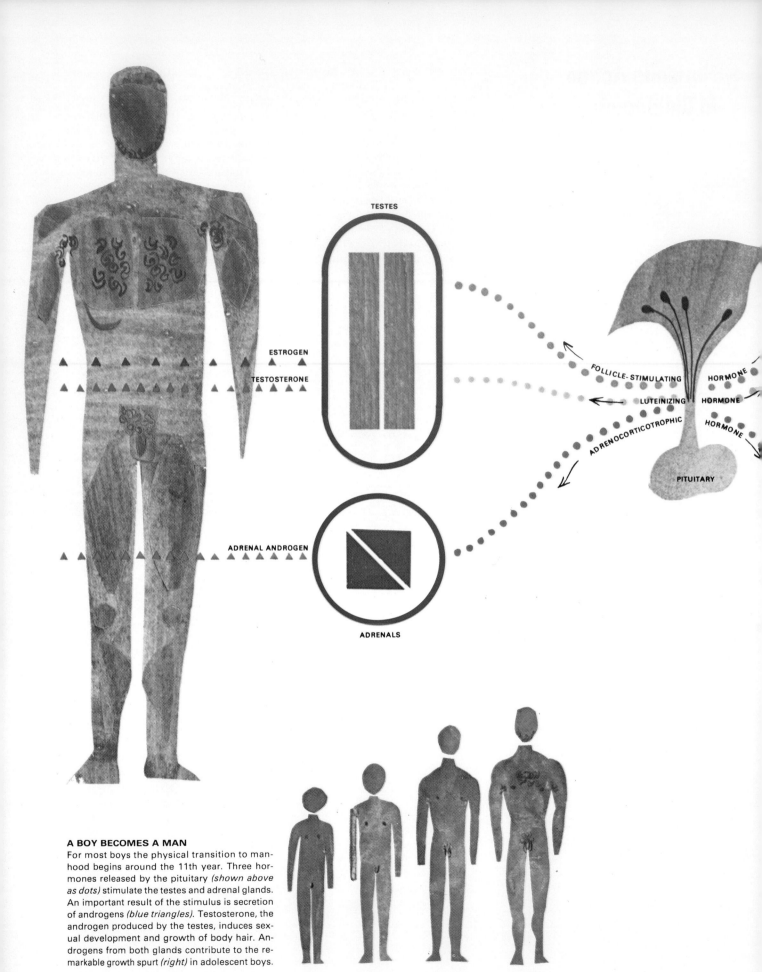

TESTES

ESTROGEN

TESTOSTERONE

FOLLICLE-STIMULATING HORMONE

LUTEINIZING HORMONE

ADRENOCORTICOTROPHIC HORMONE

PITUITARY

ADRENAL ANDROGEN

ADRENALS

A BOY BECOMES A MAN

For most boys the physical transition to manhood begins around the 11th year. Three hormones released by the pituitary *(shown above as dots)* stimulate the testes and adrenal glands. An important result of the stimulus is secretion of androgens *(blue triangles)*. Testosterone, the androgen produced by the testes, induces sexual development and growth of body hair. Androgens from both glands contribute to the remarkable growth spurt *(right)* in adolescent boys.

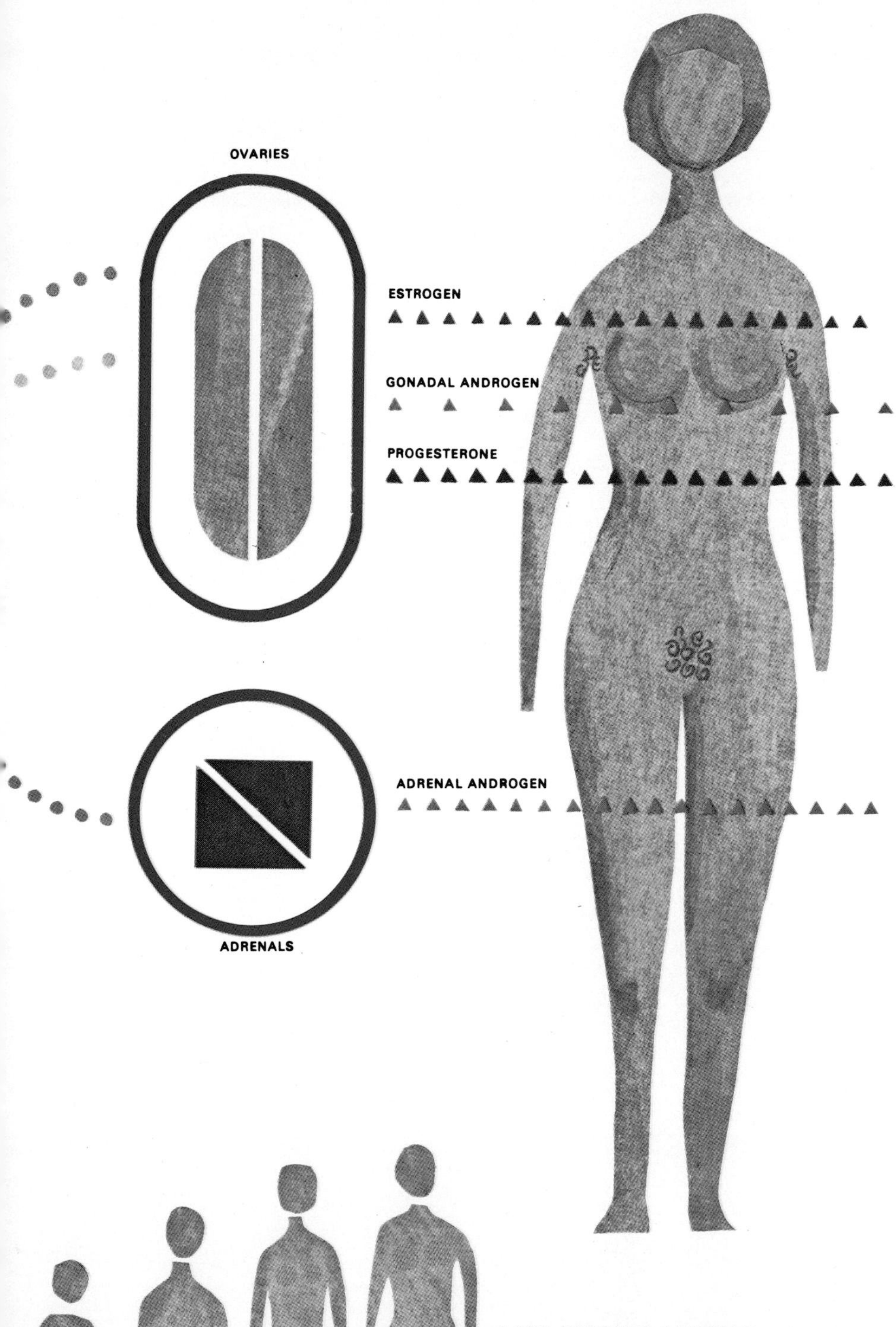

OVARIES

ESTROGEN

GONADAL ANDROGEN

PROGESTERONE

ADRENAL ANDROGEN

ADRENALS

The Hormones in Adolescence

The major changes of adolescence, sexual maturation and accelerated growth, are both brought about by marked changes in hormone secretions. In both sexes, the process, schematically diagramed on these pages, begins when the hypothalamus signals the pituitary to take up a new role. The pituitary thereupon begins secreting increased amounts of two trophic hormones—they are the same in both sexes—that stimulate the gonads, which have been almost inactive since before birth. The adrenals' activity also rises.

At this point, the process diverges in the two sexes. In boys, the trophic hormones spark the growth of cells that will produce spermatozoa; one also stimulates other cells to produce the male sex hormone, testosterone. In girls, the process is different. Egg-cell production also requires the efforts of the trophic hormones, but the apparatus that matures the eggs produces not one but two sex hormones, estrogen and progesterone, at different stages in its cycle. While each sex has its own distinctive sex hormones, each also produces small amounts of the other sex's hormones.

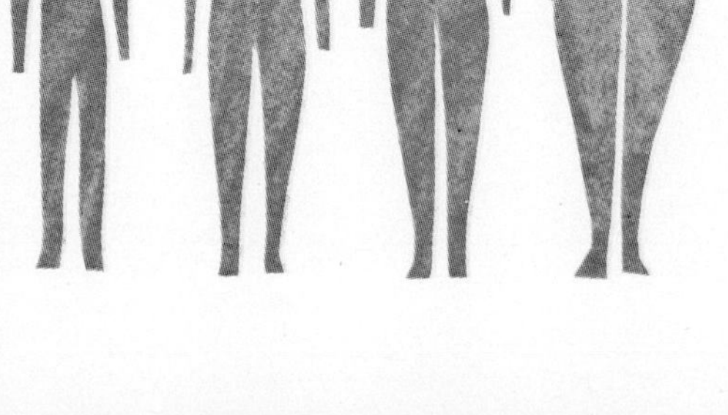

A GIRL BECOMES A WOMAN
Development into womanhood is triggered by pituitary hormones at about age nine. Under their stimulus the adrenals and ovaries secrete androgens *(blue triangles above),* which quicken growth *(left)* just as they do in boys. The ovaries also secrete estrogen; this substance stimulates the development of the breasts and of the rounded female form. It may also be a factor in terminating growth earlier in girls, by hastening complete ossification of the long bones.

The Complexities of Womanhood

Every 28 days or so, a woman's body prepares itself for the growth of a new organism. Except during pregnancy, this cyclical process *(right)* repeats itself regularly for about 35 years after puberty. It is controlled by one of the body's most intricate feedback systems, in which four hormones enter and exit, advance and retreat, like performers in a classical ballet. Each hormone presides over one step in the process, and in addition triggers the next step.

The sequence begins with the pituitary's secretion of follicle-stimulating hormone (FSH). This causes the Graafian follicle in the ovary to grow and secrete the hormone estrogen. The estrogen cuts back the pituitary's production of FSH and sets it to making luteinizing hormone (LH). This in turn triggers the follicle to release its ovum and to evolve into the *corpus luteum*, which secretes progesterone (and a little estrogen). The new hormone prepares the uterus to receive the egg if it is fertilized and also cuts LH production. If fertilization does not occur, production of both estrogen and progesterone drops. This causes the uterine lining to slough away and permits FSH production to start, beginning the cycle once more. If the egg is fertilized, however, a fifth hormone joins the cast and the plot changes *(far right)*.

Knowledge of this intricate hormonal interplay led to the development of oral contraceptives. Containing estrogen and progesterone, they function by inhibiting the cyclic secretion of FSH and LH, in turn preventing an ovum from being released and thus making conception impossible.

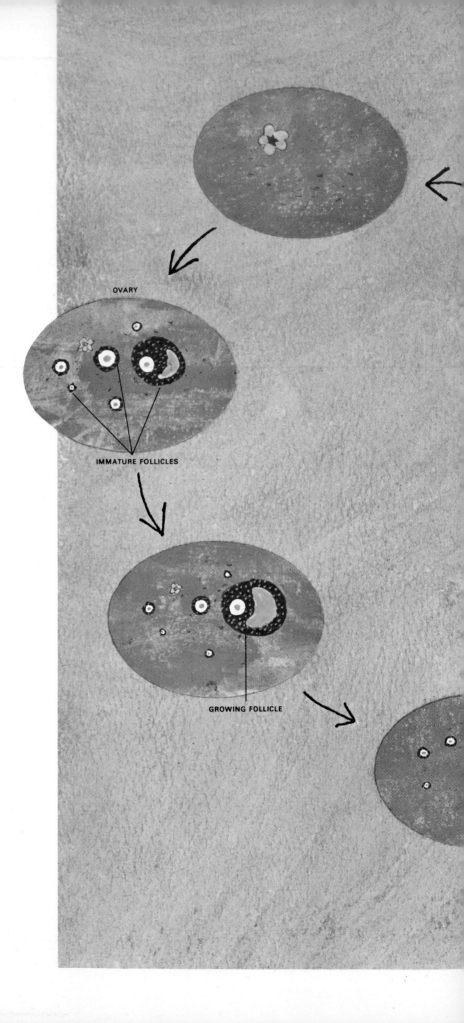

OVARY

IMMATURE FOLLICLES

GROWING FOLLICLE

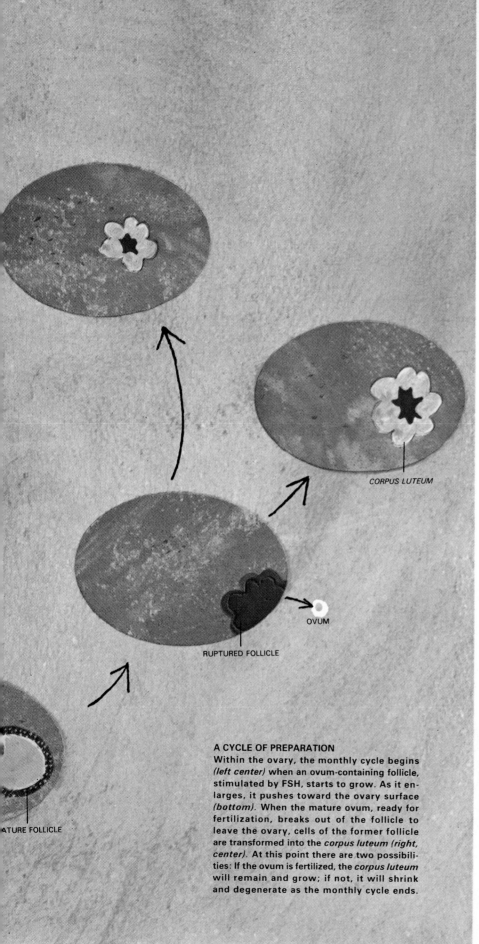

CORPUS LUTEUM OF PREGNANCY

CORPUS LUTEUM

OVUM

RUPTURED FOLLICLE

ATURE FOLLICLE

THE BEGINNING
When the clump of cells from the fertilized ovum implants itself in the uterus *(below, white mass),* it soon secretes a new hormone *(squares).* This causes the *corpus luteum (above)* to produce more estrogen as well as progesterone. Without these, pregnancy could not continue.

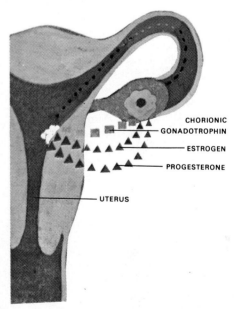

CHORIONIC
GONADOTROPHIN

ESTROGEN

PROGESTERONE

UTERUS

A CYCLE OF PREPARATION
Within the ovary, the monthly cycle begins *(left center)* when an ovum-containing follicle, stimulated by FSH, starts to grow. As it enlarges, it pushes toward the ovary surface *(bottom).* When the mature ovum, ready for fertilization, breaks out of the follicle to leave the ovary, cells of the former follicle are transformed into the *corpus luteum (right, center).* At this point there are two possibilities: If the ovum is fertilized, the *corpus luteum* will remain and grow; if not, it will shrink and degenerate as the monthly cycle ends.

Hormones That Shape a New Being

During the growth of an embryo from a cluster of cells to a fetus, the complexities of hormonal action reach a peak. Involved are the mother's endocrine system, the gradually maturing glands of the embryo and also the placenta. The placenta, which serves the embryo as a sort of combined lung, liver, kidney and intestine, secretes hormones as well.

By the third month of pregnancy, the *corpus luteum* in the ovary atrophies as the placenta takes over the job of supplying estrogen and progesterone. For this purpose it absorbs incomplete hormones of various sorts from adrenal glands of the mother and the budding adrenals of the fetus, and transforms them into usable ones. The finished products are important to both mother and fetus. In the fetus, estrogen stimulates sexual development, assisted in male fetuses *(shown here)* by a male hormone from the fetal testes. In the mother, estrogen prepares the breasts for nursing. Progesterone serves as a semiprocessed material for the immature fetal adrenals, which convert it into adrenocortical hormones. It also promotes changes in the mother's uterus to accommodate the growing fetus.

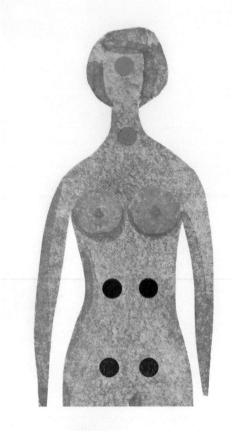

● PITUITARY

● THYROID

● ADRENALS

● OVARIES

PLACENTA, MOTHER AND FETUS
During pregnancy a woman's endocrine system *(above)* operates in a special way: Her pituitary continues to stimulate the thyroid and adrenals to produce their normal hormones, while the endocrine glands of the fetus function separately. The mother's ovaries, however, are quiescent. Estrogen and progesterone secreted by the placenta *(right)* prevent the pituitary from making the hormones that would activate the ovaries. The placenta's hormone factories are its syncytial cells, lining the villi where materials are exchanged between mother and child.

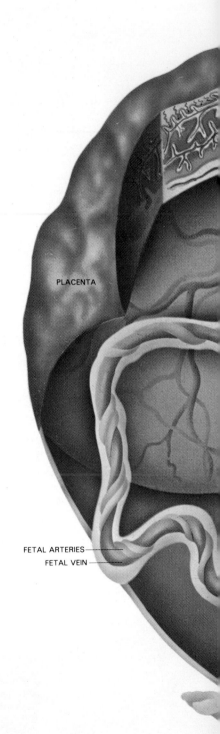

PLACENTA

FETAL ARTERIES

FETAL VEIN

148

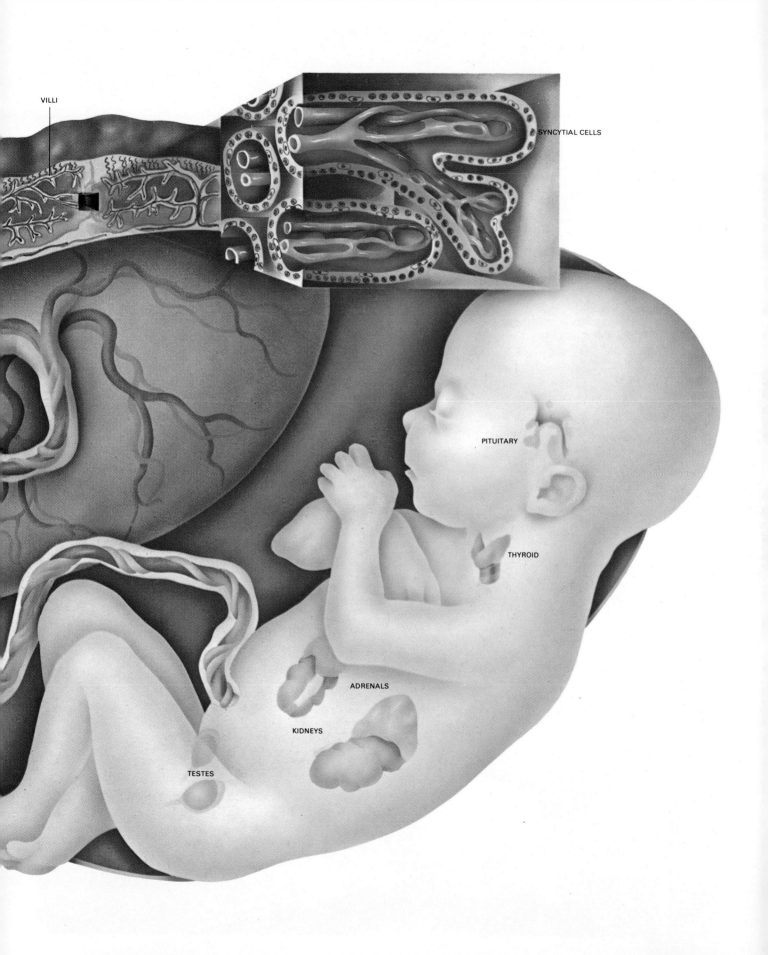

VILLI

SYNCYTIAL CELLS

PITUITARY

THYROID

ADRENALS

KIDNEYS

TESTES

7
Flaws in Development

THE HUMAN BODY is far more intricate than the most sophisticated products of man's technology. A giant computer or a space rocket embodies millions of skilled man-hours, yet neither encompasses the multitude of different parts or the manifold possibilities of one baby. If an engineer were ordered to devise a reliable process for manufacturing so elaborate a structure by the millions, he would quickly take to tranquilizers. Yet the human growth process, despite its complexity, works perfectly most of the time. If it did not, Homo sapiens might degenerate into a race of monsters and become extinct. When growth does go awry, it creates a giant or a dwarf, a child with six fingers or one with two heads, an albino or a hemophiliac—or worse.

The overwhelming majority of aberrations occur, or begin to occur, before birth. Once a child is safely born, only a catastrophe can seriously distort the growth process. Malnutrition or severe illness can temporarily or even permanently flatten the growth curve, but can seldom do more than that. The few serious aberrations that originate after birth, such as some of the cases of sexual precocity described earlier, are caused for the most part by disorders of the endocrine glands.

The embryo is far more vulnerable to noxious influences. An infectious or toxic agent can interfere with it, or it may suffer from defective genes. The result in either case is apt to be one of the many aberrations summed up in the phrase "congenital defects." These words cover one of the largest, loosest and certainly most tragic categories of disorders that afflict man. Most conspicuous are the gross malformations that have given the words their grim aura: Siamese twins; hydrocephalics, with distended heads; anencephalics, without brains; people with a missing limb, a harelip or a clubfoot. Malformations of this sort have shocked and fascinated men since the Stone Age, when shamans drew pictures of two-headed creatures on the walls of caves. Clay tablets from Mesopotamia describe deformities of the ears, nose, mouth, sex organs and limbs. Historians believe that the Babylonians took congenital defects as omens and kept these records with the aim of divining the future.

Over a thousand different defects, ranging from monstrosities to color blindness, have been catalogued, and nobody pretends that the list is complete. Any tissue from skin to bone, any organ from heart to kidney, any function from the manufacture of a vital enzyme to the synthesis of hair and skin pigment may be defective.

One of the few things that can be said collectively about this heterogeneous group of disorders is that it takes an enormous toll in human life and human potential. No worldwide statistics have been compiled, and projections based on small-scale studies are misleading because the figures vary widely and inexplicably from race to race and region to region. For example, whites suffer from anencephaly seven times as fre-

A VICTIM OF THALIDOMIDE
Like thousands of other unfortunate children, this boy is a victim of thalidomide, a sedative his mother took in her second month of pregnancy—the crucial period when the growing embryo is especially vulnerable. Luckily, the drug does not seem to affect the brain; with therapy and the help of artificial limbs, most thalidomide babies can lead nearly normal lives.

quently as blacks, while blacks are seven times as apt to be born with extra fingers. Even in the U.S., a country abundantly supplied with vital statistics, figures on growth aberrations contain a large component of guesswork. Many defective embryos are lost through spontaneous abortions early in pregnancy, but these are seldom recorded or even recognized. Furthermore, many defects are difficult to spot at birth, and some emerge only after many years. A man born with a defective gene may begin to develop in his forties the symptoms of speech disturbance and mental deterioration that characterize the degenerative disease of the nervous system known as Huntington's chorea.

Some startling figures

The statistics that are available show that the problem is serious. In 1946, Columbia-Presbyterian Medical Center in New York City carried out a study of nearly 6,000 pregnancies from the fourth month of fetal life through the first year after birth, tabulating all the malformations and congenital diseases that turned up. Of the infants born alive, about 4 per cent, or one in 25, had suffered serious disorders ranging from heart defects to mental retardation. A slightly smaller percentage showed mild defects. For the general population in the United States the incidence of severe defects is somewhat lower—about 2 per cent. In 1977, close to 60,000 of the 326,000 live-born babies were in this category. Understanding, preventing and treating birth defects are therefore urgent matters.

Researchers now look for the causes of birth defects in three general areas: defective genes, abnormal arrangements of the chromosomes and unfavorable factors occurring in the uterine environment during pregnancy. One of the subtlest gene defects, and also one of the first to be fully understood and effectively controlled, is a type of severe retardation now called phenylketonuria, or PKU. The control of PKU dates from the day in 1934 when a Norwegian physician, Asbjørn Følling, was visited by a mother and her two retarded children. The woman had noticed a peculiar musty odor clinging to both children, and asked Følling if the odor had anything to do with the youngsters' being retarded. In the course of his examination, Følling tested the children's urine and found a peculiar substance in it. After lengthy analysis, he identified the substance as a chemical relative of phenylalanine, a common compound present in almost every protein that man consumes, including mother's milk. With this clue, he and researchers in other countries were able to identify the cause of the retardation as a defect in body chemistry. In PKU victims, the enzyme that normally metabolizes phenylalanine is defective or deficient. Undigested phenylalanine accumulates in the tissues, and gives the urine and sweat a peculiar odor. The phenylalanine

SIAMESE TWINS were observed as early as the 16th Century when these engravings were done by the Swiss physician Jacobus Rueff. Like many of his contemporaries, Rueff believed that malformations of this sort were manifestations of divine punishment.

increases with every meal eaten to the point where it and its by-products injure the brain.

Because physicians could not repair the defective enzyme, they sought to counter its effects by providing its victims with a diet containing a minimum of phenylalanine. This could be done only by tampering with the protein content of their food—and it was not easy. During the first major attempt, in England soon after World War II, workers laboriously processed food for a three-year-old girl victim. Even so, they were barely able to finish each batch by mealtime. The accumulated poisons disappeared from her tissues, but the result was discouraging. Though the child did in fact become more alert, she remained retarded. The damage already done to her brain cells was irreversible. Clearly, PKU infants had to be identified and treated as early as possible.

The first effort in this direction was the "diaper test." At three to four weeks a PKU baby's urine is detectably abnormal. A little ferric chloride dropped on his wet diaper forms a blue-green ring. But detection at even three to four weeks was sometimes too late.

Finally, in 1961 a young American doctor, Robert Guthrie, developed a much more sensitive blood test that reveals the defect when the baby is only a few days old. PKU victims can be started on the necessary diet before any significant amount of phenylalanine has accumulated in their systems and while the brains are still normal. By the age of five or so, when the important period of brain growth has ended, they can generally eat ordinary foods. Many U.S. hospitals now routinely use this test on all babies, and in many states it is mandatory.

Once researchers were able to identify PKU, and distinguish it from other kinds of mental retardation, they soon discovered another important fact about it: It runs in families. From the way it is inherited, they have concluded that it results from a single defective gene. Those who inherit this gene from both parents are normal before birth, except for one defective liver enzyme. But this seemingly trivial defect can warp the entire mental development of the child.

Major ills from minor causes

Most hereditary birth defects, it is now believed, stem from equally minute causes. In a few cases, the specific chemical defect is known. In sickle-cell anemia, a blood disorder, it has been pinpointed even more precisely: alteration of a single link in the long chain molecule of hemoglobin, the protein that carries oxygen in the bloodstream. The chemical basis of most hereditary disorders, however, is still uncertain.

Hereditary defects include glandular disorders such as cystic fibrosis, which causes the production of an abnormally thick, gluey mucus that blocks the lungs' air passages and also prevents essential digestive en-

CHANG AND ENG were the conjoined twins from Siam who became so world-famous in the 19th Century in exhibitions that persons similarly afflicted were afterward called "Siamese twins." They settled in the U.S., married and fathered 11 normal children.

153

zymes from leaving the pancreas. Others are defects ranging from minor anomalies—harelip, cleft palate and extra fingers, all of which can be repaired by plastic surgery—to irreparable conditions such as a malformation of the inner ear that causes congenital deafness. Because they can be inherited, they must involve genes that supply faulty patterns for some of the body's chemical operations. But all the precise operations and enzymes involved are still unknown.

Scrambled instructions

Not all genetic defects are inherited. In some embryos the hereditary instructions that govern growth are initially all present and correct, but these instructions become garbled as they are passed from one cell to another during cell division. Mishaps of this sort usually involve not a single defective gene but a sweeping rearrangement of the cell's genetic material. Not surprisingly, the resulting defects are usually grave.

The true nature of these disorders has been ascertained only since 1956, with the development of techniques to make accurate observations of human chromosomes. Then it became possible not only to count the chromosomes (the normal number is 46) but also to identify each of the 23 pairs of chromosomes contained in human cells. During the growing embryo's repeated cell divisions, the chromosome pairs constantly split and separate, operating with the orderly precision of a crack drill team. But it happens that some chromosomes get out of step. Three French scientists in 1959 examined cells from children with a very serious growth disorder called Mongolism, or Down's syndrome. They found 47 chromosomes instead of 46. The presence of this extra chromosome is disastrous. Though those who have it often appear normal at birth, all of them quickly develop broad faces with flat, low-bridged noses and skin folds over the eyes. Many victims of Down's syndrome are born with heart disorders and lack nose bones or teeth. All are mentally retarded, most of them seriously.

Soon after this discovery of a disorder linked to a chromosomal aberration, several others turned up. Most of them involved too many or too few of the chromosomes that determine sex. Normal females have two sex chromosomes that are known as X chromosomes; normal males receive one X chromosome from the mother, and a smaller Y chromosome from the father. The aberrations found in sex chromosomes suggest the almost unlimited possibilities of error in the chromosomes' elaborate maneuvers during cell division. Females have been found with only one chromosome or with three; males, instead of the normal XY pattern, may have XXY, XYY, or even XXXXY. Some of these chromosomal anomalies produce serious derangements of development, and a few have been blamed for personality abnormalities. One result

A MEDICAL MISNOMER, the term "Mongolism" was popularly applied to a serious congenital growth disorder on the assumption that a peculiarity of eye development that resulted from the malady (correctly known as Down's syndrome) made "Mongoloids'" eyes similar to those of Mongolians. The so-called "Mongoloid" child has a skin fold in the corner of the eye *(far right)*. Actually, the eye of a Mongolian is distinguished by a curved, overlapping eyelid *(center)*. Except for the fold, the eye of the child with Down's syndrome is formed in the same way as any European's *(left)*.

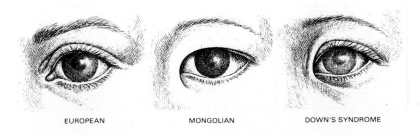

EUROPEAN   MONGOLIAN   DOWN'S SYNDROME

is often infertility, but many women who have three X chromosomes are fertile and apparently normal in other respects. Indeed, many three-X-chromosome cases are believed to go undetected.

Study of chromosome problems indicates that the replication and division of chromosomes can go wrong at any stage. In some cases the mistake occurs even before conception, in the parent's sex cells. A chromosome may break in two and one of the fragments become permanently attached to another chromosome. Or the division may be uneven, giving too many chromosomes to one cell, too few to another. Aberrations can also occur during embryonic development. Some people have been found to have two different kinds of cells in their bodies, one with normal chromosomes and one without. In these "mosaic" individuals, the original egg cell must have been normal. The defect was created at some later stage in the process of cell division. In one case, a boy with body characteristics associated with Down's syndrome but with a normal I.Q. was found to have skin cells containing an extra chromosome, but with a normal complement of chromosomes in his blood cells.

The abnormal victims of chromosomal troubles provide investigators with an opportunity for "mapping" chromosomes—that is, for discovering which chromosomes govern which areas of growth. For example, victims of Down's syndrome are known to develop leukemia—excess production of white blood cells—more than three times as often as normal people. This may be related to their chromosomal abnormality. Some leukemia patients have been found to have a defect in one of the chromosomes known to be involved in Down's syndrome: A bit has broken off it and become attached to a different chromosome. It seems likely that some of the genes in this chromosome are concerned with the production of white blood cells.

Influences within and without

Only about 40 per cent of birth defects can be definitely classified as either hereditary or environmental. Hereditary factors, including defective genes and aberrant chromosomes, account for about half of these. The other 20 per cent result from external agents that act on the embryo during its long, slow process of maturation in the womb.

Experimenters in embryology have learned how to induce birth defects in animals by subjecting the mother to radiation, vitamin deficiency or inadequate oxygen. Not surprisingly, they found that the earlier the mother was subjected to such damage, the worse the defect. Anything that attacks an embryo when its cells are relatively few in number is almost bound to wreak havoc. To show that prenatal influences could produce birth defects in the laboratory, however, did not prove that it happened in real life. That proof came in 1940, when Australia was hit by the most severe epidemic of German measles it had ever known. Since the disease is a mild one, the victims showed no immediate aftereffects. By the end of the year, the birth of defective babies in alarming numbers was noted. Some were stillborn. Many of those who survived had the horrifying multiple defects that pointed to damage during the first, most vulnerable months: They were blinded by cataracts, they were deaf, they had malformed hearts and were retarded. Altogether, some 350 defective infants were born. And nearly all of these were born to women who had contracted German measles seven to eight months before. Since then, studies by embryologists and pediatricians have identified the German-measles virus as the culprit. About 50 per cent of mothers who have German measles during the first two months of pregnancy will pass the infection onto their embryos. The infection carries with it a very high risk of prenatal death or severe defects.

Any viral infection during early pregnancy is now considered suspect. Mumps and influenza have come under particularly strong suspicion, but evidence gathered by health authorities does not indicate they are definitive dangers. A vaccine developed for German measles is generally administered to large groups of children in the hope of eradicating the virus at the source. Heavy alcohol consumption during pregnancy has been found to be associated with reduced fetal weight, mental retardation and insufficient development of certain facial features. Smoking during pregnancy also reduces fetal weight and increases the possibility of perinatal mortality—death at about the time of birth.

The danger of radiation

Radiation, long known to cause congenital defects in animals, came under increasing suspicion in human cases after World War II. Fifteen pregnant Japanese women who had been within a mile and a half (2.4 km) of the Hiroshima atom-bomb explosion produced babies with damaged skulls and brains. In the U.S. and in Britain the malformed brains and eyes of some babies have been linked to heavy doses of X-rays which their mothers received during pregnancy. The connection between the irradiation and the defects is still not clear, but physicians now use X-rays on pregnant women only for the most compelling reasons.

In the mid-20th Century, a historic disaster added drugs to the list of factors that cause dangers during pregnancy. In 1960, physicians in West Germany began noticing an unusual increase in birth defects of one particular type. The babies suffered from phocomelia (from the Greek words *phoke*, a seal, and *melos*, a limb). These children were born with seal-like, abbreviated limbs, somewhat resembling flippers. In the 10 years before 1959, only 15 cases of phocomelia had been recorded in all West Germany. But in 1960, 19 seal babies were born in the city of Bonn alone, 27 in Münster, 46 in Hamburg. By the end of the outbreak in 1961, the total had reached several hundred.

Toward the end of 1961 a persistent West German pediatrician, Dr. Widukind Lenz, began querying the mothers of seal babies and their attending physicians, asking them to search their memories for everything that had happened during pregnancy, including anything the women had eaten or drunk. Many of them recalled taking a sleeping pill that contained a newly developed sedative called thalidomide. The drug seemed an ideal one. It had no serious side effects, was completely nonaddictive and remarkably safe. More than 100 people had tried to commit suicide with thalidomide pills and failed. Because West Germany had few restrictions on the sale of new drugs, thalidomide was being distributed not only in the form of sleeping pills but also as an ingredient in cough syrups and cold cures. It was often recommended for the morning sickness of early pregnancy.

By the time Lenz had tracked down thalidomide as the villain in the case of the seal babies, its use had spread from Germany to other European countries as well as to Canada, South America, Japan and the Near East. In November 1961 the German manufacturer stopped production, but the total of thalidomide babies ultimately passed 5,000 in West Germany and at least 1,000 in other countries.

American mothers were spared the thalidomide disaster through the suspicions of Frances Kelsey, a doctor at the U.S. Food and Drug Administration. An American drug firm had applied for permission to distribute the drug in this country, but Dr. Kelsey repeatedly refused to approve the application until she had evidence of its safety. When the West German tragedy became known, the manufacturers withdrew the application. Meanwhile, however, they had already sent out millions of free pills to physicians. Fortunately, few of the pills resulted in defective children. Though there may have been others that went unidentified, the birth of only seventeen American thalidomide babies has been confirmed—seven of them resulting from thalidomide obtained abroad.

The dangers of medication

The thalidomide disaster shocked people all over the world. Drug-control laws were tightened in many countries, including the U.S. Subsequently, other drugs besides thalidomide were found to damage fetuses. They include certain hormones as well as anticancer and antimalarial agents. One of these was a man-made hormone, diethylstilbestrol, sometimes known as DES. Prescribed during the 1940s and 1950s to women who had complications during pregnancy, the drug may have been taken by several million mothers before it proved ineffective for this purpose. In the 1970s doctors discovered that two thirds of the

COURT CURIOSITIES, two dwarfs accompany the Italian duke Cosimo I de Medici in a 16th Century engraving. Regarded as funny freaks endowed with special talents, dwarfs were often kept as servants or jesters by the nobility. This practice went out of fashion in the 18th Century, when a more compassionate attitude on deformity spread.

daughters born to women treated with DES have abnormalities of the reproductive tract, and in 1980 one study suggested that sons of DES-treated women may have a higher incidence of sterility than other men.

The fact that hormonal medication during pregnancy can warp the growth of the embryo or fetus raises the question of whether a disorder of the mother's own hormones can have the same effect. Observations of mothers with certain tumors that secrete hormone-like substances suggest that it can. This finding has thus brought the study of maternal influences full circle. Some researchers are now taking a second look at the old mother-was-frightened-by-a-cow superstition that maternal impressions can influence prenatal development. Serious psychological stress, they point out, can profoundly alter the mother's hormone output, perhaps to the point where the embryo or fetus will be affected.

Research in this and other areas may yet dispel the cloud of uncertainty that still surrounds congenital defects. Physicians can prevent some of these disorders by protecting pregnant women from dangerous drugs or X-rays. In a few cases, like PKU, they can mitigate or eliminate the impact of faulty body chemistry on growth. Surgeons can repair cleft palates and remove extra fingers. In recent years, they have even repaired many defective hearts. For the majority of birth defects, however, a cure, let alone prevention, is still in the future.

When the Pituitary Malfunctions

In some human beings the most important growth-controlling gland, the pituitary, functions abnormally. The results are startling, often tragic. The two extremes of human stature are giantism and dwarfism. While other factors are sometimes involved, the usual cause for these abnormalities is the production by the pituitary of too much or too little growth hormone (hGH). Recent improvements in surgical and radiation-treatment techniques for removing or slowing the pituitary tumors responsible for an excess of hGH have greatly increased the chances for a safe and complete cure. Thousands of children whose stature is stunted because of a growth-hormone deficiency can now reach their fullest potential height with hGH injections. There is, however, a critical shortage of natural hGH available in the United States for such therapy. So that every child who is deficient can be treated, scientists are trying to create synthetic hGH.

THE LONG AND THE SHORT OF GROWTH
Extremes of growth caused by too little pituitary secretion of the growth hormone *(left)* and too much *(right)* are exhibited by two men who, curiously, are brothers-in-law. The dwarf stands just three feet high (91 cm), while the giant measures a towering seven feet eight inches (234 cm). Pituitary-caused dwarfism is much more common than the reverse—pituitary giantism.

Giantism and Acromegaly

An oversupply of growth hormone—hyperpituitarism—can produce two different conditions. Giantism, which occurs in the growing years, produces an individual of enormous size. In such cases, excessive growth is usually most noticeable in the head and legs. When hyperpituitarism strikes an adult after overall growth is complete, it causes acromegaly. Its chief symptom is enlargement of the head, hands and feet, along with lethargy and severe headaches.

Removal of the gland was once the only surgical treatment for hyperpituitarism, but this risky procedure deprived the patient of all pituitary hormones. Refinements in microsurgery *(opposite)* now allow the surgeon to remove just the diseased portion of the gland and leave the rest intact. And with early diagnosis, surgery may not be necessary at all. A small tumor can be eradicated by precision bombardment with proton radiation.

THE "ALTON GIANT"
Towering over his 5' 11'' (180 cm) father, Robert Wadlow, 20, stood 8' 10¾'' (271.15 cm) and wore size 37 shoes when photographed here in 1939. Called the "Alton Giant" after his Illinois hometown, he died at 22 following a minor injury.

THE RAVAGES OF ACROMEGALY
In 1892 this man *(left)* weighed 140 pounds (63.5 kg). Then he developed acromegaly. By 1910 *(right)* his face had become malformed and he weighed 200 pounds (90.7 kg). Doctors, ignorant of the problem, gave him pituitary extract instead of trying to reduce his pituitary activity.

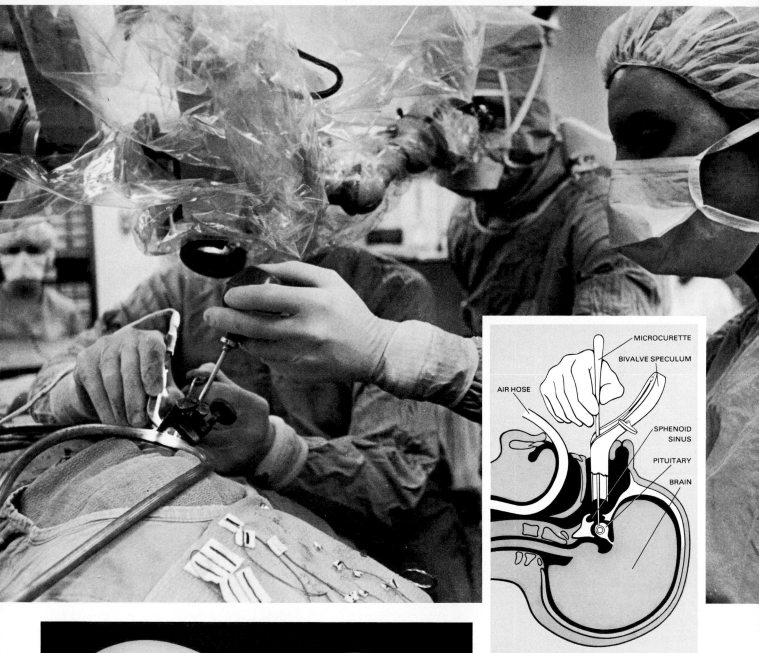

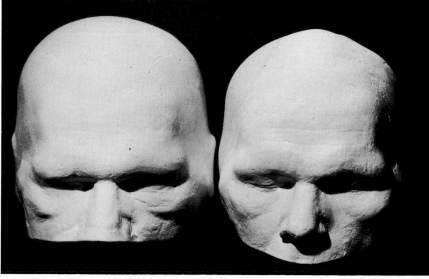

ATTACKING A TUMOR
Surgeons at the Yale University School of Medicine pinpoint a pituitary tumor with an operating microscope. The route to the gland passes through an incision in the upper gum and the sphenoid sinus behind the nose *(inset)*. A microcurette is used to cut away the diseased tissue.

REPAIRING THE DAMAGE
Two plaster casts of an acromegalic patient's head, made five years apart, show the beneficial effect of radiation treatment of the pituitary. After repeated treatments curbed the production of growth hormone, the overgrowth of the skull at the left was markedly diminished.

The Case of the Boy Who Could Not Grow

At nine months, Frank was a normal-sized baby.

Earl at 2 was as tall as his brother Frank at 4.

Mr. Hooey and Earl, 14, towered over Frank at 16.

Dwarfism of various kinds is as old as mankind, but it was not possible until the 1950s to distinguish a person with a growth-hormone insufficiency from other dwarfs. The hypopituitary person, although short in stature, is in most other respects a perfectly formed human being—such as the young Canadian, Frank Hooey *(opposite)*. The first child of Mr. and Mrs. Alex Hooey, Frank appeared normal at birth. But it soon became apparent that his growth rate lagged. By the time he reached 17, he was only four feet three inches (129.5 cm)—the height of an average eight-and-a-half-year-old at that time.

His parents had tried everything. A host of specialists had treated him, with no results. But in 1958 he was directed to Dr. M. S. Raben, a pioneer endocrinologist who was getting exciting results by stimulating growth with human growth hormone that had been extracted from the pituitary glands of deceased donors. For the results of Frank's treatment by Dr. Raben, turn to the next page.

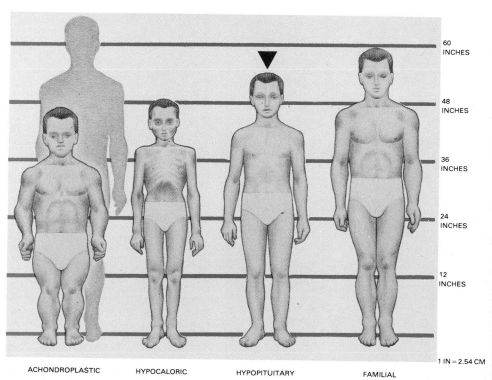

| | | | |
| 60 INCHES |
| 48 INCHES |
| 36 INCHES |
| 24 INCHES |
| 12 INCHES |

ACHONDROPLASTIC   HYPOCALORIC   HYPOPITUITARY   FAMILIAL

1 IN = 2.54 CM

THE VARIETIES OF DWARFISM
Of the four types of dwarfs (charted above at age 18, with a normal individual shadowed in background), science currently can offer substantial help only to the one with insufficient pituitary growth hormone *(arrow)*. The achondroplastic was deformed before birth; the hypocaloric was stunted by malnutrition, and the familial irrevocably inherited his small stature.

THE SMALLEST CADET
At 15, Frank was the shortest cadet ever to attend Royal Canadian Air Force camp, where he posed with a six-foot (183 cm) sergeant who stood nearly 20 inches (51 cm) taller. Frank was a bright, determined boy who participated in several of the team sports, despite his size.

163

FOR RENEWED GROWTH
Frank receives his thrice-weekly injection of
0.00010 ounce (3 mg) of hGH. Dr. Raben started Frank's treatment by giving him other hormones for eight months, then putting him on
hGH when he did not respond. Later, testosterone was added to speed final stages of maturity.

MARKING UP THE RESULTS
Frank's parents proudly record their son's new
height on the kitchen doorway. Here, at age 23,
he stood five feet six and one half inches (169.9
cm), below average but within the normal range.
The black mark behind him shows his height five
years earlier, before he started hGH treatment.

A New Life from New Growth

After five years of intensive hGH treatment, Frank was transformed into a young man of normal size. Had he been born a few years earlier, he would have been doomed to a lifetime of looking up to his peers. Fortunately, the bones of hypopituitary people do not harden at the normal age, so Frank was still able to grow.

Early diagnosis of growth-hormone deficiency by studying family growth histories, growth-rate records of the child, skeletal and cranial X-rays, and tests for hGH levels in the blood makes maximum treatment possible before the long bones harden.

But the hormone supply for treating the 2,000 or so hGH-deficient children in the United States is limited and must be rationed. HGH can be obtained only from glands removed at death. Nearly every pituitary, even one from an aged or diseased donor, contains hGH—but only enough for a week's treatment.

It takes 40 to 50 pituitaries to treat a child properly for a year, or close to 100,000 a year for all affected American children. But fewer than 70,000 are collected. These provide enough hGH to bring children to about five feet five inches (165 cm), but not enough to guarantee them the chance to achieve their full potential height.

A HIGH-STANDING BOWLER
Frank discusses a fine point of a game he likes with his teammates and his youngest brother *(far right)*. Frank's rapid growth did not sap his strength, nor did it interfere with his coordination. He rolled a hefty 16-pound (7.3 kg) ball with nearly professional skill, and won a first place trophy in a men's major-league bowling competition. He also enjoyed dancing and ice skating.

165

Recycling the Pituitary

The late Dr. Maurice Raben began his successful treatment of hypopituitary children in 1956, with injections of human growth hormone, and in the following decades thousands of patients were helped in his own laboratory and in laboratories and clinics abroad.

At the Tufts New England Medical Center, Dr. Raben and his staff obtained hGH from pituitaries gathered in the United States and in 15 foreign countries. They used a process that was called the "glacial acetic acid extraction method" and yielded about 0.00014 ounce (4 mg) of hGH from each gland. Dr. Raben's pioneering work, shown on these pages, has been followed by refined techniques and the use of frozen glands. Now twice as much hormone from each gland can be isolated—a great boon to children needing treatment, since pituitaries continue to be in very short supply.

PREPARING THE RAW MATERIAL
Using tweezers, a technician *(right)* carefully peels away the tough covering from an acetone-dampened human pituitary *(close-up above)*, the first step in Dr. Raben's process for extracting growth hormone. The glass dish in the foreground holds unpeeled glands. To obtain the hormone needed for patients, Dr. Raben's laboratory processed 40,000 pituitaries every year.

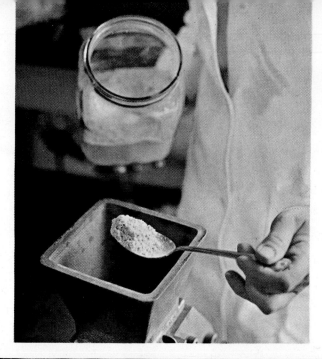

REFINING THE INGREDIENTS
In Dr. Raben's lab, dried pituitaries, already chopped up in a blender, were spooned into a flour-grinding machine to be milled into an extremely fine powder. The powder finally yielded growth hormone in the course of a complicated extraction and chemical purification procedure.

WEIGHING THE END PRODUCT
Dr. Raben, his brow furrowed in concentration, meticulously measures a supply of growth-hormone powder on a sensitive electric balance. During the extraction process great care was taken not to waste any of the hormone powder so desperately needed by his young patients.

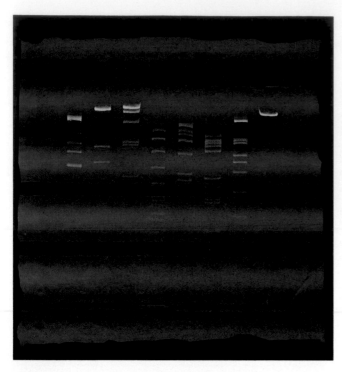

AN ENZYMATIC BREAKDOWN
Stained bacterial DNA, broken into segments with enzymes, glows on an ultraviolet light box. The segment of DNA that contains the synthesized hGH gene is then divided into still smaller fragments by four chemical reactions.

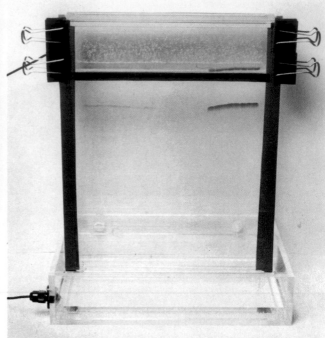

ELECTROMAGNETIC SEGREGATION
Radioactively labeled DNA fragments migrate through an electromagnetized gel according to length. When the lower dye band reaches bottom, X-ray film is exposed to the gel, allowing the hGH gene's DNA sequence to be verified.

A New Source of HGH

Genetic engineering may one day provide all the hGH needed to treat growth disorders. Scientists at the University of California, San Francisco, use techniques of recombinant DNA, or gene-splicing, so that *E. coli* bacteria can make the hormone.

In the first step, the DNA that contains hGH sequences is synthesized from messenger RNA obtained from a human pituitary tumor. Then, by chemical means, scientists extract from a bacterium a ring of DNA called a plasmid and link it to the hGH gene. This hybrid, or recombinant, plasmid is then reintroduced into the bacterium. Since bacterial cells reproduce themselves rapidly, a large population containing an exact duplicate of the hybrid plasmid soon exists. All of them can manufacture hGH, along with their own usual substances.

Bacteria-produced hGH is chemically identical to the hormone produced by the human body, but whether it is biologically active remains to be proven. Larger quantities must be accumulated and purified before it can be tested, first with laboratory animals and later with human beings.

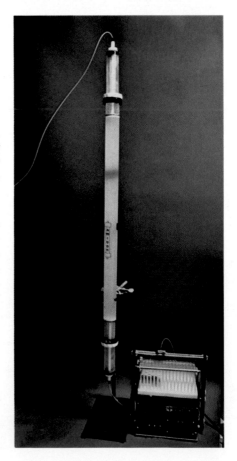

SEPARATION BY SIZE
HGH and other bacteria proteins move down through this chromatographic column in order of their size. A blue band identifies molecules that are smaller than hGH, which is drawn off into the fraction collector shown at right.

As research director John Baxter watches, members of his team prepare equipment for a new round of growth-hormone production.

8
"Tampering" with Nature

FOR CENTURIES biologists studied growth by patient observation but could do virtually nothing about what they saw. Now they are finding ways of improving and controlling growth that would have seemed fantastic a generation ago. Current investigations suggest that future methods of improving the quality of livestock will make selective breeding seem clumsy and primitive. There may be substances that suspend the aging process and prolong youth. Biologists may even learn to grow "test-tube babies" from fertilized egg cell to birth in the laboratory.

These investigations involve experiments that tamper with nature. Normally, human beings cannot be used as subjects of biological experiments, so the experimenter must find an animal similar to man, and one which can be raised in the laboratory. This is what Dr. Gertrude van Wagenen, of the Department of Obstetrics and Gynecology at Yale University, set out to do in 1931, when she bought a rhesus monkey at a pet store. The rhesus makes a fine proxy for the study of human growth. Like all primates, it resembles man in physical structure. The female rhesus has a menstrual cycle of about 28 days, like that of a human female. Because it has a gestation period averaging five and a half months and reaches physical maturity in three to five years, experiments can be carried on over several generations in a relatively short time.

Over the years, Dr. van Wagenen increased her stock of rhesus proxies. By 1955 there had been 354 pregnancies and three sets of twins, and the monkeys had become a local institution—the "Yale Obstetrical Colony." The life cycles of nearly a hundred monkeys were meticulously followed, in thousands of measurements and X-rays, to the age of seven. It was only after this work, which set the standards of normal growth and development for the colony, that experimentation could begin.

Some of the first experiments concerned the process of maturation. Students of human growth have long known that the androgens, hormones produced in the testes and adrenal glands, promote maturity in the human male. Dr. van Wagenen proved that the same was true of monkeys. Treated with the androgen testosterone, young males grew at twice the normal rate and matured 12 months earlier than usual. Then Dr. van Wagenen treated young females with the hormone and got some curious results. They too matured faster; they had their first menstruation at half the normal age, and by that time had reached the size of normal pubertal monkeys. Then treatment was stopped. The monkeys continued to develop normally in every respect, even bearing infants.

The Yale experiment has shed new light on the maturation of the human female. Although estrogens are known to bring about puberty in girls, this experiment suggests that they may not be the sole agents. The adrenal glands of females normally secrete small amounts of androgens, which promote changes in skeletal growth at adolescence. How

THE NEED FOR MOTHER LOVE
In a University of Wisconsin experiment exploring emotional needs of the young, a psychologist carefully watches the behavior of a baby monkey clinging to its mother, an emotionally disturbed animal that often ignores or strikes her child. When offered the terry-cloth substitute mother, seen here outside the cage, the baby monkey will still choose its real mother.

androgens encourage a girl's passage into womanhood is still unknown.

Dr. van Wagenen used the Yale Obstetrical Colony to explore physical growth. At the University of Wisconsin, another monkey colony serves as a population for the study of psychological development. At Yale, Dr. van Wagenen had found that infant monkeys raised on the bottle had a lower mortality rate than infants nursed by their mothers. At Wisconsin, Dr. Harry F. Harlow and his colleagues, setting out to build a monkey colony of their own, followed Dr. van Wagenen's example. They separated newborns from their mothers, bottle-fed them, and raised them in separate cages. The monkeys grew up healthy, but they were emotionally disturbed. They would "sit in their cages and stare fixedly into space, circle their cages in a repetitive manner, clasp their heads in their hands and arms for long periods of time. Often the approach of a human being [became] the stimulus for self-aggression."

Real and surrogate mothers

Suspecting that this behavior might be caused by a lack of mothering, Dr. Harlow supplied the baby monkeys with surrogate mothers: wire frames covered with terry cloth and topped by crudely fashioned monkey heads. All the infants formed deep attachments to their "mothers," huddling against them most of the day. As infants, these monkeys appeared psychologically healthy. But as adults, they were nearly as withdrawn and antisocial as the motherless monkeys, and would not mate.

The researchers then tried a new experiment. They raised one group of monkeys with natural mothers and a second with terry-cloth mothers, but brought infants belonging to the same group together for part of every day. At first the mothered group was more active and seemed to be growing more normally. Then the terry-cloth group began to catch up. By the time the animals were two years old most of the differences between them had disappeared. As adults, the members of the terry-cloth group were almost as normal in their social and sexual life as those of the first. The most striking difference between the groups was that about two-thirds of the females raised with surrogate mothers either abused or neglected their first-born infants.

Harlow's experiments led him to suspect a basic pattern of psychological development in monkeys. During the first months of its life, an infant monkey depends completely upon its mother. About the third or fourth month, when the mother normally begins to reject her child from time to time, an infant-infant relationship assumes considerable importance. In fact, further experiments at Wisconsin have shown that this relationship is essential for normal development. Young monkeys deprived of interaction with either their mother or their peers become abnormally aggressive adults that shun the company of other monkeys.

Van Wagenen and Harlow experimented with the chemistry and environment of their animals after birth. Other scientists have worked with animals before birth to discover the extent to which the egg is influenced by its uterine environment and the extent to which its development is determined by heredity. At the Royal Veterinary College in London, Ann McLaren and Donald Michie took mice with five vertebrae in the lumbar region of their spines and mated them with others whose lumbar regions had six vertebrae. Some of the mothers were of the five-bone strain; others were of the six-bone strain. If heredity alone had determined the characteristics of the offspring, which parent was five-boned and which was six-boned would not have mattered. But more than heredity was at work: The majority of animals in each litter had the same number of vertebrae as the mothers. When McLaren and Michie took hybrid fetuses from the wombs of six-bone mothers and implanted them in females with five bones, most of the offspring resembled their foster rather than biological mothers. Apparently, the uterine environment exerts a great influence on some aspects of growth.

Transplanting embryos

In 1960, scientists in Cambridge, England, transplanted eight fertilized eggs from the uterus of a pedigreed sheep to the uterus of a rabbit. The rabbit was flown to South Africa, arriving four days after the operation. The eggs were removed and each one was transplanted into the uterus of a nonpedigreed sheep. In six cases, the transplant did not take; but the other two sheep bore fine pedigreed lambs. This was not a stunt. It cost less to send a rabbit to South Africa than a lamb, and the rabbit, unlike the lamb, did not have to spend time in quarantine. Using rabbits as "mailing bags" has been largely replaced by a still more convenient technique—shipping frozen embryos. Sheep embryos can be frozen for as long as two and a half years, then thawed and transplanted to the wombs of foster mothers.

Normally, a sheep or cow produces five to 10 offspring during its lifetime, but in this same period an animal of high genetic quality can be stimulated with pituitary hormones to produce hundreds of eggs. Transplanters remove these eggs to the wombs of females of inferior quality. Though expensive and not always successful, this technique may eventually allow one superior animal to produce hundreds of offspring.

Fertilized mouse eggs can survive *in vitro*—in an artificial environment—for at least 12 days. In experiments at the Johns Hopkins School of Hygiene and Public Health, Dr. Yu-chih Hsu kept mouse embryos not only alive but undergoing developmental changes. They developed into a ball of cells called a blastocyst and attached themselves to the sides of the glass dishes in which they were grown, just as normal embryos attach themselves to the wall of their mother's uterus. The laboratory embryos also showed signs of a brain, spinal cord, vertebrae and a heart. After this stage—equivalent to about half the normal gestational period for mice—the embryos degenerated. Biologists are now working to bring mammalian embryos to full term in the laboratory.

The powers of regeneration

Another rewarding area of growth research is regeneration. Some lower animals are nearly indestructible: The hydra, for instance, can be cut into several pieces, and each will grow into a whole organism. Even higher animals and man show traces of regenerative powers. A broken bone knits and, in a child, begins to grow again. Skin grows over a wound (if the damaged area is not too large), and the muscles and connective tissues beneath repair themselves. Scientists learned much about the "what" of regeneration before they understood the "how." Watching a salamander regenerate a limb, they saw the process begin when the skin heals over the cut end. Beneath the new skin undifferentiated cells appear, multiplying with almost cancer-like freedom. At about two weeks the bud of a new limb can be seen, resembling the limb bud of a fetus. By the third or fourth week the beginnings of an elbow and a foot are visible. Inside the new limb, cells are becoming muscle, tendon and bone. About a week later, toes appear, and the limb becomes functional.

Identification of what triggers regeneration was first made more than a century ago. In 1823, an English investigator named Tweedy Todd amputated a salamander's leg, then cut the nerve running to the stump. The limb did not regenerate. Long after Todd's death, 20th Century scientists confirmed that the nerve at the site of a regenerating part is necessary to the process. If the nerve is cut, regeneration will not begin; if it is cut after regeneration has begun, growth ceases. The nerve need not even be cut: A nerve-paralyzing drug will stop regeneration as effectively as surgery. In short, anything that stops the continuous action of the nerve seems to stop regeneration.

In 1944, Dr. Meryl Rose of Smith College studied the effects of repeated injury to an adult frog's foreleg. First he amputated the leg, and then subjected the stump to daily dipping in a strong salt solution. The stump responded to this version of rubbing salt in an open wound by producing an incomplete leg—a surprising result, since normally an adult frog cannot replace even part of an amputated limb. With frogs, at least, it seemed that increasing the extent of an injury increased the degree of regeneration—but just how could not be explained at the time.

Several years after Rose had performed his experiment, Marcus Singer of Cornell University pursued the answer to a primary question about regeneration: Why do such animals as tadpoles lose regenerative power

A STUDY IN REGENERATION by embryologist Paul Weiss in 1925 showed that a limb must regenerate outward from the point of loss. In the experiment, diagrammed here, the humerus bone of a salamander's foreleg *(left, color)* was first removed surgically. After the wound healed, Weiss amputated the limb through the region of the missing bone *(center)*. Convincing evidence of unidirectional regrowth was provided when the lost limb grew back without any new bone appearing in back of the cut *(right)*.

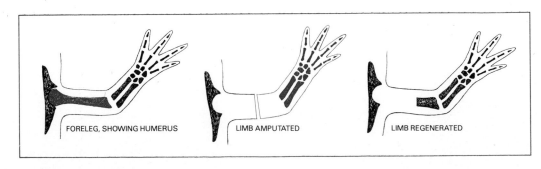

FORELEG, SHOWING HUMERUS   LIMB AMPUTATED   LIMB REGENERATED

as they grow older, and why do higher animals have so little of it? Perhaps, reasoned Singer, it is the number of nerve fibers, as compared with other kinds of tissue, that decides whether regeneration will take place. At Princeton University, J. M. van Stone showed that as a tadpole matures, the ratio of its nerve fibers to the cells of other tissues steadily decreases. Singer devised an experiment that reversed this process. He amputated the front leg of an adult frog and dissected out the large sciatic nerve of the frog's rear leg, leaving only the root attached. He then pulled the sciatic nerve through the frog's body to the stump of the amputated leg. If Singer's theory was sound, the number of nerve fibers at the site now exceeded some unknown number—the number needed to start regeneration. And in the next three months the frog did grow a new front leg—deformed but recognizable. But how had the nerves stimulated this healing and regeneration? Dr. Singer believed that they contributed a stimulating chemical. In later experiments, he injected an extract of nerve tissue into the amputation sites of animals that normally do not regenerate. The extract, later called "nerve growth factor," produced increased cell division—but no true regeneration.

Healing with bioelectricity

Another group of researchers, following a different tack, has investigated "bioelectricity" produced by the nerves as a possible force behind regeneration. Over a century ago scientists noted a "current of injury"—a very weak direct current—that is generated around damaged skin, but it was thought to be simply a pathological symptom. However, Dr. Robert O. Becker of the Veterans Administration Hospital in Syracuse, New York, believed that this current might be related to the role of nerves in regeneration. He amputated legs from frogs and salamanders and discovered a curious difference in the electrical currents the two species produced. In the frog, a positive current began immediately after amputation and persisted until the wound healed. The salamander, at first, also produced a positive current, but within a few days it shifted to a negative current that persisted until a new limb was complete.

This evidence suggested that bioelectricity was critical in regeneration, an idea given support by another researcher, Stephen Smith of the University of Kentucky. He implanted a tiny electrode generating a weak negative current in the stump of a frog's leg. The stump did not merely heal over; instead, there emerged from it a new but deformed extremity. Using Smith's techniques, Becker has stimulated partial limb regeneration in rats—the first time this kind of complex regeneration has been achieved in mammals. Finally, in 1975, Smith regenerated a complete frog's limb by implanting a battery-operated device.

The common factor underlying all these experimental observations is bioelectricity. Rose's frogs reacted to repeated injury by generating larger electrical currents, and Singer got similar results by increasing the number of nerve fibers at the amputation site. With adequate bioelectric stimulation, certain mature cells return to a primitive state, then redifferentiate into the specific types of cells required for the missing part. Bioelectricity has already been put to work in humans to stimulate the healing of bone fractures. It may prove that both chemical and electrical factors are crucial in healing and regeneration, since the line between the two is often blurred in other body functions.

The mechanisms of metamorphosis

A tadpole loses its regenerative power as it turns into a frog, and it also changes its form. This transformation, called metamorphosis, is not uncommon in the animal kingdom. A butterfly shifts from an egg to a caterpillar to a closely wrapped, dormant chrysalis and finally—by metamorphosis—to the adult insect. Metamorphic growth, surely the most dramatic style of growth in nature, has begun to provide insights into the nature of all animal growth. When a tadpole turns into a frog, its tail gradually vanishes; in the language of biology, the tail is "resorbed." Finally, a mere stub, it falls off. The cells of the shrinking tail seem to destroy themselves in a sort of mass cellular suicide.

In the early 1950s Belgian scientist Christian de Duve's research on rat liver cells led him to the conclusion that the cells must contain particles that galvanize the autodigestive process. In 1955 he and Alex B. Novikoff, of the Albert Einstein College of Medicine in New York City, saw the particles under an electron microscope and identified them as minute bags of digestive fluid. De Duve and Novikoff named them lysosomes—or, more graphically, "suicide bags." It is now known that most animal cells contain lysosomes, which function as the cell's digestive system. Sometimes a lack of oxygen, exposure to carcinogens or genetic programing triggers the lysosomes to leak enzymes through the lysosomal membrane and digest the cell's contents. But this is not necessarily disastrous. Living bodies must, at times, get rid of some of their cells. Indeed, "ungrowing" is often as important to development as growth itself. In higher animals, lysosomes may play a part in the process that accompanies all growth and at last puts an end to it—the process of aging.

British zoologist V. B. Wigglesworth, who has spent a lifetime studying metamorphosis, discovered a substance that may ward off age. Working with the tropical blood-sucking bug *Rhodnius prolixus*, Dr. Wigglesworth found that when he cut the head from a larva about to molt to another larval stage, the body metamorphosed into an adult. He reasoned that the head must contain some inhibiting substance that kept the insect in the larval state. Careful dissection revealed two tiny glands

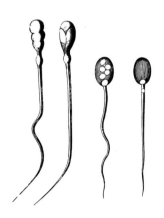

THE DISCOVERY OF SPERMATOZOA, though credited to the 17th Century Dutch microscopist Anton van Leeuwenhoek, actually was made by one of his students, who pointed out the male reproductive cells to him. Leeuwenhoek made accurate drawings *(above)* of what he saw through his homemade lenses. The larger pair above is from a dog, while the smaller came from a rabbit. In each pair, the left-hand sperm is living and mobile.

in the larva's head. It is these glands that secrete the substance, called the juvenile hormone, that Dr. Wigglesworth was looking for. Ordinarily, insect larvae go through a series of molts, shedding their outgrown exoskeletons, before finally emerging as adults. The juvenile hormone is present until this final stage. But if the glands of a young larva are implanted into a larva in the last stage before metamorphosis, its metamorphosis is postponed. Dr. Lawrence Gilbert of Northwestern University has found that the juvenile hormone prevents lysosomes from forming in certain insect tissues such as the epidermis, which secretes the exoskeleton. This suggests that the juvenile hormone prolongs youth by delaying the destruction of cells and their differentiation into adult form.

Drawing together the strands of knowledge

Decades of research have opened new windows of knowledge on every stage of growth and have brought within reach the power to control biological events in ways unthinkable a few years ago. The most astonishing instance of this new expertise was the birth in 1978 of Louise Brown, the first baby in the world to be conceived in a laboratory and carried to term in her mother's body. To achieve this event, two British researchers, gynecologist Patrick Steptoe and physiologist Robert Edwards, drew together many different strands of knowledge about mammalian embryology and the human female's reproductive cycle.

In the mid-1960s researchers working with mice, rabbits and hamsters had learned to fertilize mammalian eggs successfully *in vitro*. At about the same time, Steptoe and Edwards were working on fertilizing human eggs *in vitro* with a practical goal in mind—to help women unable to conceive because their Fallopian tubes did not function properly, preventing the passage of an egg from the ovary to the uterus. Years of further experimentation resulted in a procedure that carefully orchestrated the many factors involved in a successful pregnancy.

The first step was to obtain an egg from the ovary. A laparoscope was inserted through the mother's abdominal wall. A tiny telescope equipped with a light source, the laparoscope allows the ovary to be examined for ripe eggs. The egg was then extracted and placed in a solution of blood serum and nutrients that took the place of fluids in the Fallopian tubes, where fertilization normally takes place. Next, the egg was exposed to sperm and after several hours examined microscopically to be sure that it had been fertilized and appeared to be normal. The fertilized egg was transferred to yet another mixture of nutrients, where in the course of the next two and a half days it divided to form an eight-cell morula. During the fertilization and cell-division processes, the readiness of the mother's uterine lining for accepting the embryo was monitored.

In their previous attempts at implantation, Steptoe and Edwards had waited until the blastocyst stage—when the embryo had 64 cells—before introducing it into the uterus. But new research on rhesus monkeys had suggested that at an even earlier stage implantation was possible. So the eight-cell morula was gently removed from its nutrient medium with a plastic cannula and inserted into the uterus in precision timing with the state of its lining. After reaching the blastocyst stage *in vivo*— in the mother's body—the embryo implanted itself in the uterine wall and developed in the following months into a healthy fetus.

Though the birth of Louise Brown aroused controversy as well as scientific interest, the techniques of *in vitro* fertilization of human eggs may well give researchers new tools to study other aspects of growth and development such as genetically transmitted diseases and cell differentiation. Refinements of these techniques may also allow parents to determine a baby's sex. It is now possible in the laboratory to identify a Y, or male, sperm. Unlike the X sperm, it absorbs a fluorescent dye called quinacrine. When treated semen is viewed under a fluoroscope, the Y sperms are discernible by a tiny yellow dot. No reliable way has yet been found to segregate X sperms and Y sperms, but scientists believe that it will someday be possible. Then, by using one or the other for artificial insemination, parents will indeed be able to decide whether to have a girl or a boy—and an age-old dream of mankind will be fulfilled.

Determination of Size and Shape

The way a person grows, the size and shape he becomes, are determined by the complex and often obscure interaction of two agents, heredity and environment. Everyone inherits from his parents a genetic blueprint that specifies what kind of physique he will have, how much his bones can grow, what color his eyes will be. And then his environment, in the form of climate, diet or disease, works on these genetic possibilities, encouraging some, inhibiting others. Sometimes heredity and environment collaborate over long periods of time to develop a particular characteristic, such as great height. Sometimes a harmful environmental factor like malnutrition acts directly to disrupt normal growth patterns. Man can govern his own growth to some extent by controlling his diet and health. But there are so many variables at work that though some generalizations can be made, it is quite impossible to predict exactly how any individual will grow.

THE TALL, THIN DINKA
The man shown leaning gracefully on his spear on the opposite page is a member of the Dinka tribe, one of several Nilotic tribes in tropical Africa. They represent a genetic adaptation to the demands of environment: Almost without exception the Nilotics grow to be extraordinarily tall and thin. This is a specialized physique that helps them live successfully in their very hot climate.

DISPOSABLE HOUSING
Despite their size, the Dinka make do with small, temporary huts along riverbanks during the dry season. When the annual floods wash the huts away, the Dinka must move to higher ground.

HEAD AND SHOULDERS HIGHER
A Shilluk from south Sudan stands out in a market crowd of north Sudanese. The Shilluk, like other Nilotic tribesmen, have more or less normal torsos with disproportionately long legs. They intrigue visitors with their habit of standing for hours, crane-fashion, on one foot.

Shaped by a Harsh Land

In the blistering Nile Basin of southern Sudan live the Nilotic tribes, Africa's tallest people. Their extraordinary height, in some tribes averaging close to six feet (183 cm), is a clear example of the interaction of heredity and environment as it affects human growth. The climate in southern Sudan is so hot, with dry-season temperatures frequently above 100° F. (38° C.), that humans more compact in build would be uncomfortable living there. Centuries of genetic adaptation have provided the Nilotics with their particularly tall, thin physique that allows the body to dissipate more heat through greater surface areas than it could with any other shape.

The isolation of these tribes, whose members in the past almost never interbred with shorter peoples, has been a factor in establishing their hereditary trend toward extreme height. The results of generations of genetic purity are strikingly apparent in the Dinka and the Shilluk, the two Nilotic tribes that are shown on these pages.

A DANCE AND A DIET
Four lanky Dinka boys do a ritual ox dance, holding sticks to represent the horns of oxen, which are the tribe's most prized possession. Cattle-herding is the principal occupation of the boys, and the animals contribute to a high-protein diet that helps the Dinka stay slender.

181

DIMINUTIVE NEW GUINEANS

Territorial Officer Allan Johnston towers over two Papua New Guinean women and a man, none of them taller than four and a half feet (137 cm). They are in the lower range of stature for the island's population, which as a whole tends to shortness. Completely unrelated to the true Pygmies of Africa, these New Guineans are more heavily muscled and have Asiatic features.

The Mystery of Smallness

In the Ituri rain forest of Central Africa live the Mbuti Pygmies, a tribe whose members average less than four and a half feet (137 cm) in height. Unlike the lanky physique of the Nilotic peoples, which is clearly the outcome of genetic and environmental interaction, the Pygmies' diminutive stature does not seem to be an advantageous adaptation to climate. One theory holds that their size resulted from mutations preserved by centuries of inbreeding. Scientists have discovered that Pygmies have the same blood levels of growth hormone as taller people, but their tissues and organs are less responsive to it. The same mechanism may be present in other pygmoid peoples, such as the New Guineans on the opposite page.

HOME OF LILLIPUTIANS
In a forest encampment a Pygmy woman uses a large pestle to prepare food that she has gathered. In spite of their small size, Pygmies are strong. Men win their hunting spurs by killing an elephant singlehandedly: They run underneath the animal and pierce it with a spear.

A VISIT TO THE OUTSIDE
Two four-foot-four-inch (132 cm) Pygmies are measured for clothes by a five-foot-eight-inch (173 cm) tailor in a village near the Pygmies' home. Pygmies often visit neighbors, and their women sometimes marry into other tribes, but Pygmy men rarely take wives from outside.

183

DARRELL CHAMBERS 5' 10"

LEROY BUCKINGHAM 5' 9"   ④ LARRY BUCKINGHAM 5' 6"   ⑤ VICKI LYNN CHAMBERS   MAXINE EZELL BEATTY 5' 6"   ④ SANDRA BEATTY   ④ KIRK BEATTY 6' 0"

③ JANELL BEATTY BUCKINGHAM 5' 0"   ④ SHARON BUCKINGHAM CHAMBERS 4' 11"   ③ NEWELL BEATTY 5' 8½"   ④ TERRY BEAT

1 IN = 2.54 CM

FOUNDERS OF A FAMILY
Alba and Mack Beatty, at right *(and right center in group picture above),* had two sons and three daughters whose average height (5'4"; 163 cm) is close to their parents' average (5'3"; 160 cm).

IN BETWEEN
At 5'6" (168 cm) Larry Buckingham *(far right)* is between his parents in height (5'9" and 5'0"; 175 cm and 152 cm). On the average, a mother's and father's statures affect their son's height equally.

BIGGER THAN BOTH
Defying statistics, six-footer (183 cm) Kirk Beatty *(far right)* is taller than either of his parents. His height may have been boosted by the particular mix of genes he inherited from his parents.

184

① MARY WRIGHT 5' 2"
DORIS KAVANAUGH BEATTY 5' 2"
② MACK BEATTY 5' 8"
④ LAURA FORNEY
④ CYNTHIA FORNEY
④ DENIS FORNEY
④ MARCIA McCRACKEN
④ BRENDA McCRACKEN
④ MELODY McCRACKEN
HOWARD BEATTY 5' 7"
② ALBA WRIGHT BEATTY 4' 10"
RUSSELL FORNEY 5' 7"
③ NORMA BEATTY FORNEY 5' 2"
ROBERT McCRACKEN 6' 1½"
③ MARLINE BEATTY McCRACKEN 5' 1½"

THE GATHERED CLAN
The large family gathering shown above during a reunion at Garden Grove, California, in 1965 was headed by 83-year-old Mrs. Mary Wright, and included one great-great-granddaughter. Circled numbers indicate family generations.

The Chancy Art of Predicting

From the height of his parents a child's mature height can be predicted to within about three and a half inches (9 cm). After a child is two years old, a more accurate forecast is possible. A calculation based on the parents' heights, the child's height and weight, and his rate of skeletal growth yields a prediction with a three-inch (7 cm) margin of error. The chances are 95 per cent that a child will mature within these limits. But because innumerable genetic and environmental factors affect a child's growth, he may confound everyone and wind up far taller—or shorter—than expected.

NEW PROSPECTS FOR HEIGHT
Darrell Chambers (5'10"; 178 cm) and Robert Mc-Cracken (6'1½"; 187 cm), who married into the Beatty family, are much taller than most of their male in-laws. The average adult height of the Beatty family is still well below the American average, but continued intermarriage with tall types like Chambers and McCracken will almost certainly boost the height of future generations.

185

Mankind on the Way Up

The past several centuries have witnessed pronounced increases in the height of populations all around the world. For example, most modern soldiers *(right)* would have a hard time fitting into medieval armor. Houses built in New England 300 years ago seem quaint today because of the diminutive size of everything, particularly the height of doorways. In 1920 the average student at Harvard University was one and a quarter inches (3.18 cm) taller and 10 pounds (4.5 kg) heavier than the average student had been a generation earlier.

Scientists still have not pinpointed the exact cause of this increase, documented first in Europe and somewhat later in less developed areas. Environmental changes such as improvements in public health, medical services, nutrition and child care are unquestionably involved to a large degree, but there seem to be genetic factors at work, too. For instance, industrialization and increases in the size of human beings seem to go hand in hand. Industrial expansion takes relatively inbred country people and transports them to cities, where they intermarry. Apparently the mixing of genetic stocks tends to produce bigger children, a phenomenon known in plants and animals as hybrid vigor.

HEIGHT ON THE RISE
The height of the average Englishman between the 11th and 14th Centuries is estimated from careful measurements taken of bones exhumed from several graveyards in Great Britain. The American soldiers' heights are based on the medical records of millions of Army inductees.

MEDIEVAL ENGLISHMAN
5' 6'' (168 cm)

WORLD WAR I U. S. SOLDIER
5' 7 3/4'' (172.09 cm)

WORLD WAR II U. S. SOLDIER
5' 8 1/2'' (174 cm)

U. S. SOLDIER AFTER 1958
5' 8 9/10'' (175 cm)

187

Deprived
by Diet

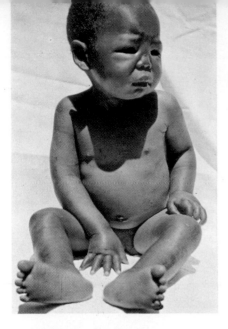

WAY BEHIND SCHEDULE
Elizabeth Zwane, an underdeveloped three-year-old girl from Johannesburg, South Africa, is a victim of kwashiorkor. Her skin is lighter than it should be, and her hair is too sparse. Most of these effects could still be cured by proper diet.

Scientists have more than enough evidence of the crippling effects of bad diet on the genetic potential for human growth. Millions of people, even whole races, are shorter than they might be or are malformed in other ways because a chronic shortfall in protein, calories, or both in their early years has kept them from reaching their full genetic growth potential.

One of the most serious nutritional diseases is protein deficiency, known by the Ghanaian name of kwashiorkor. It afflicts children who do not get enough meat, fish, dairy products or vegetables of the proper kind. This deficiency inhibits the growth not only of bone and muscle but also of hair, pigment cells and even the brain. The most pernicious form of this disease is found in infants whose diet is suddenly switched from their mothers' milk to a starchy staple such as millet, rice or sweet potatoes. If this debilitating menu is improved in the early years, the child will respond by growing more quickly to catch up with his growth schedule. The longer a child remains malnourished, the greater the chances that he will be irreparably damaged and unable to realize his genetic expectations.

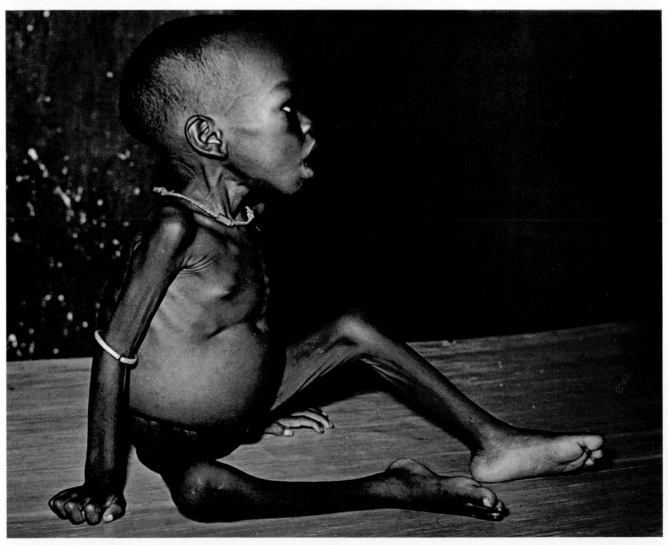

The distended stomach and emaciated limbs of this 18-month-old girl of Upper Volta in Africa are typical effects of kwashiorkor.

YOUNGER BUT TALLER
Two boys of the Guatemala highlands are proof that good diet improves growth in areas where malnutrition is endemic. The boy on the right, 42 months old, has been raised on the local starchy diet and is as tall as most children of his age in the area. The other boy, only 27 months old, has had his regular diet supplemented with a special protein-rich substance.

AN ANCIENT RITUAL
Two sumo wrestlers of an earlier age are shown in this 18th Century print. The sport is 1,500 years old and, like many aspects of the Japanese culture, it is a highly formalized ritual.

Super Size from Forced Feeding

Japan's huge sumo wrestlers provide graphic proof of the effect of diet on a man's size and shape. Sumo wrestling places a great premium on bulk: The contest is decided when one opponent is either thrown down or forced out of the ring. Although sumo recruits are usually bigger-than-average youths, the huge-bellied, heavy-hipped bodies deemed crucial for success must be carefully created through a unique program of diet and exercise.

To achieve their optimum weight of over 300 pounds (136 kg), wrestlers consume a heavy load of calories every day in a special diet—but not before earning the feast. They train every morning on an empty stomach, going through practice bouts to develop powerful legs and hips, the ultimate sources of sumo might. There follows a huge noon meal, which turns mostly to bulk because there are no workouts for the rest of the day. Such a regimen helps make sumo wrestlers symbols of strength and appetite to their countrymen, but they pay a high price for their ponderous prowess: great vulnerability to such ailments as diabetes, liver and kidney trouble.

A MONUMENTAL MEAL
One of the greatest wrestlers in sumo history, former Grand Champion Taiho, eats during his prime as his lesser colleagues wait their turn. In a typical two-meal day, wrestlers consume some 18 pounds (8 kg) of rice and *chanko nabe,* a stew of meat, poultry, fish and vegetables. Liquid consumption can also be huge: One wrestler guzzled 24 quarts (25.3 l) of beer at one sitting.

A MAN OF SUBSTANCE
Settling close to 400 pounds (181 kg) into a squat in practice, a wrestler big even among professionals prepares to hurl his body at an opponent. Sumo's body-building method produces bottom-heavy behemoths with low centers of gravity which make them difficult to push around and almost impossible to topple.

How a Human Face Takes Shape

The human face begins to be structured quite early in the womb. The process continues for a long time, until maturity. Two pits that will become the nasal passages are present by the fourth week. Beneath them are lobes that will join together to become the jaws. At five weeks rudimentary eyes have appeared on either side of the head, and the nose structure has moved below the facial midline. By the end of the second month the face already has a recognizable nose, complete upper and lower lips, cheeks and eyelids, and a basically human appearance. The ears, too, have started to form.

STEPS IN THE FASHIONING OF FEATURES

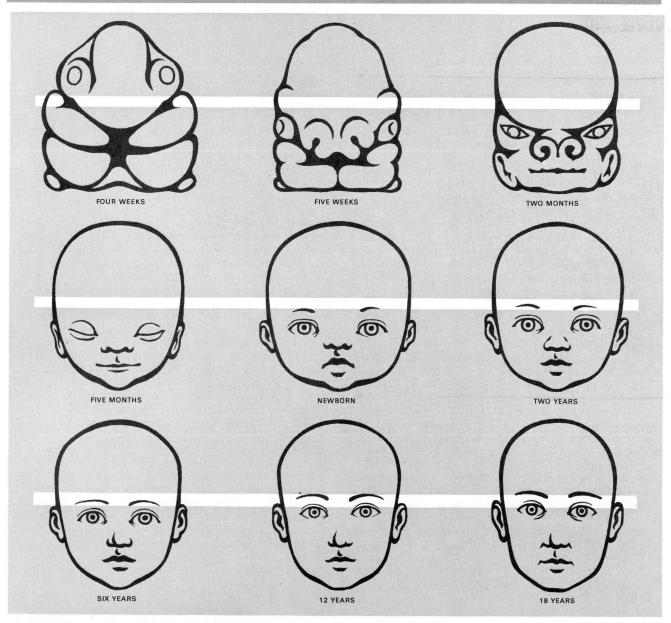

FOUR WEEKS   FIVE WEEKS   TWO MONTHS

FIVE MONTHS   NEWBORN   TWO YEARS

SIX YEARS   12 YEARS   18 YEARS

FROM FOUR WEEKS TO 18 YEARS

While most of the shaping of a face takes place within the womb, the facial proportions shift subtly between birth and adulthood. The eyes are already two thirds full size at birth and seem disproportionately large throughout childhood. Their growth is almost complete by age 12. The face becomes narrower during the years between childhood and adolescence as the jaw and chin rapidly lengthen and the "baby fat" disappears.

FURTHER READING

General

Bonner, J. T., *Morphogenesis: An Essay on Development*. Atheneum, 1963.

Ebert, James D., *Interacting Systems in Development*. Holt, Rinehart and Winston, 1978.

Falkner, F., and J. M. Tanner, eds., *Human Growth* (3 vols.). Plenum, 1978.

Harrison, G. A., and others, *Human Biology*. Oxford University Press, 1977.

Novikoff, Alex B., and Eric Holtzman, *Cells and Organelles*. Holt, Rinehart and Winston, 1976.

Pfeiffer, John, and the Editors of Time-Life Books, *The Cell*, 2nd ed. Time-Life Books, 1980.

Tanner, James M., *Foetus into Man*. Harvard University Press, 1978.

Taylor, Gordon Rattray, *The Biological Timebomb*. New American Library, 1969.

Thompson, D'Arcy Wentworth, *On Growth and Form*. J. T. Bonner, ed. Cambridge University Press, 1961.

Prenatal Development

Ashley Montagu, M. F., *Life Before Birth*. New American Library, no date.

Guttmacher, Alan F., *Pregnancy, Birth and Family Planning*. New American Library, 1973.

Hall, Robert E., *Nine Months' Reading*. Bantam, 1973.

Nillson, L., *A Child Is Born*. Delacorte/Seymour Lawrence, 1976.

Postnatal Development

Malina, Robert M., *Growth and Development: The First Twenty Years*. Burgess, 1975.

Mead, Margaret, *Coming of Age in Samoa*. Morrow, 1971; *Growing Up in New Guinea*. Morrow, 1976.

Roche, Alex F., *Skeletal Maturity of Youths*. National Center for Health Statistics, 1978.

Schell, Robert E., and Elizabeth Hall, *Developmental Psychology Today*. CRM/Random House, 1979.

Sinclair, David, *Human Growth after Birth*. Oxford University Press, 1978.

Tanner, J. M., *Education and Physical Growth*. University of London Press, 1978.

Control of Growth

Asimov, Isaac, *The Genetic Code*. New American Library, no date.

Moore, John A., *Heredity and Development*. Oxford University Press, 1972.

Watson, J. D., *Molecular Biology of the Gene*. Benjamin-Cummings, 1976.

ACKNOWLEDGMENTS

The editors of the revised edition of this book are indebted to Dr. John D. Baxter, Director, Doris Coit, Dr. Walter Miller, Laboratory Staff, Endocrine Research Division, University of California, San Francisco; Dr. Robert Becker, Chief of Orthopedic Surgery, Veterans Administration Hospital, Syracuse, N.Y.; Dr. Jo Anne Brasel, Clinical Study Center, Harbor-UCLA Medical Center, Los Angeles; Dr. George B. Chapman, Chairman, Department of Biology, Georgetown University, Washington, D.C.; Dr. William Collins, Chief of Neurosurgery, Yale School of Medicine, New Haven, Conn.; Dr. Alfred Coulombre, Chief of Neuroembryology, National Institutes of Health, Bethesda, Md.; Dr. Edmund S. Crelin, Chief of Anatomy, Department of Surgery, Yale School of Medicine; Dr. Arto Demirjian, Director, Giselle Talbot-Donnelly, Developmental Researcher, Staff, Center for Research in Growth and Development, University of Montreal; Dr. Frank Falkner, Director, Child and Family Health, University of Michigan School of Public Health, Ann Arbor; Dr. Stanley Fowler, Assistant Professor, The Rockefeller University, New York City; Dr. Lawrence I. Gilbert, Chairman, Department of Biological Sciences, Northwestern University, Chicago; Dr. Karl E. Hellstrom, University of Washington, Seattle; Dr. Jules Hardy, Director, Department of Neurosurgery, Notre Dame Hospital, University of Montreal; Mrs. Beatrice Lacey, Acting Scientific Director, Dr. Cameron Chumlea, Mrs. Virginia Crandall, Chief, Section of Development, Dr. Alex Roche, Chief, Section of Physical Growth and Genetics, Dr. Roger Siervogel, Pam Williams, Staff, Fels Research Institute, Wright State University School of Medicine, Yellow Springs, Ohio; Dr. C. H. Li, Director, Hormone Research Center, University of California, San Francisco; Dr. Daniel Linkie, Department of Obstetrics and Gynecology, Columbia University College of Physicians and Surgeons, New York City; Dr. Rhoda Metraux, Institute for Intercultural Studies, The American Museum of Natural History, New York City; Dr. Robert Malina, Professor of Physical Anthropology, University of Texas at Austin; Dr. Luigi Mastroianni Jr., Chief, Department of Obstetrics and Gynecology, Hospital of the University of Pennsylvania, Philadelphia; Dr. Anne McLaren, MRC Mammalian Development Unit, University College, London; Dr. Albert Parlow, Harbor-UCLA Medical Center; Dr. Salvatore Raiti, Director, The National Pituitary Agency, Baltimore, Md.; Dr. Alan Rosenfeld, Professor, School of Public Health, Columbia University; Dr. Stephen J. Suomi, University of Wisconsin Primate Center, Madison, Wis.; Dr. Ian Tattersall, Physical Anthropology, The American Museum of Natural History; Professor James M. Tanner, Director of Child Health and Growth, Institute of Child Health, University of London; Dr. Louise B. Tyrer, Medical Director, Planned Parenthood Federation of America, New York City; Dr. Louis Underwood, Department of Pediatrics, University of North Carolina School of Medicine, Chapel Hill; University of California, San Francisco—News and Public Information Services; Dr. Richard Wilen, Department of Obstetrics and Gynecology, Yale School of Medicine; Webb Associates, Yellow Springs, Ohio; Dr. Ronald Wilson, Director, University of Louisville Twin Study, Louisville, Ky.

Consulting editors for the first edition were the late René Dubos, Emeritus Professor of Pathology, The Rockefeller University; Henry Margenau, Eugene Higgins Emeritus Professor of Physics and Natural Philosophy, Yale University; and the late C. P. Snow, novelist and a fellow of Christ's College, Cambridge University, England. The following persons and institutions also provided valuable assistance: Dr. Melvin M. Grumbach, Professor of Pediatrics, University of California, San Francisco Medical Center; Dr. Alexander Bearn, Professor, The Rockefeller University; Dr. John Tyler Bonner, Department of Biology, Princeton University, Princeton, N.J.; CARE, Inc., New York City; Frank J. Darmstaeder, Curator, The Jewish Theological Seminary of America, New York City; Dr. Raphael David, Associate Professor of Pediatrics, New York University School of Medicine; Belle Fieldman, Thomas J. Watson Library, Metropolitan Museum of Art, New York City; Dr. Stanley M. Garn, Dr. John I. Lacey, Dr. Michael Lewis, Dr. Lester W. Sontag, Director, Fels Research Institute; Dr. Alan F. Guttmacher, Director, Planned Parenthood Federation of America; Institute of Nutrition of Central America and Panama (Guatemala); Dr. Stanley James, Babies Hospital, Columbia Presbyterian Medical Center, New York City; Dr. John H. Lawrence, Associate Director, Lawrence Berkeley Laboratory, University of California at Berkeley; Dr. Choh Hao Li, The Hormone Research Laboratory, University of California at Berkeley; Dr. Margaret Mead, Curator of Ethnology, The American Museum of Natural History; National Academy of Sciences, National Research Council, Washington, D.C.; The National Pituitary Agency; Dr. Charles Noback, Professor of Anatomy, Columbia University College of Physicians and Surgeons; Dr. Paul R. Packer, Department of Obstetrics and Gynecology, Albert Einstein College of Medicine, New York City; Bradley M. Patten, Department of Anatomy, University of Michigan; Dr. Maurice S. Raben, Tufts New England Medical Center, Boston; Dr. John W. Saunders Jr., Chairman, Department of Biology, Marquette University, Milwaukee; Dr. Harry L. Shapiro, Department of Physical Anthropology, The American Museum of Natural History; Dr. Landrum B. Shettles, Department of Obstetrics and Gynecology, Columbia University College of Physicians and Surgeons; Dr. Gertrude van Wagenen, Department of Obstetrics and Gynecology, Yale School of Medicine; Alice D. Weaver and librarians, Rare Book Department, New York Academy of Medicine; and Dr. I. Bernard Weinstein, Institute of Cancer Research, Columbia University.

INDEX

Numerals in italics indicate an illustration of the subject mentioned.

PICTURE CREDITS

The sources for the illustrations which appear in this book are shown below. Credits for the pictures from left to right are separated by commas, from top to bottom by dashes.

Cover—Arnold Newman

CHAPTER 1: 8—Bill Ray. 11—Drawings by Leslie Martin. 15—Henry Groskinsky courtesy The New York Academy of Medicine Rare Book Room. 17, 18, 19—Drawings by Samuel Maitin. 20—Electron micrograph courtesy Dr. Bernard Tandler, of Sloan-Kettering Institute for Cancer Research. 20 through 27—Drawings by Samuel Maitin.

CHAPTER 2: 28— Dr. Landrum B. Shettles courtesy *The American Journal of Obstetrics and Gynecology.* 30, 31—Adapted by Nicholas Fasciano from *Human Embryology* by Bradley M. Patten, second edition, copyright 1953, Blakiston Division, McGraw-Hill Inc.; used by permission. 34—Henry Groskinsky courtesy The New York Academy of Medicine Rare Book Room. 35, 36, 37—Drawings by Nicholas Fasciano. 38, 39—Drawings by Eric Mose from an illustration in *Scientific American,* November 1957. 41, 42, 43—Drawings by Samuel Maitin. 44, 45—Julius Weber except background and drawings by Samuel Maitin. 46—Drawing by Arnold Holeywell—courtesy Clay Adams Inc., New York City—drawings by Samuel Maitin (4). 47—Julius Weber. 48, 49—Professor Etienne Wolff (2), Professor A. A. Moscona (3)—drawing by Samuel Maitin adapted by permission from *Animal Growth and Development* by Maurice Sussman, copyright 1960, Prentice-Hall. 50—Drawing by Samuel Maitin from an illustration in *Scientific American,* November 1963. 51—Howard Sochurek—Dr. John W. Saunders Jr. 52—Ulrich Clever. 53—Claus Pelling courtesy Max Planck Institute for Biology.

CHAPTER 3: 54—Courtesy Bayer, Staatsbibliothek, München. 57—Drawings by Nicholas Fasciano. 59—Drawing by James Alexander. 60—Drawings adapted by Otto van Eersel from a drawing by Mrs. Audrey Besterman from *Science of Man 3* by permission of the British Broadcasting Corporation. 63 through 75—Lennart Nilsson.

CHAPTER 4: 76—Courtesy H. B. Osgood. 78—Drawings by Matt Greene. 81—Drawing by Otto van Eersel. 89 through 95—Enrico Ferorelli, courtesy Fels Research Institute. 96—Ted Church, courtesy University of Montreal Research Center for Growth and Development; Enrico Ferorelli, courtesy University of Montreal Research Center for Growth and Development. 97—Courtesy University of Montreal Research Center for Growth and Development. 98 through 103—Enrico Ferorelli, courtesy University of Montreal Research Center for Growth and Development.

CHAPTER 5: 104—Lisa Larsen. 107—A. Y. Owen courtesy The Oklahoma Historical Society. 110—Drawings by Otto van Eersel. 115—Henry Groskinsky. 116—Lilo Hess, Loomis Dean. 117—Andreas Feininger. 118, 119—Andreas Feininger, Douglas Faulkner—courtesy New York Public Library. 120, 121—Douglas Faulkner, Tom

McHugh from Photo Researchers Inc.—Lawrence Chang. 122—Ivan Massar from Black Star (2)—courtesy New York Public Library. 123—Ivan Massar from Black Star except top right Gareth W. Coffin, U.S. Bureau of Commercial Fisheries Biological Laboratory, Boothbay Harbor, and the Maine Department of Sea and Shore Fisheries 124—Tuggener-Foto, Zurich. 125—Marvin E. Newman. 126, 127—Left from *On Growth and Form* by Sir D'Arcy Thompson, abridged edition, Cambridge University Press; right, Roy Pinney from Photo Library Inc. 128, 129—Carroll Seghers II, Myers from Alpha Photo Associates.

CHAPTER 6: 130—Phil Brodatz. 133—Drawing by Patricia Byrne courtesy Dr. Stanley M. Garn. 135—Courtesy The Royal College of Surgeons of England. 136—Drawing by Nicholas Fasciano. 139—Seymour Mednick. 140, 141—Drawings by Elliot Herman. 142, 143—Drawing by Samuel Maitin, drawing by Vic Taylor. 144 through 147—Drawings by Samuel Maitin. 148, 149—Drawing by Samuel Maitin, drawing by Elliott Herman.

CHAPTER 7: 150—Courtesy The Anna Clinic, Hannover. 152—Henry Groskinsky courtesy The New York Academy of Medicine Rare Book Room. 153—Courtesy New York Public Library. 154—Adapted by Leslie Martin courtesy Clemens E. Benda, *The Child with Mongolism,* Grune and Stratton, 1960. 157—Phil Brodatz courtesy Watson Library, The Metropolitan Museum of Art. 159—London *Daily Mirror.* 160—Left Wide World; right from *The Pituitary Body and Its Disorders* by Harvey Cushing, J. B. Lippincott, 1912. 161—Dr. Anthony N. van den Pol, Yale School of Medicine; inset, drawing by Bill Fox; Jon Brenneis. 162—Courtesy The Royal Canadian Air Force. 163—Left courtesy Anna Hooey; right drawing by Otto van Eersel. 164, 165—Horst Ehricht. 166, 167—Ivan Massar from Black Star. 168—Tom Tracy, courtesy Endocrine Research Division, University of California, San Francisco. 169—David Powers, courtesy Endocrine Research Division, University of California, San Francisco.

CHAPTER 8: 170—Dr. Robert Sponholtz. 174—Drawing by Leslie Martin from B. I. Balinsky, *An Introduction to Embryology,* W. B. Saunders Co. 176—Roy Hyrkin. 179—Dr. Lino Pellegrini. 180, 181—Tony Archer—R. Faust, Dr. Peter Fuchs, Göttingen. 182—Jens Bjerre. 183—Colin Turnbull courtesy Department of Anthropology, The American Museum of Natural History. 184, 185—J. R. Eyerman. 186, 187—Eric Schaal. 188—Dr. E. Kahn courtesy Harlem Hospital—Pierre A. Pittet. 189—I.N.C.A.P. 190—Courtesy Art Institute of Chicago; Frederick W. Gookin Trust Fund—T. Tanuma. 191—T. Tanuma. 193—Otto van Eersel based on drawing from CIBA *Symposia,* page 1,469, formerly published by CIBA Pharmaceutical Company, Summit, N.J.

Printed in U.S.A.